PILGRIMS TO PATRIOTS

A Grandfather Tells The Story

ALEX BUGAEFF

Copyright © 2012 Alex Bugaeff
All rights reserved.
ISBN-10: 1478266848
EAN-13: 9781478266846

To

Hannah Katharine Makuch

And

Atticus Carter Makuch

CONTENTS

FOREWORD

This is the real story of our nation's founding – 200 years from Pilgrims to Patriots. That time was like a foundry where a way of life was cast and forged from the raw material of a striving people and a land that was ready for all possibilities. People who see the founding as a bunch of old men sitting in a conference hall for a few days are misinformed. The real story is much longer and takes longer to absorb, but it's worth it.

At one time or another, my kids and their friends have mentioned their wish to learn more about how our nation was born. As I traveled the country doing training for school systems, I found that schools weren't trying very hard to teach it. When they did, the history of our founding was given short shrift in favor of the study of social ills.

Today, George Washington and the other Founding Fathers are treated more as outdated curiosities than as heroes. The Constitution, if it is studied at all, is depicted as irrelevant, if not an obstacle, to the needs of modern society. The hardships that our ancestors endured to create the better world that we now enjoy are taken for granted.

I wrote this book to correct the weakness and one-sidedness that seems to prevail in current descriptions of our founding. I have tried to do it by presenting the history of the period in as balanced a way as I know how. Granted, I have chosen what to include and exclude as any other historian must, but I have tried to let my "filters" show.

My aim is to bring the founding story into the everyday lives of parents and grandparents and, through them, into the lives of their children and grandchildren.

In a series of story times, a grandfather, "Gomps," sits down with his two grandchildren and tells them the story of our country's and their heritage. Using simple language and dialog with them, Gomps makes the story understandable and exciting.

Our nation was 200 years in the making. It was not dreamed up in a few months of theorizing and debate, as many contend. Our ancestors came to the New World for freedom. They lived, fought and died for freedom, and they governed themselves under the principles of freedom from the beginning.

From the beginning, our ancestors wrote constitutions, too. Constitutional rules were written in the charters given them by the King even before they left England. The Pilgrims wrote a constitution - the Mayflower Compact - before they set foot on New World soil. The Governor of the Massachusetts Bay Colony, John Winthrop, wrote and published a constitution before his voyage left England. And our forefathers continued to write constitutions as they needed them for settlements, colonies, States, and the new nation.

Our ancestors understood the importance of rules of governance for applying the principles of freedom. As James Madison said, "If men were angels, no government would be necessary." The trick was to come up with a set of rules that would protect against tyranny while allowing as much freedom as possible.

Their first try was the Articles of Confederation. It didn't work very well. I believe, although I have no historical basis to support it, that the Continental Congress approved the Articles as much to honor Benjamin Franklin, who wrote its blueprint, as they did to satisfy various contending interests.

Armed with their experiences under the Articles, the Founders were ready to put it all together. And, of course, the result was a masterpiece - the U.S. Constitution.

But by itself, the Constitution was not enough to produce and sustain the success that our nation has achieved. Speaking about democracy in other countries, John Bolton, former U.S. Ambassador to the United Nations, said that holding democratic elections is not enough to create a democratic system. Institutions of democracy are needed to put the results of elections into practice and to protect them.

That's what the 200 years of struggle did for our ancestors and for us. At the same time as they were developing constitutions, our ancestors were setting up and living under the institutions that supported them. They created legislatures and passed laws. They created a democratic military form – militias. They created courts of law. They created political parties. They created governments at all levels. And the customs within which it all flourished became commonplace.

Our country was also successful because of who we were and are. The ancestors who came here were ambitious, not meek. They were risk takers. They were not submissive. They were dreamers and doers. They wouldn't settle for good enough. They wanted the best.

Our country attracts and encourages people with those kinds of attributes even today, and, like Winthrop's constitution for the Mas-

sachusetts Bay Colony, the U.S. Constitution both warns and beckons
— this is who we are and this is how we do it.

I encourage parents and grandparents to read this book for themselves. I encourage them to read it to their children and grandchildren
or to tell the stories to them in their own story times. I also encourage
children and grandchildren to read it on their own, although I did not
write it with children as the primary audience.

Above all, I wrote the book I wanted to write. I wrote it in a style
with which I am comfortable. I have shared our nation's history in
stories that I wanted my grandchildren to hear. Hopefully, they will
gain a deep appreciation for our founding and will pass the stories
along to their children and grandchildren.

Alex Bugaeff

Stafford Springs, Connecticut

I

MOLLY PITCHER,
REVOLUTIONARY WAR
CANNONEER

It was the Fourth of July, in the afternoon. My grandchildren, Hannah, 11, and Carter, 9, plopped down on the sofa on either side of me. Their grandmother, Peach, was in the kitchen.

"Hi, Gomps. We're bored," Hannah announced.

"So, I see," I replied, "and you'd like me to do something about it, I take it."

"We thought maybe you could tell us a story," Carter said.

"What kind of story?" I asked.

"Something exciting," Hannah replied.

"How about a story from the history of our country?" I said.

"Aw, history is boring," Hannah groaned.

"Oh, I don't know," I said. "The word 'history' is kind of the same as 'story,' don't you think? What makes for an exciting story to you?"

They thought for a moment, and then Hannah blurted, "The people are interesting and you don't know what's going to happen."

"How about you, Carter?" I asked. "What makes a story exciting for you?"

"The people are in like a scary place and something bad could happen, but they get out of it at the end."

"OK," I said. "What if I told you that the early history of our country has all that and more? Would you give it a try?"

Both kids thought for a moment. Then Hannah said, "OK, but a short one."

"Carter?" I asked. "Are you good with that?"

"Yeah, I'm good, but make sure it's short."

"All right, then," I said, "I'll tell you the story about a woman in the Revolutionary War."

☙

"Her name was Molly Pitcher. At least, that was her nickname. By the end of this story, she becomes *Sergeant* Molly Pitcher."

"Sergeant?" Hannah asked. "A woman could be a sergeant back then?"

"This one did," I replied. "But we're getting way ahead of ourselves. Let me tell you a little bit about her first.

"Her real name was Mary Ludwig. She was born to German parents in the Pennsylvania countryside in 1754. As soon as she could work, she did chores on her parents' farm. She carried hay bales and water buckets when she grew big and strong enough. Then, at 13, she married William Hays, a local barber."

"13?" Hannah blurted. "That's too young to get married, Gomps."

"Today it is," I replied, "but back then it wasn't. Both boys and girls grew up faster, married younger, and often died younger, too."

"Yipes," she said. "I didn't know that. So what happened next?"

"In 1777, William joined the Continental Army to fight in the Revolutionary War," I continued. "He was put in an artillery regiment and became an artilleryman."

"What's artillery?" Carter asked.

"Cannons," I replied.

"Cool," said Carter, "and, what did he do?" Carter continued.

"He was a rammer," I replied. "He stood at the mouth of the cannon with a long wooden pole called a ramrod. He twisted rags on the end, called a sponge, and cleaned the barrel. Then he loaded the cannon. Get the idea?"

"Cool!" Carter said.

"So what about Molly — or Mary?" Hannah said impatiently.

"In those days some wives followed the troops, to help them with their clothing and cooking and tend to their sicknesses and wounds. They set up their own camps at a safe distance from the troops and Mary was one of them. She went with William's regiment from place to place.

"In the winter of that year, General George Washington had the Army's camp set up in Valley Forge, Pennsylvania. The weather was bitterly cold and the troops were suffering. General Washington's wife, Martha, set up a wives' camp to help the troops deal with their misery. Since William's regiment was there, Mary served with Martha's group."

"Then Mary knew Martha Washington!" Hannah exclaimed.

"We don't know for sure, but she probably did," I replied.

"In February, William's regiment trained for the fighting that would start again in the spring. He practiced with the ramrod to clean the embers and dirt quickly from the cannon barrel with the sponge, a job that needed lots of water to do. And since artillery was hot work, even in winter, he and the other artillerymen needed drinking water, too.

"Mary volunteered to bring the water to him in buckets. The women who did this were called 'water girls.'"

"That sounds hard. Was she strong enough, Gomps?" Hannah asked. "I thought she was only 13."

"By now she was a young woman of 23," I reminded her, "and I'm sure she was strong enough. Remember, she had worked on her family farm doing the same kind of thing.

"When spring came," I continued, "the Army left Valley Forge to take up the fight against the British where they'd left off the year before. William's regiment fought on one battleground after another. In each battle, Mary and the other water girls were right in the middle of the action, running up to the cannons with their buckets.

"In June, the Continentals and the British fought a major battle in Monmouth, New Jersey. The temperature soared to 100 degrees, and the heat from the cannons made it even hotter. The fighting continued through the day, with one side and then the other gaining ground.

"Then, William went down – he was hit! Without missing a beat, Mary put down her buckets, grabbed William's ramrod and took over for him. She had seen how to do it in the training at Valley Forge.

"First, the sponge to clear the barrel. Then, the gunpowder – ram it in. Then the hay wad – ram it in. Then the cannonball – ram it in. Then she stood back, held her ears, and BOOM!

"She kept up the firing for the rest of the day. The smoke stung her eyes and the smell of gunpowder burned her nose. Musket shot and cannonballs were whistling past her left and right, and one went right between her legs!"

"Oh, no," Carter exclaimed. "Did she get hurt?"

"Nope," I replied, "but part of her skirt was torn away. Still, she kept on firing, and in the end . . . we beat the British."

"Yay!" both kids shouted.

"Gotta say," Hannah said, "that was pretty good."

"Ah," I said. "But that's not the end of the story.

"During the battle, General Washington had seen what this brave water girl was doing. When it was over, he made her a sergeant. From then until her death many years later, she was known as Sergeant Molly."

"Wow," exclaimed Hannah. "She was brave. And strong. But how did she get the name Molly Pitcher?"

"Good question," I replied. "In those days, Molly was a common nickname for Mary. So she was already called Molly.

"'Pitcher!' was what William and the other artillerymen called out when they needed a drink – a pitcher of water. They yelled, 'Molly, pitcher, pitcher!' At least, that's how the story goes."

"What happened to her?" Carter asked.

"After the war," I replied, "she had a big family back in Pennsylvania and lived a long life."

"How about William?" Carter asked.

"He healed completely from his wounds and went back to Pennsylvania with Molly," I replied.

"Is that the end of the story, Gomps?" Hannah asked.

"Of that story, yes," I said.

"I gotta admit," she said, "maybe history isn't so boring after all. Thanks."

"Yeah, thanks, Gomps," Carter added. "Could you tell us another story like that some time?"

"You just name the day," I replied.

And with that they went back out to play before leaving for the fireworks.

2

WHERE WE CAME FROM

About two weeks had passed, and the kids were visiting Peach and me for the night. After dinner we went to the living room for family time. They plopped down again, and Hannah spoke.

"Gomps, we liked that story about Molly Pitcher. Could you tell us another one?"

"Sure," I said. "What kind of story would you like?"

"Tell us about our country back then – the wars and stuff," Carter said.

"Oh, Carter," Hannah sighed, "that's all you care about – war and guns."

"So?"

"So, I'd like to know about more than just the wars and guns," she said. "I'd like to hear about the whole thing."

"The whole thing?" I asked.

"Yeah."

"Well, it's a big story," I said. "It's about people who wanted to be free: free to be what they wanted to be, worship God the way they wanted, and have something to say about the laws they lived under.

This meant a way of living that had never been tried before, so it wasn't easy. There are battles, and killing, and starvation, and hardship in this story. Are you up for it?"

"Yes!" they chimed in unison.

"OK," I said, "but if you have a question, I want you to ask it right away. OK?"

"OK!"

"Here we go, then," I said. "The story starts almost 800 years ago, with a king."

"A king?" Carter exclaimed. "We don't have a king."

"Carter, you can't ask questions so soon," Hannah scolded. "Gomps just started!" Carter stuck out his tongue. Hannah threw a fake punch at him.

"Hey, you two, knock it off," I said. "Hannah, it was OK for Carter to ask his question, even if it was right at the beginning. You, too. That's part of the deal.

"And Carter is right about the king," I said. "We don't have a king. But our story started in England, and *they* had a king."

"Oh, OK," said Hannah.

"In fact, kings were the problem," I continued. "They had power to do whatever they wanted and to make the people obey them. England was a country where you stayed in your class and kept your mouth shut."

"What do you mean, 'stayed in your class'?" Carter asked. "Weren't you even allowed to go to the bathroom?" Hannah poked him.

"Your social class," I said. "The working people were called commoners, the working class. If your father was a working man, you could only be a working man. That was your class, and you stayed that way for life.

"If your father was a nobleman, you would be a nobleman."

"What's a nobleman?" Carter asked.

"They were the upper class - the dukes and earls and barons," I replied.

"I thought they were royalty," he frowned.

"No," I replied, "royalty are the king and queen and their family."

"Oh, I get it."

"I knew that," Hannah sniffed. Carter let it pass.

"Great," I said. "But the life of a noble wasn't all peaches and cream. The king had castles and a court and wars to pay for, and he needed money to do it. So he taxed his people in every way he could, especially the nobles, because the commoners didn't have much.

"In fact, the king was taxing the barons so heavily that they had nothing left for themselves. Life was tough enough, living in those drafty castles. So they got together and stood up to him."

"They had guts to do that!" Hannah exclaimed. "Wouldn't he just kill them?"

"He would if he could, I suppose," I replied, "but there were too many of them, probably almost a thousand.

"So, in the year 1215, the barons got together and demanded changes. They wrote their demands in a document called the Magna Carta, which is Latin for 'the great charter.' Have you heard of it?"

"Nope," replied Hannah.

"Me either," said Carter.

"The Magna Carta laid the foundation for the rule of law in England, even over the king," I said. "It took away some powers from the king, and it gave the nobles and commoners new rights and freedoms. And it created a group of 25 barons who could overrule the king if necessary."

"He agreed to that?" Hannah interrupted.

"Well, he signed it," I replied. "And then he turned right around and ignored it."

"And then?" Hannah leaned forward.

"War," I said. "It was the king against his nobles."

"I knew it!" Carter rejoiced. "Who won?"

"I guess you could say the nobles won," I replied, "because less than a year later, the king was leading his army against them and he got sick and died."

"Yipes!" Carter exclaimed.

"What happened to the Magna Carta?" Hannah asked. "Did it die, too?"

"No, Hannah, it remained important to the English people," I replied. "Over time, some kings ignored it, and most of it was thrown out and replaced by newer laws, but one rule was kept: that even a king is not above the law. And the Magna Carta became the closest thing to a constitution that the English people would ever have."

"What do you mean, Gomps?" asked Hannah. "England doesn't have a constitution?"

"Not like we do," I replied. "Our constitution spells out all the parts and powers of our government in one place. The powers of the English government are spread out over many laws, court decisions, treaties, rules of Parliament, and royal powers."

"What's Parliament, Gomps?" Hannah asked. "Is that where English laws are made?"

"That's right," I replied. "The word Parliament comes from the French word for talking – 'parlez.' Parliament started with that group of 25 barons in the Magna Carta. Later, people were elected to Parliament by voting similar to ours. They also have a Prime Minister who is somewhat similar to our President."

"Does a king have to obey Parliament?" Carter asked.

"I suppose he could go against them if he really wanted to," I replied, "but Parliament has gained enough power that kings respect it."

"Got it," Carter concluded.

"You all set, Hannah?" I asked.

"Yup, I got it," Hannah replied.

"Good. Now we jump forward 300 years to King Henry VIII."

"Up to this time, England had been a Roman Catholic country. Catholic Popes had been trying to control English kings in religion and politics for centuries.

"But Henry VIII was not a king who was about to be controlled by anyone, even the Pope. Henry created his own religion – the Church of England – and made himself the head of it.

"This started a long struggle for power between Henry and the Catholic Church. In the end, Henry kicked the Catholic Church out of England and made the Church of England the official religion — they called it the 'established' religion. And he commanded everyone to worship in it."

☙

"Next, we go to the year 1600," I said. "From this point on, England had a lot of kings — so many that they're hard to keep track of. So for the most part I'll just call them 'the King,' but in 1600, England had a Queen — Henry the Eighth's daughter, Elizabeth I. She had only a few more years to live, but she was part of our story."

"Yay," said Hannah. "Sergeant Molly, and now a Queen — I like this story."

"But in 1600, the Queen had problems," I said.

"What kind of problems?" Hannah asked. "How could a queen have problems?"

"Well, England had been at war, off and on, with most of the countries in Europe — France, Germany, Spain, Portugal, Holland — and at this time, it was Spain.

"Spain was one of the world's great powers back then. They sent explorers sailing around the world to discover new places and to claim them as Spain's property. They called the Americas the New World.

"England was trying to keep Spain from taking over the New World. To do that, they had to build a navy big enough to match Spain's. This cost the Queen a lot of money, and, since England was a smaller country than Spain, it was harder for her to keep her navy going."

"How did she get the money?" Hannah asked.

"Bet you can guess."

"Taxes!" Carter burst out.

"Right," I replied. "Like the kings before and after her, the Queen was still collecting taxes from everyone, nobles and commoners alike.

"The Queen also collected taxes on things that her subjects bought and sold from other countries — what we call 'trade.' Taxes on trade are called *tariffs*."

"What if people didn't want to pay taxes?" Hannah asked.

"The royal army would come and take it from them," I replied.

"Whoa," they both said in unison. "That doesn't sound fair."

"Maybe," I said, "but that was how kings and queens operated."

"What if a person didn't want to give up their money?" Carter asked. "Or what if they didn't have any?"

"They might have been sent to prison or they might have been killed if they fought back," I replied.

"Killed?" Hannah blurted. The kids' eyes went wide, and they got quiet.

"I warned you that there would be killing in this story," I said. "You still OK with it?"

"Oh, yeah," they both answered.

But Hannah wasn't satisfied on the tax collection part. "That's awful that a person could end up dead for not paying," she observed. "Didn't the Magna Carta protect them?"

I shrugged. "That was one of the parts of it the kings ignored."

"What happened to those soldiers?" asked Carter.

"Nothing," I answered. "They were doing what the king or the queen wanted."

"That wasn't right," Carter protested.

"Now you're starting to get where our country comes from," I said. "The idea that people have basic rights took a long time to sink in.

"Anyway, the Queen's army and navy cost a lot of money. So besides taxes and tariffs, the Queen also tried to take treasures from other countries, especially gold.

"The Spanish explorers had found gold in parts of the New World, and when they brought it back, the English navy would attack their ships and take the gold.

"Sometimes the Queen didn't have enough ships, though. So she paid pirates to go after them."

"She paid pirates?" Carter interrupted.

"She did," I replied. "Pirates were probably the first government contractors. She gave them licenses and called them 'privateers.'"

"Arrr," growled Carter, squinting as if he had an eye patch.

"But the Queen's money problems didn't end with ships and armies, or even with all those castles and servants and advisors she had to pay for. Now she had a big problem with the Church of England. Being the established religion meant that ministers' salaries and other Church expenses had to be paid for. In return, the Church leaders had to preach in favor of the King (or Queen) and convince Parliament to go along.

"But not everybody wanted to go along. People of other religions, including the leftover Catholics, wanted to be able to worship their own way. So when they dared to go to their own churches, what do you think the Queen did?"

"Sent in the army?" Carter blurted.

"You better believe it," I said. "The people of other religions had to worship in secret, and if word got back to the Queen, she'd send the army after them again. It was risky, and some were killed or kicked out of the country."

"Gomps?" said Carter.

"Yes?"

"When do we get to the good part?"

"This isn't good?" I asked.

"Yeah, but I'm tired of hearing about England," Carter continued. "I want to hear about us."

"OK, but do you want to stop now and start up again another time?"

"Yeah, I guess so," Carter replied. "I like the story, but I'm tired of sitting."

"Me too," Hannah admitted.

"OK," I said. "Let's have some lunch."

3

HOW IT ALL BEGAN

A week later, my daughter, Mandy, and her husband, Mark, had me over for dinner. We had just finished when Carter asked, "Gomps, could you tell us more of the story?"

"Which story is that?" I asked.

"The one about our country."

I glanced over at Mandy and Mark. They smiled and gave me a nod: *Take it away!*

"OK," I said. "Where were we?"

Carter jumped right in: "You were going to start telling us about us."

"OK," I said. "Let's get to America.

"In fact, some other Europeans had gotten to America before we did. Columbus was here for a short time and soon after, France sent a couple of ships. The Vikings had been here hundreds of years before either of them. Europeans and English had been fishing off the coast of New England for a number of years. And, the Spanish had small settlements in Florida and what we now call New Mexico.

"Well before 1600, word had gotten around in England that the Spanish were bringing back gold from the New World. They had taken it from the great Indian empires of Peru and Mexico, but many people, including Queen Elizabeth, believed that gold was everywhere. Some said that the roads here were paved with gold. It turned out not to be true, of course, but that got a lot of people interested.

"There were other reasons for people in England to be interested in the New World. The English economy could not grow much more on its own. Their island didn't have room for many more people, so there was little chance for people to expand their businesses. Only the oldest sons of the nobility could inherit land, and there wasn't any more around for the taking. Commoners could not rise above their social class. No matter how hard they worked, there was little chance for them to get ahead in life.

"But, in the New World, there was plenty of land for population growth and farming, and there were raw materials, like timber, fish, and furs – in other words, plenty of opportunity to make money.

"So businessmen were very interested, and gradually many ordinary people became interested, too. They realized that the New World offered them the chance to make a new life. To them that meant two things: freedom of opportunity to earn a better living and freedom of religion to worship as they chose. For those freedoms, some people were willing to take a leap into the unknown.

"The first trips were set up by a noble, Sir Walter Raleigh. He was an experienced sailor who had connections with the Queen and the ability to get money from investors, mostly other nobles. They would pay for the ships, supplies, and crews, and in return, he promised to share the profit."

"That was a pretty good deal for the investors, wasn't it, Gomps?" Carter asked. "They did nothing and got some profit anyway."

"You're right, Carter," I said, "but with one big 'if.'"

"What's that?" Carter asked.

"If the idea didn't work, they could lose all their money," I explained. "And nobody could be sure that it would work. There were no cities, no roads, no ports in the New World. The investors risked their money, but the men who went there risked their lives. That's why those first businessmen who dared to go were called 'adventurers.' Today, we would call them 'entrepreneurs' and the investors, 'venture capitalists'."

"You mean like with Facebook and Google?" Carter asked.

"Very sharp, Carter," I said. "The big difference is, explorers in cyberspace might lose their shirts, but they won't freeze to death."

"I get it," he said.

"So, in the 1580s, Sir Walter Raleigh got permission from the Queen to go and claim land in the New World. That permission came in the form of a license called a Charter.

"If he claimed it, could he keep it?" Hannah asked. "What would she get out of it?"

"She needed big bucks!" Carter broke in.

"Carter!" Hannah exclaimed.

"Well, she did, didn't she, Gomps?" Carter insisted.

"But you didn't have to interrupt like that," Hannah persisted.

"OK," Carter admitted.

"Can I go ahead now?" I asked.

"Yeah." "Yeah."

"Good."

"You're both on the money," I replied. "She did need big bucks and she figured she could get them by taxing everyone who earned money from the venture. If they found gold, she'd get 20%. Get the idea?"

"Got it." "Yup."

"But, Sir Walter didn't go to the New World himself," I continued. "The Queen wouldn't let him — she wanted him around. He just got the investors to cough up the dough.

"Sir Walter put together three voyages - all to Roanoke Island, off the coast of what we now call North Carolina. He named the area Virginia in honor of Elizabeth, who was called 'the Virgin Queen.' All three voyages failed."

The kids were silent, thinking about what that might mean. "Did they all die?" Carter finally asked.

"The first two times, the settlers gave up," I replied, "and those who survived went back to England. Two years after the third voyage, someone sailed back from England to check on the settlers and found that all the people — about 120 men, women, and children -- had disappeared."

"Disappeared?" Carter exclaimed. "What happened?"

"No one knows for sure," I replied. "Some think they fled to a safer place and married into friendly Indian tribes. Others think they were made slaves by Indians or killed. In any event, they were never seen again, and they left very few traces behind."

"Ooooh," they both murmured.

"It was almost 20 years before the English tried again," I continued, "and by that time – 1606 to 1608 – the whole cast of characters had changed. The Queen had died and was replaced by King James. Sir Walter was in jail – the King didn't trust him – and a new group of investors calling themselves the Virginia Company of London approached King James to ask for a charter."

☙

"Knowing that the Roanoke Island settlement had failed, the Virginia Company tried a different place - on what is now the southern Virginia coastline. They hired three ships to take the new settlers across the ocean. The longest ship was 116 feet and the shortest was only 50 feet."

"Wow," exclaimed Hannah, "those ships were little. How did they make it all the way across?"

"They sound small, don't they?" I replied. "But people had been sailing around the world in ships like these for years. There were 39 crewmen among the three ships and about 105 passengers, so it was crowded. The passengers were all men - no women."

"No women?" Hannah yelled. "Why no women? I bet they could have done just as good a job. Maybe better."

"Maybe they could have," I said, "but the English had fresh memories of the Roanoke Island disaster. The women who went over on that voyage had all disappeared, and maybe they had been slaughtered. The leaders weren't sure that they could protect women. Besides, they weren't sure that women would be able to hold up under the conditions in the New World."

"I coulda fought off those Indians and done the work, too," Hannah insisted, arms folded.

"I'm sure you could have," I said, looking over at a smiling mom and dad.

"Now about those passengers," I continued, "they included adventurers, investors, nobles and their servants, and workers of every type — carpenters, bricklayers, coopers, laborers, and other tradesmen. There were also four boys."

"Boys?" Carter asked. "What did they do?"

"They worked right alongside the men," I replied. "There were no laws back then that kept children from working, and, in fact, in poor families children were expected to work to bring in money."

"Hmmph," both Hannah and Carter muttered.

"Plus, there was one more passenger," I went on. "You might recognize his name: Captain John Smith."

"Wasn't he in love with Pocahontas, or something like that?" Hannah asked.

"Where did you hear that?" I asked.

"Either in school or in the movie," she replied.

"Well, they did know each other, but not the way you think." I said. "We'll get to that part of the story, but first, I'm going tell you a little bit more about John Smith.

"The English adventurers knew from the Roanoke voyage that there would be Indians there and they could be warlike. They also knew that the groups of passengers crowded onto the ships might fight among themselves. So they needed someone with military experience to organize defenses and to help keep the peace. They chose Captain Smith.

"Captain Smith was a good choice. As a teenager in England, he had run away from home and ended up in Austria, where he joined their army and fought in what is now the country of Turkey. In fact, he had been captured there and made a slave until he escaped."

"Wait a minute, Gomps," Hannah interrupted. "John Smith was a slave? Was he black?"

"Yes and no, Hannah," I replied. "Yes, he had been a slave, and no, he wasn't black. He was white."

"I thought only black people were slaves," Hannah replied.

"No," I replied, "throughout history people of many races have been enslaved. Do you know what slavery is?"

"I thought I did," she said.

"Slavery is not an easy thing to hear about," I said. "You sure you're ready for it?"

I looked over at their mom and dad to see if they were OK with it. Mandy shrugged as if to say, "It might as well be now, when we can tell the whole story." Mark nodded with a resigned look on his face.

"OK," I said. "Then, next time we'll take a hard look at it."

4

SLAVERY

"Slavery is when someone is held captive against their will," I
started off the next week, "and made to work without pay.
A slave is treated as property, like a thing, rather than as a person.
A slave owner can buy or sell slaves. Whole families can be held
in slavery, and any children born to slaves are considered slaves
and the property of that slave owner. If a slave tries to escape, the
owner can track them down and beat them or even kill them.

"Today, slavery is illegal just about everywhere in the world, but it
was common and accepted in many places for centuries. The Jewish
people were enslaved by the Egyptians thousands of years ago. And
Egyptians enslaved pretty much anyone they captured in war.

"African tribes have enslaved other Africans at different times in
history. The Portuguese and Spanish made slaves of both whites and
Indians, as well as Africans. Arabs and other Middle Eastern groups
have had slaves of their own race and other races, including whites.
That's what happened to Captain Smith. And, of course, whites have
enslaved blacks in a number of places."

"That's gross!" exclaimed Carter. "Why would anyone do that to
another person?"

"It is the worst kind of thing, isn't it?" I agreed. "I guess there are two main reasons. The biggest seems to be that slaves are a source of cheap labor. The second is that it can be a kind of prison. Let's say that your tribe conquers another tribe and you capture a lot of their warriors. You could just kill them, or you could make them slaves and force them to work for you. If you let them go, chances are they would regroup and attack you again."

"There's no excuse," Hannah concluded.

"You're absolutely right, Hannah," I said. "And we'll have a lot more to say about slavery later on, because it was a sickness that almost killed our country before it was 100 years old."

"One more thing," Carter asked. "Did England have slavery?"

"You've been doing some quick thinking, Carter," I replied. "No, they didn't have slavery, but they had something almost like it. They called them 'indentured servants.'"

"Sounds like people with false teeth," he joked.

Everyone laughed.

"Good one," I said. "Indentured servants were people who were rented or rented themselves out to other people for a period of time. An indentured servant had to do whatever their master wanted them to do, like a slave. But at the end of the rental time, the indentured servant would be free."

"Why would anyone *want* to be an indentured servant?" Hannah asked.

"A young person might want to take up a skilled trade like carpentry, and would indenture himself to an experienced carpenter in order to learn," I replied. "A famous man, Benjamin Franklin, indentured himself to his brother to learn the printing trade. And sometimes a family would indenture one of their children to a rich family."

"Their own children?" Hannah yelled.

"Exactly," I said. "Suppose they were very poor and had six children. They would indenture their strongest child to a rich family in return for enough money to help the rest of the family."

"What would a kid have to do?" Carter asked.

"The short answer is whatever their master said," I replied. "In reality, most indentured children did manual labor like cleaning floors, carrying firewood, or cleaning barns. And they had to work all day, every day."

"You said they were servants for a period of time, Gomps." Hannah asked. "How long was that?"

"It was up to the master and the servant, or the servant's family," I answered. "But usually it was somewhere around four to seven years."

"And this was in England?" Carter continued.

"Yes, it was quite common back then," I replied. "In fact, some of the nobles on the Virginia Company's voyage brought indentured servants with them – which will bring us back to our story next time."

"This was kinda short, Gomps," Hannah observed.

"I know, Hannah," I said, "but I didn't have much time tonight and I'd like you to have a chance for the slavery story to sink in, anyway."

"OK," they both said.

5

VOYAGE TO THE NEW WORLD

"The voyage to Virginia set sail from London, England in 1606," I began again the next week. "It took them four months to get here. The weather was warm and the seas were calm, so not many got seasick, but they all suffered from spoiled food and bad water.

"Some of the passengers argued and fought the whole way. In fact, for trying to stop the fighting, Captain Smith was accused of mutiny and put in chains for the rest of the voyage! They thought he was trying to take over the ship."

"How did he get out of it?" Carter asked.

"It was a close call," I replied. "You could be hanged for mutiny, and some wanted to hang him on the spot. But a few of the strongest leaders knew that they would need him, so they stopped it.

"When the ships finally got to our coast, they sailed past Roanoke Island and made their way to the mouth of a river in Virginia.

"Finally, Captain Smith was able to convince the leaders to give him his 'day in court,' and they held a trial right there on the ship shortly after arriving. He won his case and was freed. You'll hear a lot more about him in a few minutes.

"Now, I want to tell you something else about this trip. So far, I've talked about it as a business adventure, and that was the most important reason for the voyage. But there was another side to it.

"The King, being a Christian, wanted the settlers to spread Christianity while they were here. So there was a section in the Charter that the settlers would try to convert the Indians to Christianity. In fact, the first thing the settlers did when they jumped ashore was to plant a wooden cross in the sand.

"Then the adventurers began to set up their settlement. Remember, this was 400 years ago. They made crude huts or set up tents, and they cooked over open fires. There were no toilets, running water, furnaces, air conditioning, electric lights, power tools, or screens; no supermarket, no radio or TV, no showers. They just had the hand tools they brought with them. It was cold in the winter, hot in the summer, and buggy all the time. Their little settlement had no protection from any of it.

"Now, this settlement was right in the middle of Indian territory. The tribes there made up the Powhatan Nation, and the chief was named Powhatan."

"Gomps, you keep using the word 'Indian.' Aren't we supposed to call them Native Americans?" asked Hannah.

"Yes, Hannah, we do call them Native Americans today," I replied, "but back then, there was no 'America' yet. The English and Europeans thought there was a passage through the New World to the country of India, a sort of shortcut, and they thought that the people here must have come from India, so they thought of them as Indians."

"*Was* there a passage to India?" asked Carter.

"No, but many thought there must be," I replied, "kind of like they thought the roads would be lined with gold."

"But what about the Panama Canal?" he persisted.

"So you've been studying your geography," I replied. "That's a great question. The Panama Canal is a passage to the Pacific Ocean and to India, all right, but it didn't exist at that time. It wasn't created until about 1900, three hundred years later."

"Aha," said Carter.

"Now, the English settlers had no real protection from the Indians, at least at the start," I continued. "In fact, they were told in the Virginia Charter to try to get along with the Indians and not to fight with them.

"Once they got here, they met Chief Powhatan, and he seemed somewhat welcoming. He showed them how to get food and water and even suggested a good campsite.

"But some of the leaders were suspicious of him. So they chose their own campsite, and it was a disaster."

"How come, Gomps?" asked Hannah.

"They chose a swamp!" I replied.

"Ha ha, a swamp? Why did they do that?" Hannah and Carter both asked.

"Well, first, the swamp was pretty dry at the time of year they arrived," I replied. "And they didn't know that it would flood when the summer rains came.

"Also, the leaders thought that Indians were dumb and didn't know a good campsite when they saw one.

"On top of that, many of the leaders were nobles. Back in England, they were used to having everything done for them, including their thinking. The fact that they knew next to nothing about the New World didn't faze them — until they were proven wrong.

"So they pitched camp in a swamp. And within one year, over half of the original voyagers had died — mostly from disease and starvation.

"Plus, some of the settlers were stealing from the Indians, some stopped working, and the squabbling among them continued.

"And it turned out that there was a warlike side to Chief Powhatan. He was welcoming them at the same time that he was plotting against them. Many times, he ordered his tribes to attack the settlement, and there is even evidence that he tried to poison them."

"Couldn't the Indians just have killed them?" Carter asked.

"How do you mean?" I replied.

"Well, there were a lot more Indians," he continued. "Didn't they way outnumber the English?"

"The English had guns," I replied.

"I didn't know there were guns back then," he said.

"Well, there were," I said. "Imagine what it looked like to the Indians. These strangely dressed guys pointed sticks at them that spat fire and went boom. Then, one of the warriors mysteriously fell to the ground bleeding.

"Still, things were not going well for the English. A better leader was needed to help make decisions, make peace with Powhatan, and get everyone working. And who do you think took the lead?"

"Captain John Smith," Carter said.

"That's right, Carter. How did you know that?" I said.

"A few minutes ago you said we would hear more about him. It sounded like he would be the guy."

Pretty smart, I thought to myself. Just then, Mandy cleared her throat. "Gomps, this is a great story, but it's bedtime for these two."

6

CAPTAIN SMITH LEADS THE VIRGINIA SETTLEMENT

"Who wants a story?"

"Me, me," Hannah and Carter both shouted. This time they were over at our house for the night.

"What'll it be?" I asked.

"We want to hear about what happened to Captain Smith. Don't we, Hannah?" Carter said.

"Definitely," said Hannah.

So much for history being boring, I thought.

"OK," I said, and everyone settled in.

"When we ended the last time, the Virginia settlement was in trouble. Some of the settlers weren't working, and they all were suffering from food shortages and bad water. They were fighting among themselves, and Chief Powhatan was attacking them.

"While all this was going on, the settlers tried to show the investors some early progress by starting a little lumbering business. They shipped the lumber back to England, where it was sold at a profit.

"While the lumber encouraged the investors in England, the time spent lumbering kept the settlers from building better living quarters in the settlement. And so some members of the group began to suffer and die from the bad conditions there.

"One of those who died was the group's supply officer. Captain Smith was made the new supply officer, and he was horrified when he saw what had happened.

"The leaders had decided on a communal living system, meaning they shared everything. They kept all their supplies together in one place, and as members of the group caught fish, shot game, and brought in crops, those were added to the common stores. Then each member of the group took what they needed from the supplies.

"What's wrong with that, Gomps?" Carter asked. "Isn't it fair to share what you have?"

"Where did you hear that?" I asked.

"In school," he replied.

"It's OK, if you choose to share what you've earned, like your allowance," I continued, "but what if you have to?"

"You mean *have* to give some of my money?"

"Yeah," I replied. "How would you like that?"

"I wouldn't," he replied.

"Well, that's what they started out with in the settlement," I said. "The problem was that the ones who had stopped working still took from the supplies. They figured, 'Why work when we can just take what we want?'"

"The others would be working for *them*," Carter said.

"That's about it," I said.

"No wonder it didn't work," he concluded.

"So Captain Smith made a new rule that only those who worked could take from the supplies," I continued. "Later, when even that didn't work, he stopped the common supply altogether, and each settler had to provide for himself. These changes helped get the settlement on its feet enough so that they could give it a name. And they named it 'Jamestown,' after the King at the time.

"Not long after, Smith was also put in charge of building houses and improving relations with the Indians. Because of his army service in Austria and Turkey, Smith found he could learn other languages quickly. It had not taken him long to learn the Indians' language - Algonquian.

"Smith's ability to speak with the Indians made it possible to trade with them. He offered spare tools and building materials in exchange for food, and that seemed to smooth things over.

❧

"As the settlers learned, though, relations with the Indians were not always easy. On one of his trading trips, Captain Smith was captured and held in captivity for several days. The Indians had seen him wandering around their camp and thought he might be spying.

"At the next tribal meeting, Chief Powhatan was to decide whether Smith should be killed or kept alive, and who should be standing next to the Chief but his daughter . . .?"

"Pocahontas?" they both shouted.

"So she *was* a real person," Hannah marveled. "I wasn't sure."

"Pocahontas was real, all right," I said. "She was about ten or eleven years old at the time and smart just like her father. And she was headstrong, too.

"Chief Powhatan had apparently decided to have Captain Smith killed, but Pocahontas took a liking to the Captain, and the legend has it that she rushed over to him and put her arms around him to save him. With that, the Chief changed his mind and allowed Captain Smith to live."

"Did that really happen, Gomps?" Hannah asked. "It sounds too good to be true."

"I wasn't sure about it myself," I replied, "but apparently it's true. At least, we know that she persuaded her father to spare his life. Captain Smith wrote about it in a letter shortly afterward, and so did Pocahontas."

"Pocahontas wrote it? Come on, Gomps," Carter said, "how could she do that?"

"Remember, I said that Pocahontas was smart?" I said. "She had visited the English settlement and learned English."

"No way," Carter said.

"Really?" asked Hannah.

"Yup," I said. "She was able to spend a lot of time there and learn all about the ways of the settlers. And she learned how to read, write, and speak English.

"Now, here's something even more unbelievable about Pocahontas. After spending a number of years visiting with the settlers, she decided to become a Christian!"

"No way," said Carter.

"Way," I said. "That has been proven by her writings and by eyewitness reports in letters and documents, both in Jamestown and in England. Her conversion to Christianity and her ability in English probably helped the two sides to get along."

"Whoa, what do you mean, England, Gomps?" Hannah asked with a look of disbelief on her face.

"She ended up in London, England, believe it or not," I exclaimed.

"No way," they both shouted.

"Way," I repeated. "But there's still more to her story before she got there, because a man came into the picture."

"Captain John Smith!" Hannah and Carter announced together in triumph.

"Ha, ha, gotcha!" I laughed. "You might think so, and that is the legend, but it isn't true. Smith and Pocahontas were never interested in each other romantically. The man who came into her life was named John Rolfe."

"Never heard of him," said Hannah. "Who was he?"

"John Rolfe was a member of the settlement," I explained. "His only child, a daughter, had died, and then his wife. During Pocahontas' many visits there, she and John fell in love."

"Eventually they got married and went to London, but before they did, he had a vital mission he wanted to carry out.

"Rolfe was a gardener, a farmer of sorts, and he had been experimenting with a plant that he thought could become profitable. He had planted it on a trip to South America and in the Caribbean islands. He had brought seed with him to Virginia, and he was convinced that the soil and weather there would be perfect for it."

"What plant was that?" Carter asked.

"Tobacco," I replied.

"Oh, no," groaned Hannah. "That stuff's horrible."

"Yes, but they didn't know that," I said. "It actually grew wild in the New World, and many Indian tribes considered it a sacred plant. Columbus's sailors had brought some seeds back, and by the time of our story it was popular, but scarce, in the Old World, so it was expensive. Rolfe believed that he could find a way to grow it as a crop in Virginia and ship it back to England for a profit. But there was just one problem."

"What?" Carter asked.

"To grow a lot of it, he needed lots of workers – more than there were in Jamestown or than he could get from England. The Indians wanted no part of tobacco farming, so there was only one other source of cheap labor."

"Uh oh," said Hannah. "From the way you said that, I'm afraid of what you're going to say next."

"What do you mean?" asked Carter.

"You'll see," said Hannah.

"I'm afraid so," I said.

"The year was 1619 – just 13 years after the Virginia voyage set out from England. Rolfe and others were expanding their tobacco farms and needed workers. Just then, a Dutch ship – the *Treasurer* – docked at Jamestown and offloaded 20 Africans."

"Oh, no! Slaves!" the two groaned.

"How did they get the Africans in the first place, Gomps?" Hannah asked. "Did they get them right from Africa?"

"Mostly, yes," I answered.

"But how? They didn't go willingly, did they?" she persisted.

"No," I said, "but it gets a little complicated. Some of the Africans had been captured and enslaved by other tribes during wars. The chiefs of the conquering tribes found out that slaves had value to the Europeans."

"They would do that to their own people?" Hannah asked.

"Each tribe saw themselves as different from the others," I said. "So to them it didn't seem like they were capturing their own people. And slavery among tribes had been practiced for a long time before this, so they understood what they were doing.

"At the same time, Europeans, probably starting with the Portuguese, were exploring Africa. They found out about the value of slaves, and they, too, captured Africans. The worst seemed to be the Spanish. They had been capturing Africans during their explorations for quite a while.

"After the Africans were captured, they were sold in African ports for delivery to the New World. The captains of the ships that took them were called slave traders, and the whole system was called the slave trade."

Hannah shivered. "Can we get back to the story now, Gomps?" she asked. "I don't want to hear any more about capturing slaves."

"OK," I said, "but slavery is an important part of the story, and we have to face it. But for now, let's get back to the Virginia settlement."

"Tobacco was profitable and helped make the Virginia Company a success. At that point, the Company settlement was made an English colony — the Virginia Colony."

"What's a colony, Gomps?" Carter asked.

"A colony is a land area that is used by another country for profit. The colonizing country may have conquered the area or just moved in. The colonizing country then ruled the colony as if they owned it."

"Can they just do that?" Carter continued. "Aren't there laws?"

"Sometimes the area wasn't even a country, like the New World," I replied. "Or it might have been a country, but was too weak to defend itself, like India.

"The profit to the colonizing country can come from raw materials . . ."

"Like gold?" Carter interrupted.

"Yes, like gold, or copper, or even lumber," I replied. "The profit can also come from crops or manufacturing or trade — anything that the colonizing country thinks there will be a market for at home."

"But it sounds like they don't always profit," said Hannah.

"That's right, Hannah," I replied. "Sometimes it ends up costing the colonizing country more to run the colony than they get in profits. So there's a risk in doing it."

"Why would it cost them more?" Hannah asked.

"Well, there was the cost of troops to take over; the cost of running the place, once you've taken over; the cost of running the businesses; and the cost of shipping what you've produced."

"Then why do it in the first place?" asked Carter.

"There was a lot of money to be made when it was done right," I replied.

"So, when you said that Virginia was made a colony, you meant that the King saw money in it?" asked Hannah.

"I think he had that in mind all along," I answered. "In fact, in the adventurers' writings, they called it a colony right from the beginning. And, the King's charters said that he would get 20 percent of any gold or silver that was found."

"Did the King send troops?" asked Carter.

"Yup. As time went on."

"And they set up a government?"

"Yup."

"Before you go any further, Gomps, I have a question," said Hannah.

"Sure," I said.

"You said that Pocahontas converted to Christianity. Were there any other Indians who did?"

"You have a good memory, Hannah," I replied. "The answer is, 'Sorta.' The settlers believed that non-Christians only needed to hear about Jesus Christ and they would want to become Christians, too. But the facts were that even though Pocahontas had converted, not many others did. The Jamestown settlers were more interested in profits, anyway. This was not the case, however, with the next settlers in the New World – the Pilgrims."

Carter and Hannah sighed and were quiet. I had a feeling they had enough to think about for a while.

"But we'll save that for next time," I said. "Peach? What's for dessert?"

"How about apple pie and ice cream?" she said.

"Yay!" we shouted. And off to the table we went.

7

THE PILGRIMS RISK
EVERYTHING

It was the end of August — the Dog Days of summer. The day had
been hot and humid and the air was still. The kids were visiting
for the night, and I waited until late at night before starting the story
again.

"Don't tell your mom and dad that we're up so late, OK?" I said.

"Not to worry, Gomps," Hannah winked.

"They won't hear it from me," Carter said.

"I'll tell you more of our country's story, if you'd like," I said.

"We like," said Carter.

"OK," I said. "Last time, I think I was going to start telling you
about the voyage of the Pilgrims."

"Who were they?" asked Carter. He glared at his sister, daring her
to object to his asking a question so soon, but she ignored him.

"Remember that some of the English people coming to the New
World were looking for freedom of religion?" I asked.

"Yes," said Hannah.

"Well, the Pilgrims were the first. To understand their story, we have to go back to England again."

"OK," said Carter, "but not for too long."

"When we talked about the King," I said, "we said that one of the things he did was to try to make everyone worship in the Church of England. King Henry the Eighth had established it as the official religion, and he and his daughter Queen Elizabeth and kings that followed wanted to make sure that it had power like the Catholic Church had had. But the Pilgrims had beliefs that were different from the Church of England."

"Different how, Gomps?" Hannah asked. "Weren't they Christians, too?"

"Oh, they were Christians, all right," I replied, "but a different branch. They called themselves Separatists. The Pilgrims wanted to separate from the Church of England and worship in their own way. They believed in living a simple life, guided by the Bible and not by church leaders.

"They also believed that the Church of England had become hopelessly corrupted. It was accepting money from the King to pay priests and to run the churches and monasteries. In return, the Church leaders were urging their members to support what the King wanted.

"In order to avoid that, the Pilgrims were one of those groups that had to worship in secret. When the King caught them, they were chased out, or thrown in prison, or beaten.

"It got so bad that a number of Pilgrims decided to move to another country. They had heard about the New World and thought it might be the place for them.

"There was just one problem: most of them were poor commoners. They were laborers, carpenters, shopkeepers, and the like. There were no nobles among them and they didn't have the money to pay for the trip. So they made a plan.

"They had heard that Holland (also called the Netherlands) was a place that was much more accepting of other religions. So, in 1608, just two years after the Virginia group had sailed, the Pilgrims decided to leave England and stay in Holland to save up for their voyage.

"The Pilgrims thought it would take only a few years to save up, but it wound up taking twelve years. During that time, they suffered from poor housing and starvation."

"How come?" exclaimed Carter.

"They could speak very little Dutch," I replied, "and they had a hard time finding jobs.

"Yet, after nine years in Holland, the Pilgrims began to plan the voyage. They still didn't have enough money, so they turned to businesspeople back in England. And they ended up with an arrangement very much like the one the Virginia voyage used: investors and adventurers.

"At the time of sailing, Pilgrims made up about half of the total group, and adventurers made up the other half. The investors put up most of the money.

"Meanwhile, the main investor had gone to the King to get a charter for the land they were going to settle. Do you think the King gave it to them?"

"I don't think so," said Carter.

"Why not?" I asked.

"The Pilgrims were big trouble and he wasn't sure he could control them," he answered.

"Hannah?" I asked.

"I think he did," she said. "They were causing so much trouble he was happy to get rid of them."

"You're both right," I said. "He was happy to get rid of them, all right, but he put things in the charter that said that they would still be his subjects and they would still have to obey English law. And, of course, he would still be able to tax the businesses that they set up there and collect on any gold or silver they found.

"Oh, and one other thing," I added. "The charter described the boundaries of the land that the King was granting, and they called it — ta-dah — New England."

"Ahhh," said Carter, rubbing his chin. "It all becomes clear to me now."

"Oh, Carter," said Hannah. "Stop the act. Just because you're reading Sherlock Holmes doesn't mean you have to pretend to know everything.

"But, Gomps, I have a question," Hannah continued. "Who owned that land?"

"Excellent question, Hannah," I replied. "Technically, no one owned the land. Indians were here first, but owning land wasn't part of their way of living. They lived on it and used it, but tribes came and went as food was available and as one tribe conquered another.

"No other European country had claimed this region, either. So the King thought he was free to claim it as his and to grant rights to it as he saw fit.

"All of these arrangements had taken three more years. It was now 1620, and the Pilgrims in Holland were getting ready to leave. The investors had arranged for two ships to take them to the New World. One was a small ship, the *Speedwell*. The second, the larger one, is the one everybody knows the name of. 'The Pilgrims came over on the . . .'?"

"*Mayflower*," Hannah replied.

"Bingo!" I chimed.

"First, the Pilgrims had to go from Holland to England. There they would be joined by the adventurers. The *Speedwell* took the Pilgrims from Holland to the English port they would be leaving from. The *Mayflower* was waiting there to take on the adventurers and most of their supplies for the journey."

"We saw the *Mayflower*!" Hannah exclaimed. "When Peach took us to Plymouth."

"OK, but have you ever heard of the *Speedwell*?"

"Nope," Carter said.

"Hannah?"

"Me neither."

"That's not surprising," I said. "The *Speedwell* barely made it to England!

"The Pilgrims loaded up in Holland, and by the time they got to Southampton, the *Speedwell* had sprung leaks. It turned out to be a tub. No way could it make it across the ocean.

"So the leaders had to change the plan. They decided that everyone would go on the *Mayflower*."

"Everyone?" asked Carter.

"Yup," I replied. "The Pilgrims and the adventurers and - are you ready for this? The animals."

"Animals?" said Carter.

"Yup, they brought dairy cows along with them, and probably sheep!"

"Cows?" Hannah exclaimed. "How did they keep cows on the ship?"

"They kept them tied," I said, "probably below the main deck. It doesn't sound easy, does it?"

"How big was the *Mayflower*, anyway?" Carter continued.

"You know," Hannah answered. "We saw it. Remember? It didn't look big enough for all those people and animals, too."

"In fact, it was 94 feet long, 26 feet wide, and 11 feet deep," I said.

"I remember going on it," Carter said. "It seemed pretty big to me."

"Well," I said, "some of the Pilgrims decided they didn't want to go, so what started out as 150 people was down to about 100, plus 50 adventurers and crew. Still, they had all their belongings, food and water, plus the animals and food for them. Then you had the ship's crew, as well. The *Mayflower* was really cramped."

"I'll say," said Hannah. "I'm not sure I would have wanted to go, either, especially after the other ship almost sank."

"You couldn't have gone anyway," said Carter. "You're a girl."

"That's where you're wrong, Carter," I said. "That's how they did it on the Jamestown voyage, but this was a different kind of deal.

"The Pilgrims weren't limited to just men. Whole families had stayed together in Holland for all those years, and they had every intention of staying together in the New World. So women and children went, too."

It was Hannah's turn to stick out her tongue at her brother.

"So off they sailed in the *Mayflower* in August, 1620. Unfortunately, they didn't get far, even in the *Mayflower.*"

"What happened?" asked Carter.

"The *Mayflower* wasn't ready for the trip, either," I answered. "It turned out that the masts were too big and the sails put too much strain on the hull. It started to leak and didn't sail right. So it was back to port for repairs and smaller masts.

"That took another three weeks. By that time, it was early September. And that created two problems that nearly doomed the whole thing.

$$\sim$$

"The first problem hit them soon after the repairs were done. They were now sailing across the Atlantic Ocean at a stormy time. While the Virginia voyage had been relatively calm, the *Mayflower* was battered by high seas, rain, cold, and high winds.

"Most of the passengers had never been on the open ocean, so a lot of them got seasick."

"Yuck." Carter made a sour face. "This is getting worse and worse!"

"Imagine what it must have been like on board. Men, women, children, and animals all jammed into this little ship with food, water, equipment, and belongings crammed into every nook and cranny. People slept on tiny cots, in hammocks, or just on pads on the decks."

"Uh, Gomps," Hannah interrupted. "I don't know how to ask you this, but . . . what about toilets?"

"There weren't any, not as we know them," I answered.

"No toilets?" they yelled. "How did they go to the bathroom?"

"They had what they called chamber pots," I replied, "like soup pots. I'll leave the rest to your imagination."

"Eeeyew," they both exclaimed with horrified looks on their faces.

"And the cows," Carter said. "What about the cows?"

"Shovels and buckets, I guess."

"Oh, gross," they both yelled, as they squirmed in an effort to escape the image of it. "What did they do to clean up?"

"They tied a rope to a bucket, threw it over the side and brought up sea water. That's what they used to wash themselves, their clothes, the chamber pots, and the decks."

"That thing must have stunk!" said Carter.

"You're not kidding," I said. "Now add to that all the people who were seasick, and you've got what must have been a floating sewer. And, as on the Jamestown voyage, some of their food and water went bad. I don't know how they made it. But they did."

"How long did it take?" Hannah asked.

"About two months," I replied. "They first made land on the ocean side of what we now call Cape Cod, Massachusetts, in November. Their plan was to sail to the mouth of the Hudson River, but they ran into shallows on the way and couldn't get any farther.

"So they went back to Cape Cod and spent the next month looking for a good place to start their settlement.

"They finally chose a small harbor on the mainland across Cape Cod Bay from where they first made land. They called it Plymouth. The land was rocky, but it was protected from the worst of the ocean weather and had good fishing.

"Just before they landed, they decided that they needed some kind of plan for their government."

"Didn't they get that from the King before they left?" Hannah asked.

"Nope," I replied, "the King got lazy and just added a page to the Virginia Charter. But the Virginia Charter wouldn't work for the Pilgrims, because it focused on the business side of the settlement and not on religious freedom.

"So the Pilgrims wrote their own charter. They called it the Mayflower Compact. It was short and sweet, stating that they were binding themselves together under God to form a government of 'just and equal laws.'

"The Mayflower Compact amounted to the first constitution. Once the Compact was done, they elected their first governor and wrote the first laws. Then they went ashore."

"Is that where Plymouth Rock is?" asked Carter.

"Well, we're not sure that there was a rock where they landed, but that's the place, yes."

"What do you mean, no rock?" Carter protested.

"There is no mention of it in any of the original documents about the landing," I replied.

"But that doesn't mean it wasn't there, does it?" said Carter, pressing the issue.

"It could have been," I said. "Maybe we need to talk about how we know so much about all these things.

"Back in those days, people wrote down what happened to them every day, kind of like texting or diaries. They called these books 'journals.' Many of those journals have been preserved so that historians can study the actual pages, even today.

"One of the Pilgrims who kept a journal was William Bradford, who became the second governor of Plymouth Colony. His journal covered 27 years, from the time before they sailed until 1647. So we can read from that journal his descriptions of what happened."

"Have you read it, Gomps?" Hannah asked.

"Yes, in fact I have, Hannah," I replied. "Not the actual original, but a modern published version of it. You can borrow it, if you would like."

"I'd love that!" she replied.

"Then you will have it," I said. "As for Plymouth Rock, it wasn't until 1741, more than 120 years later, that someone chose that boulder to mark the spot. Later, it was moved by the Town of Plymouth to the place where you saw it on your visit there."

"Gomps?" Hannah asked. "What about the Indians? The Virginia voyage met them right away. Did the Pilgrims meet Indians, too?"

"A good question, Hannah," I replied, "but it will have to be a subject for another day.

"And, I think it's cool enough now so you can sleep. Off to bed with you."

"OK, Gomps," they chimed. "Thanks for the story."

And off to bed they went.

8

MEETING INDIANS

It was story time again. "Where were we going to start this time?" I asked the kids.

"You were going to tell us about the Pilgrims meeting the Indians," Carter replied.

"Then I will," I said.

"During the Pilgrims' exploration of possible landing sites, they sometimes caught glimpses of Indians. A few times, small groups of them shot arrows from a distance, but never really got close. The Pilgrims didn't even have to fire their guns.

"In fact, when the Pilgrims explored inland they found a number of Indian camps that had been abandoned. It turns out that only about one-quarter of the Indians in that region were left."

"What happened to them?" Carter asked.

"We're not sure," I replied. "Maybe they just went away, but more likely they died. The question is what they could have died of.

"Today, many people think that the early fishermen carried diseases that the Indians were not able to resist. A few think they infected the Indians on purpose.

"It's also possible that diseases sprang up from among the Indians themselves. Or, that these Indians did not survive the winters. Or, it could be that other tribes had killed them off."

"So the Indians fought each other, too?" Carter asked.

"Yes, they did," I replied. "Different tribes would fight over territory, and sometimes these fights turned into wars."

"Doesn't sound so different from today," Hannah remarked.

"Well, sometimes they were able to work out their differences without a war," I said. "For example, there's a lake in Massachusetts that's called Lake Chargoggagoggmanchauggagoggchaubunagungamaugg."

"No way, Gomps," Carter interrupted. "You're making that up."

"No, Carter," I said, "I'm serious."

"I couldn't even spell it, let alone pronounce it," Hannah added. "Where is it?"

"I had to practice, myself, just to be able to rattle it off," I said. "It's in the Nipmuc tribal area of central Massachusetts, and they call it Lake C for short. Some people say it means, 'You fish on your side, we fish on our side, and nobody fishes in the middle.'"

That got a laugh from everyone.

"Two of the big tribal groups in the region were the Wampanoags and the Mohegans," I continued. "The Wampanoags occupied the eastern Massachusetts and Rhode Island areas, and their chief was Massassoit. The Mohegans occupied the Connecticut and western Massachusetts areas, and their chief was Uncas. The Wampanoags were relatively peaceful; the Mohegans were more warlike.

"I'll talk more about the Indians later, but first I want to tell you about the first days of the Pilgrims' settlement."

"It was now December, and winter had arrived. The Pilgrims wrapped themselves in whatever clothing they could find, but they still shivered in the bone-chilling cold. They had never felt cold like this in England.

"Once they got ashore, they began to build their first shelters. The *Mayflower* was still anchored in the harbor, so many of the settlers slept on the ship while they were building on shore."

"We saw their houses when we visited Plymouth Plantation, Gomps," said Carter. "Were those their first ones?"

"No," I replied. "First they built crude huts. The houses you saw came later."

"It's hard to call them houses," Hannah added. "They were just cabins with dirt floors and open fireplaces. There were no chimneys — just a hole in the roof above the fire. All their stuff must have smelled of smoke."

"Yes," I said, "those houses weren't much help. They suffered from cold and starvation through that first winter, and about a third of them died."

"A third?" exclaimed Carter. "How did the rest of them make it?"

"I'll tell you how next time," I replied. "That's all for today. My voice needs a rest."

9

TOUGH TIMES IN PLYMOUTH

I had been invited to dinner at Mandy and Mark's house, and as we finished dessert, I asked the kids if they would like to hear about the end of that first Pilgrim winter.

But before I could gather them together, Mandy beckoned me aside.

"Uh, Dad, can we speak with you for a moment?" she said.

Uh-oh, I thought, this didn't sound good. Was she going to fire me from my storytelling job? We walked into the kitchen where Mark was waiting, out of the kids' hearing.

"The kids have told us how much they are enjoying this story, and frankly, we're enjoying it, too," she said.

I breathed a silent sigh of relief.

"But the problem is that sometimes the gaps in the story are too long, and they lose the thread," she continued. "So we were wondering if we could make it a regular time."

"Sure," I said. "What did you have in mind?"

"Well, about the only time we can all get together looks like Wednesday evenings. We were thinking maybe you could come over for dinner and then tell the story after."

"Wednesday evenings are good for me," I said. "There might be weeks that I'm out of town on business, but I'd be able to let you know in advance. Would that be OK?"

"That would be fine," she said, as Mark nodded in agreement. "But one other thing."

"What's that?" I asked.

"Could Mark and I listen in?" she said. "We're learning, too. We've talked it over and, believe it or not, neither one of us was taught much of this when we went to school."

"Sure," I said, "on one condition."

"What's that, Gomps?" Mark asked.

"This story is for the kids, so you can't ask questions," I said. "You can only listen."

"OK," they chimed together.

We went back into the living room to tell the kids.

"Kids, we just spoke with Gomps," Mandy said, "and we're going to have regular story time every Wednesday after dinner unless he's away on business. Is that OK with you?"

"Yay," they both cheered. "When do we start?"

"How about right now?" I asked.

"Great!"

And everyone gathered round.

"Last time, we left the Pilgrims suffering through the first winter. Many had died, and the others were holding on for dear life.

"Finally the spring came, and they could think about planting crops. They had found a basket of corn in an abandoned Indian village when they arrived, and that corn became part of the first seed they had to plant. They also had brought wheat and pea seeds with them from England."

"Was that corn free for the taking?" Hannah asked.

"The Pilgrims thought it was," I replied. "They thought it had been left behind, but a band of Indians thought differently and attacked. The settlers fought them off and kept the corn, but it made for a bad start to their relationship.

"The Pilgrims soon discovered that the soil wasn't very good. It was too sandy to grow vegetables by itself. Luckily, an Indian chief had approached them over the winter, and he helped them. His name was Samoset. He was the chief of the Pemaquid Algonquin tribe, and he spoke some English!"

"Huh, just like Pocahontas. How'd he learn?" they asked.

"Well, the Pemaquid Algonquins were in the area of what is now the state of Maine. Fishermen from England had been landing there for some years. Samoset made friends with them and learned some English from them.

"When Samoset heard that some Englishmen had landed in Plymouth, he went to meet them. During that meeting, he told them about another Indian who spoke perfect English. His name was Squanto."

"Perfect English?" Hannah asked. "How'd he do that?"

"Squanto had been kidnapped by an Englishman who hoped to sell Indians as slaves in Spain," I told them. "He was freed by a Christian priest and made his way from Spain to England, where he lived with a shipbuilder who eventually took him to the New World as an interpreter. So he had lived in England himself."

"Did he meet Pocohontas?" Carter asked.

"That's an interesting question, Carter," I replied, "but there is no record that they ever met, although some say they did."

"That's an amazing story, Gomps," Hannah said. "It's hard to believe. Are you sure it's true?"

"Governor Bradford heard it personally from Squanto and wrote it down in his journal. Also, it has been confirmed by the journal of another eyewitness."

"Unbelievable," Carter said as he shook his head. "What happened then?"

"Well, Samoset arranged for the Pilgrims to meet with Squanto and his chief, Massasoit. It turned out that Squanto was living with the Wampanoags. His own tribe, the Pawtuxet, had been wiped out by a disease, probably smallpox, while he was in Europe.

"Massasoit and the Pilgrims made a peace agreement, and at the end of the meeting, Squanto stayed with the Pilgrims and became their interpreter and adviser.

"Now, why did I tell you about Squanto in the middle of the story about the spring planting?"

"I don't know," said Hannah, "but you're going to tell us, aren't you."

"I guess that wasn't a fair question," I replied. "Here's the reason: Squanto showed them how to fertilize their crops."

"Come on, Gomps," Carter interrupted. "There couldn't have been any fertilizer back then."

"No," I said, "but there was natural fertilizer: fish."

"Fish?" they both exclaimed.

"Yup," I replied. "Squanto showed the Pilgrims how to put a dead fish at the bottom of every planting hole. As each fish decomposed, it released food to the plants."

"I've heard that," Hannah said, "but I thought it was just a made-up story. How do you know it's true? Wait, don't tell me. Bradford's journal?"

"Exactly right," I said. "Bradford wrote it all down."

"But, enough of Squanto and farming for now."

"Remember that I said the main reason the Pilgrims had come here was for freedom of religion? Well, during this whole time, they worshipped just as they had hoped they could. They were in church every Sunday – all day."

"All day?" interrupted Carter.

"Yup," I replied. "They had worship services in the morning, ate lunch, and then went back to worship for the whole afternoon."

"Wow," said Carter, "I don't know if I could have stood a whole day of that."

"You would have," I said, "because that's what they all did. And there was more.

"They had very strict religious practices on the other days, too. They read the Bible all the time and used it to decide all kinds of things in their daily lives."

"Couldn't they decide things on their own?" Carter asked.

"They believed that people wouldn't always do the right things on their own," I replied. "They believed that their religion and the Bible were necessary in order to live in the right way."

"I've heard some religious people called Fundamentalists," Hannah said. "Is that what they were?"

"Probably about the same," I replied.

"Doesn't sound like much fun to me," Carter added with a smile. "It would make me mental. You know, fun da mental."

Hannah groaned while Mandy and Mark tried to cover their laughter.

"Good one, Carter," I said, smiling. "But do you think it's the right thing to make fun of other people's religion?"

Suddenly, Carter looked embarrassed. "Naw. It seemed funny and I said it too quick," he mumbled. "I shoulda thought about it, first. I'm sorry."

"That's OK, Carter," I said. "We've all done that.

"Now, back to the point I was making. Their religion got these people through some tough times together, so you can't say it didn't help them. We have to be thankful for their sacrifice. If it hadn't been for them, *we* wouldn't be here."

"What do you mean, we?" asked Hannah. "You mean us, personally?"

"Yes, that's exactly what I mean," I replied. "You both are direct descendants of one of the Pilgrims – John Alden. He came on the *Mayflower*, and if he hadn't toughed it out, you guys wouldn't be here."

"Peach told us about him when we went to Plymouth Plantation," Hannah added. "He was her great, great, great, great grandfather and that means he's our great, great, great, great, great, great grandfather, right?"

"That's right," I said, "although there's a few more 'greats' in there – eleven for her and thirteen for you, altogether. But there's more to tell about John Alden."

"Goody," said Hannah.

"As you know, the Pilgrims planned their living arrangements while they were on the *Mayflower*. In addition to the Mayflower Compact, they decided that they would use a communal system of ownership. Everyone would own all the land together; they would put their crops and goods into the common supply and then take what they needed from it."

"Isn't that like what they did at Jamestown?" asked Hannah.

"Yes, it was," I replied. "And the Pilgrims had the same results with it. It wasn't long before about one-third of the Pilgrim group stopped working. They had learned that they could take advantage of the supplies that others had produced and didn't have to do any of the work themselves."

"Didn't that make the others mad?" asked Carter.

"Yes, it seemed to," I replied. "In fact, Governor Bradford returned to the village from a trip one day and saw several of the lazy ones playing a game in the center of the village, right in front of everyone. He yelled at them and broke up their game, but he saw the cause of the problem.

"And their laziness caused an even bigger problem. Because so many didn't work, the group didn't have enough supplies for the next winter, and they starved again."

"Why didn't they do something?" asked Carter.

"They did, eventually," I continued, "but part of their religious belief was to be accepting of their fellow group members. So it took them longer to face up to what had to be done – three years, in fact.

"Finally, Governor Bradford had had enough. He did away with the communal system and put in a system of individual responsibility. The first thing he did was to divide the commonly held land into individual plots. Then he deeded each family their own plot.

"From then on, each family would be responsible for their own house and for growing their own crops. If they could produce more than they wanted, they could sell to others, and if they needed more, they could buy. Guess who was one of the first to get a plot of land?"

"John Alden?" said Hannah.

❧

"You're absolutely right," I said.

"Alden was a cooper, a barrel maker, by trade. He was also an adventurer, not a Separatist. He was hired in England to keep the *Mayflower's* hull in good condition on the voyage, and then to make barrels for the settlement when they arrived.

"He had met another passenger, Priscilla Mullens, before the voyage, and they had grown fond of each other. They were married a few years later, and the next year Governor Bradford deeded them their plot across Plymouth harbor in what is now Duxbury, Massachusetts."

"Cool," said Carter.

"So she was our great, great, great . . . greatgreatgreat grandmother," Hannah mused.

"Yes, and more about that in a minute. Meanwhile, the new owner-ship system worked much better than the communal system," I said. "Soon, even the lazy settlers were able to take care of themselves."

"But they hadn't done anything for three years," Hannah said. "How did they get their act together so fast?"

"Hannah, there's an old saying, 'Necessity is the mother of inven-tion,'" I replied. "Bradford knew that they'd figure out a way."

"That was cold-hearted," Hannah frowned.

"I think just the opposite," I said. "Bradford made it possible for them to be equal members of the settlement. That gave them self-respect and the respect of the rest of the group. He just gave them a good, swift kick in the pants."

"I never thought about it that way," said Hannah.

"What about the adventurers, Gomps?" asked Carter. "What happened to them?"

"Glad you asked, Carter," I replied. "Let's talk about their part of the story. These adventurers were like the Virginia adventurers. They did not go on the voyage for religious freedom, although all of them likely were Christians. John and Priscilla Alden certainly were. They went seeking their fortunes.

"But there was a difference from the Virginia adventurers, too. The land in Virginia was open and rich. The land in New England was hilly and rocky - not as good for farming. This had been well known in England for years. So this voyage attracted adventurers who were in the fishing, fur, and logging businesses.

"Some of these adventurers fished, trapped and logged them-selves. Probably more became traders, buying fish and furs from Indians, French or other Pilgrims and then selling them to merchants here and back in England.

"It wasn't long after Plymouth was established that many of the adventurers set out into the wild interior. They went up just about every river in New England by boat, fishing and trapping along the way. And the loggers hauled their equipment into the forests."

"Gomps, it sounds like these adventurers were all over the place," Hannah said. "You said there were Indian tribes all around, too. Weren't the Indians unhappy that their land was being invaded?"

"Many tribes were unhappy," I replied. "Some of them attacked the adventurers.

"And Indians were not the only threats in the wild. Not all adventurers were law-abiding, and outside the settlement there was no law to abide by. Theft, boundary disputes, and even murder were widespread on the frontier. But that's a part of the story for next time. We've been at this for long enough for tonight. I'll see you next Wednesday."

10

PILGRIMS AND INDIANS, TWO WAYS OF LIFE

The next Wednesday was the first of our regular story times. After dinner, I started right in.

"Last time, we ended with the lawlessness on the frontier," I began. "The area needed some kind of military force to keep the peace and to protect the settlers. And they needed a military leader to put it together. They had someone like that in the Virginia settlement. Do you remember his name?"

"Wasn't that Captain John Smith?" Hannah answered.

"Exactly," I said. "Good memory. The Pilgrims had a guy just like Captain Smith. His name was Captain Myles Standish. Standish had fought in the King's army. So the Pilgrims and adventurers hired him to come with them to the New World.

"Captain Standish trained the Pilgrims to fight and organized them into a temporary military force that they called the 'militia.' These were everyday people who would grab a musket at a moment's notice and get together to defend themselves or to enforce the law. When the danger was over, they put down their weapons until they needed them the next time."

"What about in Virginia?" Carter asked. "Did they have a militia?"

"Yes, they had militias there too," I replied. "Did I forget to mention that?"

"That's OK," continued Carter. "Who would they have battles with?"

"Mostly unfriendly Indians," I replied.

"Who started it?" Carter pressed.

"Well, that depends on what you mean by 'started it,'" I replied. "The Indians were here first and English came and gradually worked their way into the territory. Most Indians felt that the land was their territory and that the English had no right to push them aside. The English felt that the Indians did not have an ownership system and were just using the land to live on. Some tribes were nomadic and would occupy a territory only temporarily. And, of course, the Indians took over territory from one another through tribal wars."

"What do you think, Gomps?" Hannah asked.

"The two ways of life were so different that it's hard to say who's right," I replied. "Before the English arrived, Indians had changed the land more than most people believe. They cleared forests, mostly by burning them, to create meadows and farmland, causing soil erosion in the process. They thinned out other forests to make hunting easier. And they made roads, dams, and other earthen structures."

"That doesn't sound like the Indians we've been told about," Hannah observed.

"No, it doesn't," I replied. "Indians did a surprising amount of farming, especially the growing of corn and other crops. So much so that they stripped the soil of nutrients at each place and had to move to new areas every few years.

"Then, when so many of them died from disease, the rest couldn't keep up the work, and the forests took back over. When the Pilgrims got to Plymouth, there was little evidence of how the Indians had been using the land.

"English people, on the other hand, valued growth and improvement," I continued. "If a piece of land could best be used by building a permanent road on it or a bridge over a river, that's what they would do.

"The English used profit as a reward for producing new and better things. Indians didn't have a profit or a 'progress' motive. They thought they should just live as their ancestors did.

"There are exceptions on both sides, of course. English and Europeans have tried to protect the land to one degree or another, but probably not to the extent that the Indians did. And of course Indians adopted new things that improved their lives, like the Plains Indians' horses, which were brought over by the Spanish. Indians have invented new things and run businesses, too, but not to the extent that Europeans did. Although today, Indian gambling casinos look an awful lot like something Europeans would invent.

"In the end, what I think is not as important as what you think. Either way, the English obviously became dominant, and there's no way we would go back to the way the Indians wanted it. And, to one degree or another, I think most Native Americans today recognize that, although some of them still may not like it.

"Oh, one other thing about Captain Standish while I'm still thinking about it. It turned out that he was attracted to Priscilla Mullens as much as John Alden was. And, for a time, there appeared to be a friendly rivalry between them over her. In the end, as legend has it, she let John know that she preferred him."

"How did she do that?" asked Hannah.

"Alden was shy, and the legend says that he told her that a friend of his might like her, but didn't know how to tell her how he felt. The legend quotes her as saying, 'Speak for yourself, John.' And, that's how she told him that she liked him."

"Is that true, Gomps?" Hannah continued.

"No one knows, for sure, Hannah," I replied, "but it makes for a good quote, doesn't it? Women have been saying that to shy men ever since. And a good thing, too, because if Priscilla hadn't spoken up, you might not be here!"

$$\backsim$$

"So, on with the story.

"In the first spring after their arrival, the Mayflower sailed back to England. By this time, about 100 of the original 150 passengers had died, and a few of those who remained got discouraged and went back to England on the ship. The ship also took letters and what products the adventurers had been able to scrape together over the winter — mostly animal pelts.

"The return of the Mayflower started communications with England. Now, products, mail, food, tools, and people started going back and forth across the ocean. Plymouth was now a Colony."

"I thought it was called a Plantation — Plymouth Plantation," Carter said.

"You're right, Carter," I said. "That's how it came to be known, but it was an established settlement on foreign shores, and that meant it was a Colony."

"Were they all by themselves, then, like in Virginia?" Hannah asked.

"Not for long," I replied. "Remember that their original Charter was attached to the Virginia Charter?"

"Yes," Hannah said. "That didn't work out, did it?"

"Right," I said, "but the Jamestown group still knew about Plymouth. So, after the Plymouth group had settled, the Jamestown group sent visitors, thinking they could set up some kind of business arrangement."

"How did that turn out?" Carter asked.

"Not too well," I replied. "The Plymouth group still had big problems to solve, and the Jamestown visitors decided that Plymouth probably wouldn't have much to offer. So they went back to Virginia, thinking it was just as well that nothing had come of their effort.

"Still, the Plymouth Colony had established a foothold. Meanwhile, a different group was getting together in England for another settlement . . . but their story has to wait until next time."

"Oh, Gomps, can't you give us a clue?" Hannah begged.

"Witches!" I exclaimed. "And, that's all I'll say for tonight. Now, off to bed with you."

II

WITCHES

It was the second Wednesday in our new story time arrangement and we had just finished dinner.

"Should I start now?" I asked. "Or wait until after dessert?"

"Why don't you start now?" Mandy said. "Then we'll have dessert to look forward to."

"Fine by me," I said.

"Last time, the Plymouth Plantation was up and running and the Jamestown visitors had gone back to Virginia. Everybody with me?"

"Yup," the kids chimed together.

"So, it's on to a new group of settlers.

"Not long after the Plymouth Plantation got established, another English group was forming to come to New England. This new group called themselves the Massachusetts Bay Company, and they planned to settle in what is now Boston."

"Did they know about Boston before they left?" asked Carter.

"Well, Boston didn't exist yet, but they had reports about the area from a struggling little settlement in nearby Salem, and from fishermen along the coast," I replied. "They already knew that there was a harbor with high ground around it. So, unlike the Jamestown and Plymouth groups, they didn't have to explore to find a good place.

"This group was different from the other groups in another way. While Jamestown and Plymouth were paid for by investors, the Bay Company people were paying for it themselves."

"Paying for it themselves?" Hannah asked. "Were they rich?"

"These were successful businessmen and landowners," I answered. "So they had the money to do it.

"They had studied news from the Salem, Jamestown, and Plymouth settlements and had learned what worked and what didn't. They knew that they would need more of everything — ships, people, weapons, seed, supplies, tools, animals, and plans."

"Plans?" Hannah asked. "What kind of plans?"

"All of the groups that had gone before had just gathered together in England and set sail," I said. "When they arrived, they had to figure out who was in charge, how the laws would be enforced, how their leaders would be chosen, how money would be collected and spent, things like that. So they lost time by having to work all that out after they got here.

"The Bay Company worked these things out before they left. Everyone who thought of joining them would know the plans in advance and could decide whether to go or not.

"Before they left, the Bay Company also elected a governor. His name was John Winthrop.

"Winthrop came from a working family in England. He had given some thought to becoming a minister, but that didn't work out. In fact, he had tried a number of jobs and didn't have much luck with any of them. He had even tried to become a member of Parliament, but had not been elected."

"How could he be elected to be a governor, then, Gomps?" Hannah asked.

"Finally, Winthrop had been named one of 21 local judges in his home county," I replied. "In addition to minor cases, he wrote procedures for collecting money for the poor, for choosing police officers, for inspecting bars, and for choosing juries. He did these well, and people noticed."

"I see," Hannah said.

"So, one of the first things that Winthrop did as governor was to make arrangements for the trip," I said. "He worked with the ship captains, suppliers, families, church leaders, and voyagers. And he was among those who got the Bay Company Charter from the King.

"Another thing Winthrop did was to write the goals for the trip. He called them the 'General Observations.' The document explained their reasons for going: freedom to live a Christian life, the chance to start over, and the chance to escape the cramped conditions in England. In effect, the General Observations said, 'This is what we are going to do and why we're doing it. If it's not what you want, don't come along.'"

"Why didn't they just go to Plymouth?" Hannah asked.

"Well, the Bay Company group had religious beliefs that were a little different from the Plymouth group. The Plymouth group wanted to worship in ways that were completely different from the Church of England. They thought the Church of England could not be changed and wanted to be separate from it.

"The Bay Company group had some disagreements with the Church of England, but thought it could be fixed. They came to be called the Puritans. They wanted to 'purify' the Church of the bad practices that they felt had 'infected' it."

"Like what?" asked Hannah.

"I talked about those before when I told the story of Plymouth – the corruption and politics. Both groups saw those practices in the same way. The difference was that the Massachusetts Bay group thought they could be corrected and the Plymouth group thought they could not.

"Another reason for the Puritans not to have gone to Plymouth was that they wanted more than just religious freedom. They wanted opportunity. They wanted that fresh start in life that I keep talking about – much more so than the Pilgrims.

"So, on April eighth of 1630, off they went – 700 people this time, on eleven ships. The voyage was smooth and took two months.

"When they arrived, they stopped off first at the Salem settlement to visit with them. And a sorry settlement it was."

"What was wrong with them?" asked Carter.

"At that time, Salem was little more than a religious outpost originally settled by fishermen. There had been death and starvation there. The shelters were broken down. They were being attacked by Indians. And they were having trouble with their religion."

"Trouble with religion?" Carter echoed.

"Yes," I said. "After they had agreed to be taken over by the Massachusetts Bay Colony, some members of their group were doing things outside of the group's beliefs. And this resulted in one of the scariest chapters in this story."

"How scary?" asked Hannah, excitedly.

"Witches," I answered.

"Witches?" they shouted in unison, as their eyes got wide. "Really?" "Cool." "Wow!" "This is getting more interesting." "Tell us, tell us."

❧

"The Puritans were very strict Christians," I began, "and that included a belief in the Devil. They believed that the Devil had supernatural powers, and one of those powers they believed to be witchcraft.

"The roots of the problem were probably already there when the Massachusetts Bay Company ships arrived, but the real trouble began sixty years later, in 1692, when two cousins in Salem, girls of 9 and 11, began acting strange. They fell down, crawled around, screamed, threw things, complained of being poked with pins, and even interrupted sermons in church. The doctors couldn't find anything wrong with them. Soon after, other girls in the settlement began acting in the same ways.

"The girls claimed that they had been attacked by witches, and immediately accused three women. Ministers and other church members added to the accusations by saying that this was the work of the Devil, so everyone was quick to believe the claims."

"How could they believe them?" Hannah asked. "Didn't they know how ridiculous it was?"

"People were scared," I replied. "They kept looking over their shoulders, terrified that the next shadow or wisp of breeze would be the Devil attacking them.

"Egged on by the settlement's belief in their claims, the girls soon named others. In the end, over 60 people, mostly women, were accused. But there were a few men, too. One of them was your ancestor, Captain John Alden."

"John Alden?" Hannah asked.

"Not that John Alden. Remember, we're talking 60 years later. This was his son, Captain John Alden."

"Holy cow," Carter and Hannah said in unison.

"Was he a witch?" Carter asked.

"No," I replied. "He was a sea captain based in Boston. He stopped in Salem on his way home and was accused of witchcraft while there. He escaped and hid out in his parents' home in Duxbury until the whole thing was settled.

"Trials were held and the girls had to testify, but their stories didn't hold up. In the end, over 40 people were found innocent, including Captain Alden."

"Whew!" said Carter. "I'm glad. But what about the others?"

"Sadly, 19 people were found guilty and were hanged," I said.

"Hanged?" Carter shouted. "Couldn't they have just been put in jail?"

"People believed that as long as witches were alive, they could continue to cast spells, no matter where they were."

"I'm really getting the idea that life was a lot different then," said Hannah.

"That's right," I answered. "Modern science was just starting, and people often resorted to superstition to explain what they didn't understand.

"The most important things about this story are the power of false accusations, the danger of spreading rumors, and how easy it is to start mass hysteria. These kinds of things can get out of control fast and end up in ways no one intends."

⁓

"Now, back to 1630 and the Massachusetts Bay voyage.

"After visiting the Salem settlement, the Massachusetts Bay voyagers sailed across the harbor to what is now Boston to start their settlement. Actually, they set up several settlements, right off the bat. The main group set up in one area under the leadership of John Winthrop, but others of the group started to spread out right away.

"Unfortunately, all the groups started to get sick, and about 200 died by December of that first year."

"What did they die of?" asked Carter.

"Some had become sick from poor nutrition on the voyage – they had scurvy from a lack of vitamin C. They also suffered from diarrhea, exposure, and starvation after they arrived. The next summer, others could not stand the sweltering temperatures."

"They died from the heat?" continued Carter.

"Yes," I answered. "They discovered that the New England summers are much hotter than in England, and their clothing was too heavy."

"Why didn't they take off their clothes?" Carter asked.

"Carterrrr," Hannah replied, "can you see those Christians walking around in shorts?"

That brought a chuckle from everyone, including Carter.

"Meanwhile, more settlers and ships came," I continued. "New settlements sprouted all over New England. In fact, that's what happened everywhere along our Atlantic coastline — more people meant the need for more room, so settlers quickly moved west, north and south. Everyone except the Plymouth Pilgrims, unfortunately."

"What happened to them, Gomps?" asked Hannah.

"Well, the Plymouth Colony couldn't get out of survival mode," I replied. "Most settlers didn't share their Separatist beliefs, so there were few newcomers. Their land was not good for growing crops, and they got into boundary disputes with the Massachusetts Bay Company. After 20 years, Plymouth had only about 7,000 people and never expanded farther than about 30 miles from Plymouth harbor. By comparison, the Bay Colony had more than 20,000 people and extended over 100 miles west and north.

"To help Plymouth, the Bay Colony tried to include them in the region's affairs. In 1643, the Governor of the Bay Colony formed what was called The United Colonies of New England, or the New England Confederation, and they spelled out the rules in a kind of constitution called the Articles of Confederation.

"There were four member colonies: the Massachusetts Bay Colony, Plymouth Colony, Connecticut, and New Haven. Unfortunately, the other colonies were not strong enough to hold up their end of the bargain, and the arrangement never got off the ground."

"Wow, I didn't know that Connecticut existed that far back," said Hannah.

"Yes," I replied, "not long after the Plymouth and Bay Colony settlers had landed, some of them immediately split off and sailed up the Connecticut River and formed towns. And, at that time, New

Haven was its own colony, too. It wasn't until later that it was made a part of Connecticut.

"Unfortunately, things continued to go downhill for Plymouth, and in 1691 they agreed to be taken over by the Massachusetts Bay Colony."

"So, what happened to the Aldens?" Carter asked.

"They continued on with their day-to-day activities," I replied, "except now they were part of Massachusetts. In fact, the family served in Colony life in a number of ways in the coming years."

"Then what, Gomps?" asked Hannah.

"War with the Indians," I said.

"Really?" Carter asked, his eyes sparkling in delight.

"Yup," I said, "but you're going to have to wait until next time to hear about it. That chocolate cake is calling to me."

12

WAR WITH THE INDIANS

"Where were we, kids?"
This time Mandy had asked me to wait till after dessert to start. She didn't want the kids eating sweets so close to bedtime.

"War with the Indians," Carter said.

"I believe you're right, Carter," I said. "Settlers had been moving into areas of New England where Indians were already living. Some Indians made friends with the settlers and had peaceful relations with them. Others attacked the new settlements in the hopes of driving the colonists off."

"I thought you said most of the Indians had died or left by the time the Pilgrims got there," said Hannah.

"Very sharp, Hannah," I replied, "That was true in the area right around the Plymouth and Bay Colony settlements. In the inland areas and in Connecticut, though, the Indians hadn't suffered as much loss. So there were plenty of Indians around.

"Luckily for the Plymouth and Bay Colonies, one of the friendliest tribes was the Wampanoags, who lived in the area that is now Rhode Island. Remember them?"

"Wasn't Squanto from that tribe?" Hannah asked.

"He was living with them," I replied. "And, do you remember the chief's name?"

Hannah thought and shook her head. "Can't come up with it."

"Me either," said Carter.

"Massasoit," I said.

"Oh, yeah," both kids chimed.

"Why was it lucky that they were near Massa whatsisname?" asked Carter.

"Massasoit struck up a friendship with the colonists right away. Remember, he and his tribe helped the settlers to grow crops.

"But he had enemies, especially the Pequot tribe and their chief, Sassacus. They were in what is now Connecticut and western Massachusetts."

"Why were they enemies?" Carter asked.

"Good question," I answered. "Sassacus wanted to become the chief of a nation, like Powhatan in Virginia. So he often got into wars with the surrounding tribes to force them under his control. Massasoit was one of the chiefs who didn't want to be controlled by him.

"When the settlers spread out into the Connecticut River valley, they were moving right into Pequot territory and Sassacus felt threatened. He understood the situation immediately. He could attack the settlers and try to drive them out, but he knew they came from a larger group to the east — the colonies. Simply defeating these settlers would not solve his problem, since the colonies would just send more settlers.

"Instead, Sassacus formed a three-part plan. He attacked the settlers, but only to harass them and keep them on the defensive. At the same time, he tried to force the Mohegans, the Wampanoags, the Narragansetts, and other neighboring tribes to become his allies and attack the colonies together.

"Finally, he tried to get the French on his side. He knew that the English and French were always at odds with each other. The French had set up in what is now Canada to oppose the English settlements. So Sassacus sent some of his chiefs to Canada to persuade the French to join him."

"Why would the French do that?" Carter asked.

"He promised them all the territory in eastern New England," I answered.

"But you said he wanted to control more land, didn't you, Gomps?" Hannah asked. "Why would he give it to the French?"

"Aha, you've zeroed in on just the right question, Hannah," I exclaimed.

"He had no intention of giving them anything. He said that just to get their support."

"So what happened then?" asked Carter.

"The French saw through his plan and refused to help him. He had to fight with just the Indian allies that he could put together in New England, but those tribes were resisting his pressure to do it."

"Why?" continued Carter.

"They were more peace-loving," I replied, "and they figured out that whatever happened, an alliance with Sassacus would end up in his favor. These tribes were caught in the middle. They had the English settlers, with whom they at least had peace. And they had Sassacus and the Pequots, who planned on conquering them.

"Seeing that his offer of alliance with the other tribes wasn't working, Sassacus attacked them to try to force them to fight with him. So,
there was a War of the Indians before there was an Indian War. In the
end, the eastern tribes sided with the colonists."

"Gomps, this is getting complicated," said Hannah. "I had no
idea that there were so many arguments among the Indians. They
were more like us than I thought."

"Ha, ha," I chuckled. "You are right about that, my dear.

"By this time, both Governor Bradford of Plymouth and Governor Winthrop of Massachusetts could see what was happening.   The
fighting got worse and worse, until the colonists were forced to recognize that they were going to have to fight it out with the Pequots
or be killed off little by little. The problem was that they were not
prepared for a big fight."

"Why not?" asked Hannah.

"Well, to answer that, we have to look at the Plymouth Colony
and the Bay Colony separately. Remember that the Plymouth settlement was still small and made up mostly of devout Christians who
did not come to the New World to fight wars. And they had brought
very few guns with them."

"Didn't they have a general?" asked Carter.

"In a way," I answered. "They had Captain Myles Standish, but
he couldn't do much if the settlers wouldn't fight.

"The Bay Colony wasn't prepared for war either, but for different
reasons. They were spread out over most of southern New England
and they didn't have anyone experienced in leading them in battle."

"Why not?" asked Hannah. "Didn't you say that they planned better than the other colonies?"

"Yes, they planned the best," I replied, "but they thought they would be able to put together military forces quickly enough when they needed them. Remember that all the reports said that there were very few Indians in the area where they were going, which turned out to be true."

"What they didn't expect was how fast the first settlers would spread out into areas that did have active Indian tribes. And those settlers were devout Christians, too, and many avoided violence as much as the Pilgrims did.

"So, instead of hiring a military leader, they brought some men with just enough experience to handle the policing and defense of their towns. Kind of like sergeants, even though they called them captains, too."

"So who was in charge of everything?" asked Carter.

"Ahh, that's a great question, Carter," I replied. "They gave that job to Governor Winthrop."

"Did he have any military experience?" Carter continued. "You didn't say anything about that."

"He had none," I replied.

"None?" they both exclaimed, wide-eyed.

"None," I said. "His background was in religious ministry and in the courts, but not in the military."

"Why did they think he could be a captain, then?" Hannah asked.

"They assumed that any good leader could organize troops well enough for what they thought they would need," I replied. "And until the Pequots started to fight, that probably would have been good enough for quite a while."

"Well, obviously, that part of the plan didn't work," continued Hannah. "But that makes me think of something else."

"What's that?" I asked.

"OK, so the Bay Colony didn't have a military guy, but where was the army? You haven't said anything about them at all."

"Hannah, you have come up with one of the most important question so far," I answered.

"I have?" she said, with a mixed look of surprise and pride.

Carter looked at her enviously, wishing he had thought of it, too. "Yeah, where was the army?" he asked, hoping to get some credit.

"I thought of it first," Hannah insisted, turning to him with a challenging look.

"Relax, guys," I said, "The fact is that there were no soldiers, not in the Bay Colony, or in the Plymouth settlement, or in the Jamestown settlement, even."

"No army?" Carter shouted. "I thought you said that they had fights with the Indians!"

"They did, but not with soldiers," I said.

"Why not?" asked Carter. "Wouldn't they be better at fighting?"

"The colonists had grown up in England, where the king's army acted as the police department and patrolled among the people. Following the King's orders, his army ran roughshod over the people."

"Like how, Gomps?" asked Carter.

"Remember how the King collected taxes?" I asked.

"Yeah," Carter replied, "with the army."

"Right," I said, "and were the people happy about that?"

"I don't think so," Hannah replied.

"Right," I said. "The army had to follow orders, even if it meant hurting people. So the English people didn't like having soldiers living among them and neither did the colonists.

"And there was another reason that the colonists didn't want soldiers. The settlers didn't want an army that could be used to take away their freedom. They were afraid that someone could take over their colonies by force with a professional army."

"But wouldn't the army come from the people?" Carter asked.

"Even then, you would have soldiers who were ordered to fight," I replied. "If they were commanded to do something that the people didn't want, they would still have to do it."

"OK, so if they didn't have an army, how did they fight?" Carter continued.

"Militia," I replied. "The men in each settlement fought. They were expected to drop what they were doing, whether it was farming, or blacksmithing, or carpentry, or whatever their regular job was, grab their guns and gather together to fight."

"I thought you said they were Christians and didn't want to fight," said Hannah.

"I did say that, Hannah," I responded, "but whether they wanted to fight or not, they couldn't just let the Indians kill them. It was defend yourself and your family or die."

"When the Indians won, did they kill the settlers' families?" Hannah persisted.

"Sometimes," I replied, "but sometimes the Indians would take the women and children and make them slaves."

"Really?" asked Hannah, wide-eyed again.

"Really," I said. "So, there was a lot at stake for the settlers to defend."

"What a horrible thing," said Hannah. "I see what you were saying about slavery before. It wasn't just Africans."

"No, it wasn't," I continued, "but it was just as bad."

"Gomps, you said that this was an important question," interrupted Carter. "Why is that?"

"Because we fought with militias right into the Revolutionary War," I said. "Average citizens had to be able to fight whenever it was necessary. They called it 'taking up arms,' and that was written right into our Constitution.

"Now, getting back to the Bay Colony, you can see what a problem they had fighting an Indian nation. They needed a big military force themselves, but the only one to organize it was the Governor, and he didn't know how to do it.

"They soon realized that they needed someone to help them. And this is where another one of your ancestors came in."

"Really?" they exclaimed.

"That's right." I replied. "His name was Captain John Underhill."

"Wasn't Underhill Gramma Betty's name?" asked Hannah.

"Yes, it was," I answered. "So both of you and I are his direct descendants, as are your mom and uncle Gregor."

"Wow!" they both said.

"What did he do?" asked Carter.

"He organized the Bay Colony militias and led them in fighting the Pequots," I answered.

"I thought you said that the Bay Colony didn't have anyone like that," said Hannah, looking confused.

"They didn't," I replied. "Captain Underhill came from Long Island in the New York Colony."

"What's the New York Colony, Gomps?" Carter asked.

"Well," I answered, "I haven't gotten to that part of the story yet, but there were other settlers who came over after the Bay Colony voyage and they settled in what is now New York. Captain Underhill came with them, just like John Smith did with Jamestown and Myles Standish did with Plymouth. I'll tell you more about that in a little while."

"OK," Carter said. "So how did Captain Underhill get to the Bay Colony?"

"Word had gotten to the Bay Colony that Captain Underhill was an experienced military man and a fierce Indian fighter, so they paid him to organize their forces and lead them in battle."

"Cool," said Carter. "So we're related to a big general?"

"Well, don't be so quick to take pride in him," I said. "Let me tell you more and you can decide whether he was cool."

I had the kids' attention.

"As I said, Captain Underhill was a fierce Indian fighter. Some people believe that he ordered his troops to kill Indians in brutal ways."

"How?" asked Carter.

"Carter, maybe we shouldn't hear this," cautioned Hannah. "I don't like the sound of Gomps' voice."

"Well, Hannah," I replied, "you might as well know now."

"OK," she said.

"There were reports that he ordered his troops to hack some Indians to death and to set fire to their camps," I said.

"Oh, no," said Hannah, shivering.

"I'm afraid so," I said. "Now, on Captain Underhill's side of the story, this was a kill or be killed situation. He wrote in his journal that his goal was to get the Indians to stop attacking. He felt that he had to make a show of force to do it. He wanted to make them afraid of attacking the settlers.

"But it has also been reported that he didn't like Indians. He apparently thought of them as savages.

"Whatever you may think of him now, Captain Underhill organized the Bay Colony militias well and stood up to the Pequots. In the end, they backed off, and the settlers were able to live with them in a more peaceful way.

"So, there you have your ancestor, Captain John Underhill," I said. "What do you think?"

"Well, I guess he helped save the settlers," Carter concluded.

"Yes, but did he have to do it that way?" Hannah asked. "It's not easy, I guess, if you yourself might be killed."

"No, it's not easy," I offered, "but that's how it happened."

"Does that mean we're in an important family?" asked Carter.

"Yes and no," I answered. "John Alden and Captain John Underhill played their parts in the founding and growth of our country, but I told about them mostly as an example of how many people played a part in our story.

"Just about every person can find a family member who has played their part in our history, some early, like ours, and some more recently. We can all be proud when our family members did good things, but we're no more important than others because of it. And even if our ancestors did great things, we can't take any credit for them at all. It's up to us to do great things of our own.

"So the Pequot War was over, and the settlers were able to continue with their lives in relative peace. Next, we'll see what was happening in other parts of the New World."

"You mean like New York?" asked Hannah.

"Yup," I answered. "And it all starts with the story of how the Indians fooled the Dutch."

"How'd they do that, Gomps?" Carter asked.

"You're going to have to wait until next time," I said.

13

HOW THE NEW YORK INDIANS FOOLED THE DUTCH

Next time turned out to be two weeks later, after I got back from some out-of-town business. As before, we finished dessert before I started.

"Last time, we got to the end of the Pequot War and the coming of peace in New England," I said. "New York is next.

"Believe it or not, New York started out as a Dutch settlement. Then it was English, and then Dutch again, before becoming English for good — with a little Swedish thrown in."

"I smell war," Carter said. Hannah ignored him this time.

"Sorry to disappoint you, Carter," I said. "No war this time, but lots of warships and power struggles."

"I'll take it," he said.

"By now everything was happening fast," I continued. "Word about Jamestown, Plymouth, and the Bay Colony spread like wildfire from one European country to the next, and kings, nobility, investors, and settlers all wanted to be a part of it.

"One of the first to set up a settlement was the Dutch. In 1609 an English explorer by the name of Henry Hudson had been searching for a passage to Asia for a Dutch trading company. He sailed his ship into what is New York harbor and from there up the river that now bears his name – the Hudson.

"Hudson hadn't found the passage, so he sailed back to tell his company that he *had* found an excellent harbor and a major river. On the way he stopped in England – and got arrested for sailing under a rival nation's flag. Some historians think he might have been a spy for England the whole time, though."

"Gomps," said Carter, "I'm sorry I ever said history was boring."

"Anyway," I went on, "the Dutch members of his crew sailed his ship to the Netherlands and told their company what they had found. The company quickly sent other ships.

"The first voyage they sent was led by Captain Adriaen Block, who set up a settlement in what is now New York City. They called the colony New Netherland and the settlement New Amsterdam, after their country and its largest city - Amsterdam."

"Were there Indians?" Carter asked.

"There you go again, Carter, always looking for wars." Hannah chided.

"Am not!"

"Are so!"

"Hey, you two, knock it off." I interrupted. "Do you want to hear about this or not?"

"Yeah!" Carter said.

"Sure," said Hannah, sounding a bit less enthusiastic.

"OK," I said. "There were Indians when Captain Block arrived, but these Indians were a different story from the ones in New England."

"How so?" Hannah asked.

"These were Indians in a completely different nation – the Iroquois," I replied. "The Iroquois had tribes all over what is now New York, New Jersey and up into Canada. The Iroquois tribes in the New Amsterdam area were the Algonquins, the Lenape, and the Mohawks.

"By the time Block arrived, these tribes had already had plenty of contact with fishermen and fur traders from England and France. In fact, they traded fur pelts to them."

"Did they have wars with the Dutch?" Carter asked.

"There you go again," sighed Hannah.

"Hannah, actually that was a good question," I said. "There were armed squabbles that we call skirmishes just like there were in New England, but the Iroquois tribes figured they would do better by trading with the Dutch than fighting with them. It wasn't until later that they were involved in war, and it wasn't with the Dutch."

"Who was it with?" asked Carter.

"You're going to have to wait on that one," I answered. "But the answer probably won't be a big surprise.

"So, back to New Netherland. In 1621 the Dutch formed a new company, the Dutch West India Company, to develop its new territory. As soon as they formed the colony, the Dutch established the Dutch Reformed Church as the official religion. They also invited people from all countries to settle there.

"That opened the floodgates, as Germans, French, Belgians, Danes, Swedes, and even some English came, in addition to more Dutch. And, as in New England, they fanned out to all parts of New Netherland to seek their fortunes. They hunted and fished, set up trading posts, farmed where they could, started shops and small businesses, and generally set about creating new lives for themselves.

"Unfortunately, things happened so fast that the Dutch couldn't control it all. People from other countries were living according to their religious principles, not Dutch Reformed. And they followed their own laws and were sending their goods and profits to their home countries and not to the Dutch.

"The Dutch tried to get control by sending a new governor – Peter Stuyvesant."

"I've heard that name before," Hannah interrupted. "Wait, isn't he the one that bought New York City from the Indians for $24.00?" she asked.

"It sounds like you've been getting a little bit of history in school, yes?" I asked.

"Yeah, I think that's where I heard it," she replied.

"Well," I said, "that's probably close enough, but a few of the details are a little different. First, it was the governor before Stuyvesant – Peter Minuit – who made a deal for Manhattan. And, second, it was probably a trade of goods, like blankets and stuff, rather than cash. But that was about the value of the deal."

"$24.00," Hannah exclaimed. "That's nothing. He gypped the Indians."

"That's one way to look at it," I replied, "but you might say that the Indians fooled the Dutch.

"By that time, the settlers were living among the Indian camps. The settlers and Indians were trading with one another, and aside from occasional disagreements, the Indians considered the settlers a permanent part of the neighborhood.

"So, when Governor Minuit traded with them for some land, he gave them some good stuff and they gave up nothing, as they saw it. In their way of life no one owned the land, anyway. They continued to go about their business, ignoring the Governor and his talk of ownership."

Both kids laughed. "I like that idea better," observed Hannah. "Minuit outsmarted himself."

"Now, back to Governor Stuyvesant," I said. "He was sent in 1647 to replace Minuit so that he could get control of the situation and get the profits flowing back to the Dutch West India Company. But by this time, things were too far gone. English settlers from Connecticut had spread into New Netherland, and the colony's southern border was being crossed by . . . are you ready for this? . . . the Swedish!"

"The Swedish?" they exclaimed. "How did the Swedish get here?"

"Believe it or not, they sent a voyage to what is now Delaware and claimed it as a Swedish colony. Then they tried to move north into New Netherland."

"Holy cow," said Carter. "It's hard to keep track of everything."

"That it is," I replied. "Once people heard about the New World and what could be done there, they came from everywhere to get in on it.

"In 1650, Stuyvesant tried to patch things up by entering into a treaty with the Connecticut English. In that treaty, Stuyvesant gave up the Dutch claim to land in the Connecticut region in return for the English acceptance of the new borders. But it didn't work. When the Dutch West India Company heard about the treaty, they refused to approve it.

"In 1664, seeing that the Dutch settlement had been weakened, the King of England sent a fleet of warships commanded by his younger brother, the Duke of York, into New Amsterdam harbor, and they took over the colony. Stuyvesant didn't have the military to stop them, so he left and took his Dutch government with him.

"Six years later, the Dutch sent their own fleet back and retook it, but they still couldn't hold onto it, and in 1674 they left it to the English for good."

"Were there any battles?" Carter asked.

"There he goes again," Hannah said to no one in particular.

"Well, were there?" Carter repeated, ignoring her.

"No, there weren't, Carter," I replied. "Each time, the fleets showed up without warning and the other side was caught flatfooted."

"How come the Dutch couldn't hold it when they came back, then?" Carter persisted.

"I don't think they ever had a good idea of what it took to run the place," I said. "Neither the Dutch government nor the Dutch West India Company seemed to work hard enough at it."

"Then, why did they go there in the first place?" Hannah asked.

"I don't know for sure," I replied. "Maybe they thought that they could interfere with what England was doing in New England and Virginia. I don't think they understood how big and far away America was and how much manpower, equipment and supplies would be needed over such a long time. In the end, they just gave up."

"Huh," Carter concluded.

"Can we go ahead now?" asked Hannah, clearly impatient with Carter's interest in all things military.

"Sure," I said.

"The first thing the English did when they took over New Netherland was to change the name. Since the Duke of York was the one who led the fleet that took it over, the King named the colony after him – New York."

"And the name stuck," proclaimed Carter.

"It certainly did," I said, among general laughter.

"From that point on, the New York colony continued to operate pretty much the same way it had been. People of all countries continued to settle there. The Dutch Reformed Church was eliminated as the established church, and it was replaced by the Church of England."

"What made New York get so big?" Hannah asked.

"Two main reasons," I answered. "The first was its location. New York City was a great spot for a seaport. The mouth of the Hudson River was wide and deep, so ships of all sizes could sail in and dock there. Also, goods could be easily transported to and from the port on the Hudson and other rivers.

"The second reason was the people who settled there. They brought lots of good ideas with them and the will to work hard."

"Cool," said Hannah.

"So, New York is now off and running," I said. "Other colonies were settled quickly after that. Next time, I'll tell you about a drowning at sea, the hundred years' lawsuit, and more colonies.

"Now, I understand there's still some homework to be done before bed. So, off you go. But give me a hug first, because I'll be leaving before you finish."

"Bye, Gomps," said Hannah.

"Night, Gomps," said Carter. And they both wrapped me in a hug.

14

A DROWNING AT SEA AND THE HUNDRED YEARS' LAWSUIT

"It's been a while, hasn't it?" I said as we were finishing dessert.

Because of business trips I had to make, the kids and I hadn't had story time for three weeks.

"Yeah, we missed you!" said Hannah, as Carter nodded.

"Aw, I'll bet you say that to all your grandfathers," I said. "But it's nice to hear just the same."

I started out with a quick review.

"Last time, we talked about how New York was colonized. If you remember, the Dutch were there first . . ."

"Yeah, and the Indians outsmarted the Governor!" Carter blurted.

"So you do remember," I replied.

"The Dutch invited people from everywhere to settle there and got into trouble trying to run a place with so many different ways of life."

"Why was it so hard?" Hannah asked.

"Well, let's take laws, for example," I replied. "Suppose you had grown up in a place where something was legal and you moved to a place where it was illegal. You were so used to it being legal that you might forget and do things the old way. Or, you might ignore the new law and do it your way anyway."

"I get it," she nodded.

"So New Netherland was hard for the Dutch to run," I continued. "Then the English took over and started doing things their way."

"Did they kick out all those other people?" Carter asked.

"No, but by now they had some experience with how colonies worked and could handle it better," I replied. "So New York was now up and running.

"By this time, people in England knew that the settlements in the New World were starting to be successful. This included the English nobility, and some of them wanted in on the action. One of them was Lord Baltimore."

"Like Baltimore, Maryland?" Hannah asked.

"Like Baltimore, Maryland," I answered. "He and his family, the Calverts, were Roman Catholics. They had been trying to worship as Catholics in England, despite the King's pressure on them to change to the Church of England. They wanted to set up a place where Catholics and other Christians could worship in peace.

"In 1632, Lord Baltimore went to the King and asked for a Charter for an area in the New World, south of New York. The King gave it to him, and Baltimore organized his own operation.

"Baltimore's plan was a little different than the others. He stressed profits and, within limits, religious freedom. The land turned out to be good for farming, so he set up a system that was more like how Europe worked. There were landowners who made their own rules, and there were workers who lived and worked on each owner's land. Based on this plan, some landowners became reasonably successful.

"On the religious side, Lord Baltimore granted religious freedom, but only to Christians. In his Toleration Acts, he said that people of any other faith were not welcome, and if anyone tried to worship in another faith, they would be run out or put to death."

"Death?" they both exclaimed. "Where's the freedom in that?"

"I'm with you," I replied. "The Maryland colony survived, but it didn't prosper. Why do you think that is?"

"If you weren't a Christian, why go there?" said Carter.

"Yeah, and if he thought that way about religion, you might wonder what else he would do," added Hannah.

"I think you're both right," I agreed. "Lord Baltimore couldn't change from the Old World ways, and those ways didn't work very well anymore. The poverty in England and Europe proved that. At the same time, the New World showed what could be done if you let people work for their own good."

"So much for Maryland," I said, "next up is Delaware."

"Delaware?" asked Hannah. "They were a colony?"

"They sure were," I answered. "Not many people know it, but Delaware was one of the original colonies."

"I didn't know that," Hannah replied. "Where was it, exactly?"

"Well, today you know Delaware as the small state on the shore of the Atlantic Ocean, east of Maryland and south of New Jersey," I said. "But it didn't start out that way. Delaware probably went through more changes than any other colony."

"What kinds of changes, Gomps?" Carter asked.

"Settlers, ownership, boundaries, just about everything changed, as you'll see. It started out as a part of the Virginia Colony, at least as the English saw it. At the same time, Henry Hudson had explored it and claimed it for the Dutch."

"Here we go again," said Hannah.

"That's right," I replied.

"So England and the Dutch both thought they owned it?" Carter asked.

"That's right," I replied.

"Cool," Carter continued. "Did they fight for it?"

"Not exactly," I said. "Still another country claimed it at the same time. Do you remember Peter Minuit?"

"Wasn't he the one who got fooled by the Indians in New York?" Carter offered.

"New Netherland, at the time. That's the guy," I said. "Minuit had friends who were Swedish royalty. After he was replaced as Governor of New Netherland, he went to Sweden and talked them into claiming Delaware as theirs, with him as Governor."

"Then what?" Hannah asked.

"Peter Minuit drowned," I answered.

"Drowned? Oh, no," Hannah cried. "What happened?"

"Right after he set things up in Delaware, he sailed back to Sweden to bring more settlers and supplies," I said, "and his ship ran into a hurricane and he drowned."

"Holy cow," Carter said. "It's just one thing after another."

"I'll say," said Hannah.

"Back to Delaware," I said. "In spite of Peter Minuit's death, more Swedes came, along with Finnish people and Germans. They spread north from Delaware into New Netherland.

"Now, the Dutch didn't like this one bit. So the Swedes and Dutch had a series of skirmishes over it. Finally, Peter Stuyvesant had enough of the fighting and led a big military force down there and threw out the Swedes, once and for all."

"So Delaware ended up Dutch, then?" Carter asked.

"Not for long," I laughed.

"There's more?" Carter asked.

"Plenty," I said. "Remember that the Duke of York sailed into New Amsterdam and took New Netherland for the English?"

"Yeah," said Carter. "Ta-da — New York!"

"Right," I said. "Well, what do you think he did in Delaware?"

"Sent in the fleet!" shouted Carter.

"Yup," I said. "He sent the fleet into the Delaware River and the Dutch gave up Delaware, too. But the Delaware story still wasn't over."

"You're kidding," said Hannah.

"I'm not kidding," I said. "Remember Lord Baltimore, the Governor of Maryland?"

"Yeah," they both said, hesitantly.

"When Lord Baltimore saw that the Duke of York had claimed Delaware for himself, he said something like, 'Hey, wait a minute, my claim goes all the way to the Atlantic Ocean. Delaware is mine.'

"The Duke said something like, 'Not so fast. Where were you when the Dutch had it? Did you conquer them?'

"Lord Baltimore's answer? 'Doesn't matter. The King gave that land to me.'

"The Duke's position was, 'Well, I'm not giving it up.'

"So what do you think Lord Baltimore did?" I asked.

"Went to war?" asked Hannah.

"Nope," I replied. "He just gave up and let the Duke have it.

"But that's still not the end of it."

"There's more?" said Hannah.

"By this time," I continued, "an Englishman by the name of William Penn had gotten a grant from the King for land that included Delaware."

"Wait a minute, Gomps," Hannah said. "I thought the King gave it to the Duke. Did he give it to two different people?"

"Three, in fact," I replied. "Don't forget Baltimore's claim."

"What a mess," she exclaimed.

"It sure was," I said. "So what did the Duke say this time?"

"'I'm not giving it up?'" guessed Hannah.

"That's right," I said. "The Duke still felt he had the best claim to it, and he still occupied it. So what do you think William Penn did?"

"Did he go to war?" asked Hannah again.

"Nope," I said. "William Penn sued the Duke of York!"

"SUED HIM?" they both yelled.

"Yup," I said. "Took him to court. And guess what?"

"What?" they said in disbelief.

"Lord Baltimore heard about it and joined in the lawsuit himself," I answered.

They both began to laugh uproariously.

When they calmed down, Carter asked, "Who won?"

"None of them won. They finally agreed to cut up the area and give a piece to each one, but only after almost 100 years in court."

"A HUNDRED YEARS?" they yelled. "They were in court a hundred years?"

"They sure were," I replied. "Of course, the Duke, William Penn, and Lord Baltimore were all dead by then, but their children and grandchildren carried on the lawsuit. It was finally settled in 1776."

"1776?" asked Hannah. "Wasn't that the year of the Declaration of Independence?"

"That's right, Hannah," I said, "good for you. Delaware didn't officially become its own colony until the year we went to war with England for our independence."

"Holy cow," Carter murmured.

"I'm tired just hearing about it," Hannah said.

"Me, too," said Carter.

"I don't blame you," I said. "But that's it for Delaware. Which one should I talk about next?"

"Let's do our state, Connecticut," Carter asked.

"Good idea," I replied, "but it will have to be next time. This has been enough for tonight."

15

THE KING STARTS
RAKING IT IN

We met again the next week and I started right off.

"Last time, I mentioned Connecticut, but I didn't say how it was formed, did I?"

"Come to think of it, you didn't, Gomps," said Hannah.

"OK, then," I said. "Remember that the area that is now Connecticut was settled by people who spread out from Plymouth and the Massachusetts Bay Colony.

"In fact, there were two centers of settlement at the time — Hartford and New Haven. And for a short time each was a separate colony. But by 1636, they decided that there was strength in numbers, so they merged into one group, and Connecticut became one colony.

"There are really only two things that made Connecticut stand out at this time — a written constitution and tobacco. Connecticut is called The Constitution State. Can you guess why?"

"Because they had a constitution?" Carter blurted.

"That's right," I said. "But what was special about their constitution?"

"Were they the first?" Hannah asked.

"Exactly right!" I exclaimed. "Connecticut was the first colony to have a written constitution. They did it in 1639, just three years after the colony was formed. They called it 'The Fundamental Orders.' Then other colonies heard about it and wrote their own in the years that followed.

"Now, on to the other thing that Connecticut was known for: tobacco."

"Wasn't it grown in the south?" Hannah asked.

"Yes," I replied, "but they could grow it in Connecticut, too. The Connecticut River has a flat area on either side that has a sandy kind of soil. It turns out that this soil is very much like the soil in the south. So they tried growing tobacco there, and it worked."

"Why is that important?" Hannah asked.

"Good question," I said. "Remember that tobacco was in great demand in England and Europe at the time?"

"Oh, yeah," they both replied.

"Well, Connecticut tobacco turned out to be very good and got high prices in the Old World. That meant that tobacco growers in Connecticut made good profits, and it helped the colony to become prosperous."

"Cool," said Carter. "Anything else about Connecticut?"

"Not really," I replied. "It was more of a stopping-off place for people going between Boston and New York. In fact, that's still true to this day."

"Who's next, Gomps?" Hannah asked.

"How about New Jersey?" I answered.

"Sounds good," said Hannah.

"Great," I said. "First, let's talk about where it is. It's on the Atlantic Ocean, sandwiched between New York to the north, Pennsylvania to the west, and Delaware and Maryland to the south. So it's pretty small.

"New Jersey started out as part of Dutch New Netherland, and as we know, the Duke of York took that over in 1664.

"Like the Dutch, the Duke of York had trouble controlling all of the different groups, and he got tired of it after a while. But just then, his prayers were answered."

"How?" Carter asked.

"Along came two other members of English nobility, Lord Berkeley and Lord Carteret. They had been hearing about all of the money being made in the New World. So they asked the Duke for some of his land, and he gave them his rights to New Jersey.

"Unfortunately, Berkeley and Carteret couldn't get along with all those groups any better than the Duke could. As time went on, Berkeley and Carteret lost more and more control over the whole area until 1702, when they gave up and turned New Jersey back to the King. From then on it was a colony owned and operated by the King."

"What happened to Berkeley and Carteret?" Carter asked.

"They lost their whole investment in the operation," I answered.

"Everything?"

"Everything," I confirmed. "That's the chance you take as an entrepreneur. Sometimes you can't make the venture work and you lose money."

"Did the King do any better than they did?" asked Hannah.

"Yes, he did," I replied. "But he had much more going for him."

"Like what?"

"Well, let's take the bickering among all the groups that were there. How do you think he got them to stop?"

"He sent in the army!" Carter yelled. "Yes, yes, yes," he shouted as he danced around the room, pumping his arms. "I knew it!"

"Yes, you did, Carter," I said. "The King had the advantage of being able to send his troops into the colony to keep order and to enforce his commands. What other advantage did he have?"

Both were quiet, not coming up with any other ideas.

"OK," I said. "Did the King have expenses in operating the colony?"

"Oh, yes," said Hannah. "He had to pay the army and he had to pay for the ships to send them."

"Right," I said.

"Oh," said Hannah, as the answer suddenly occurred to her. "Taxes."

"Bingo," I said. "Just as in England, the King had expenses, and as the expenses went up, he planned to collect taxes to pay for them, except in this case, he was going to tax the colonies. And, if they didn't pay . . .?"

"The army," shouted Carter.

"Now you've got it," I said. "But there's more. Some of the settlers in New Jersey and in other colonies went into business making things."

"Like what?" Carter asked.

"Like nails, cloth, lumber, things like that," I replied. "And they found out that they could sell some of these things back in England and in Europe. So they shipped them back across the Atlantic Ocean for sale there."

"Hmmm," said Carter as he rubbed his chin again, knowingly.

"Do you remember what we called it when things were sold back and forth from one country to another?" I asked.

Both kids looked puzzled.

"That's a tough one," I continued. "We talked about it once at the beginning, but we haven't mentioned it since. The answer is 'trade.'"

"Oh, yeah," they said together.

"Now, here's where more trouble started brewing," I said. "It had to do with the kinds of things the colonists were selling in England. Were some of those things already being made by people in England?"

"Well, yeah," ventured Hannah, "Nails and cloth? Must have been."

"Then why would people in the Old World buy stuff from the New World, if it was already being made in England?" I asked.

"Must have been cheaper," she replied.

"Even with the added cost of shipping?" I continued.

"I guess," she concluded.

"That's right, even with the cost of shipping," I said. "So, how was business for the people in England?"

"Not so good," Hannah answered.

"Right again," I said. "They weren't selling as much of their stuff, and, therefore, their profits went . . .?"

"Down!" shouted Carter.

"Exactly right," I said. "If you were one of them and you saw that the King was putting money into a venture that was hurting your business, what would you do?"

"Stop making it?" said Carter, hesitantly.

"Some did, I guess. What else?"

"Go to the King?" Hannah asked, hesitantly.

"Go to the King," I confirmed.

"But, Gomps, wouldn't the King just kill them or something?" she continued.

"Well, it depends how they did it," I said. "They knew what the King needed."

"Money," said Carter.

"That's right," I continued. "And they knew how to ask. They said something like, 'We understand if the colonists want to make these things and sell them, but at least make it fair. Isn't there something you could do to raise the price equal to ours?'

"The King, being no dummy and having smart advisers, said something like, 'I have an idea. We'll put a tax on it, but we won't call it a tax, we'll call it a tariff.' And, of course, the English manufacturers smiled to themselves as they bowed and thanked him for his wisdom and quick action."

"Tariffs," said Carter. "Didn't you say something about that at the beginning, Gomps?"

"Yes, I did, Carter. But only in general. Good thinking there. I said that tariffs are a kind of . . .?"

"Tax," Carter answered proudly.

"And, tax is added onto . . . ?"

"The price," he replied.

"So, what happened to the prices of the stuff from the New World?" I asked.

"Went up," they both concluded.

"Did the English businessmen get off the King's back?" I asked.

"Sure," said Hannah. "Their prices would be no higher than the New World prices."

"Right," I replied.

"And, would the King have had more money to spend?" I asked.

"Yes," they both concluded again.

"Need I say more?" I asked.

"Nope," they both said.

"So there you have the story of how New Jersey got started," I continued. "And that will do it for tonight. Next time, we'll talk about slavery and the War of Jenkins' Ear."

"The War of Jenkins' Ear?" they shouted, laughing. "Really?"

"Really," I said. "In the meantime, you've got some homework to do, I'm sure, and then it's off to bed."

16

THE SOUTHERN COLONIES AND THE WAR OF JENKINS' EAR

The following Wednesday I got back into town early enough for dinner with the kids. We picked up right where we left off.

"Last time, we finished with New Jersey," I said. "Next, let's go to North and South Carolina. These colonies are the area south of Virginia, from the Atlantic Ocean across the first mountain range to the west. They have rich soil, rolling hills, and warm weather.

"The first settlers in the Carolinas were actually the Spanish. They had spread north from Florida, but the Indians drove them out.

"The first English activity in the area was in 1584, when Sir Walter Raleigh got a Charter to settle it. But after the Roanoke Island settlement failed, he more or less gave up on it.

"Then, in 1663, the King granted a second Charter for the area. Most of the first inhabitants were people who spread south from Virginia - English, Scotch-Irish, Quakers, and Germans. The rest came over from the English countryside.

"At the beginning, these settlers were mostly subsistence farmers."

"What's a sub —" Carter started over. "A sub-sis-tence farmer?" he asked.

"A subsistence farmer is someone who grows crops and livestock just to live on," I answered. "They and their families stay out in the countryside and basically live on their own. They produce little, if anything, for profit."

"Got it," said Carter.

"Sounds like kind of a boring life," Hannah remarked.

"It was hard," I said. "Mostly work all day, every day, and go to bed early."

"What about religion?" Hannah asked. "Were there churches they could go to?"

"Not usually," I said. "Most of the areas were not settled enough to have them. Instead, there were traveling ministers who would go from place to place and preach."

"Did they have slaves like in Virginia?" Hannah continued.

"There weren't many in the early days of Carolina," I answered. "The farms were just too small to need them. On larger farms, there may have been indentured servants from England or Indian slaves or African slaves, but very few.

"Here's something interesting about Carolina slaves: in the Carolina Charter, they were allowed to earn their freedom like indentured servants did. And, once they did, they could intermarry with whites, and their children were born free.

"Now, those were the early days of Carolina. Things changed as the tobacco farmers came in from Virginia. They discovered that the soil was just as good for tobacco as it was in Virginia.

And, of course, they needed lots of workers for the fields, and that meant . . .?"

"Slaves," they both replied.

"That's right," I said. "So the original rules for slaves in Carolina got thrown out, and the rules from Virginia were put in. Carolina slaves were now property and could no longer earn their freedom."

"Ugh," said Hannah.

"Yeah," said Carter.

❧

"In the meantime, things had been happening differently in the southern part of Carolina. English settlers were coming from the Caribbean island of Barbados, and, of all things, some French were coming from France."

"French?" asked Carter. "What were they doing here?"

"Yes, it seems odd, doesn't it?" I answered.

"France was a country dominated by the Roman Catholic Church, but not all French worshipped that way. Some were Protestants. The French Protestants were called Huguenots. And the Roman Catholics drove them out of France, so they sailed to the New World, and some of them settled in the southern part of Carolina.

"The Huguenots, too, wanted freedom of religion, so the area became known for that. Pretty soon people of other religions heard about it and settled there. There were Baptists and Quakers and even Jews."

"Did they grow tobacco there, like in Virginia and northern Carolina?" Hannah asked.

"That's a great question," I said. "They didn't. Not that they didn't try, but they found that the soil wasn't good for tobacco.

"What they did find, though, was that rice and indigo grew very well."

"Indigo?" Carter asked. "What's that?"

"Indigo is a plant that you could get dye from," I replied. "They would press the plants and a blue liquid would be squeezed out. Then they would sell the liquid to weavers to dye their cloth.

"So even though they weren't growing tobacco, they still had big farms. And that meant more slaves."

"I knew it," Hannah groaned.

"In fact, an excellent harbor there on the Atlantic Ocean became a main port for slave ships. It was called Charleston, and it's still one of the biggest ports in the South today.

"But the Africans were not the first people to be used as slaves in this area. Local Indians were captured and turned into slaves."

"I didn't know that," said Hannah.

"Not many do," I replied. "There were somewhere between 25,000 and 50,000 Indian slaves at the beginning."

"Wow, that's a lot!" exclaimed Hannah. "How were they captured?"

"Mostly by other tribes," I replied. "One tribe would conquer another and take the survivors as slaves. The farmers would then trade tools and cloth for the slaves. But after a while the tribes joined forces, attacked the farmers, and took back all their tribesmen. From then on, the surviving farmers used only African slaves."

"Did the northern colonies have slaves, too?" Carter asked.

"Yes, they did," I answered, "although nowhere near as many as in the South. Since there weren't huge plantations in the North, slaves were mostly used for household jobs, and to some extent in factories."

"So slaves were used all over," Hannah concluded.

"Yes, by those people who could afford them and saw nothing wrong with using them," I replied.

"What do you mean saw nothing wrong with using them, Gomps?" Carter asked. "I thought you said everybody had slaves."

"Well, there were people, mostly in the North, who believed, as we do, that slavery was wrong and against their religious principles. They not only didn't use them, but some spoke out against slavery and a few even tried to hide escaped slaves. They wanted slavery abolished.

"While all this was going on, there were constant disputes over who owned what territory within Carolina. Finally, in 1710, the King divided Carolina into North Carolina and South Carolina. Then, two years later, North Carolina was made an official English colony, and in 1729 South Carolina was, too."

❧

"Now let's look south of the Carolinas to Georgia. Georgia got started a little bit differently.

"About 1730, James Oglethorpe, a rich member of the English Parliament, saw the New World as a chance to try a new way of dealing with the poor and with all the people in debtors' prison. He went to the King and . . ."

"Whoa, Gomps!" Carter interrupted. "What's debtors' prison?"

"Oh, I guess I haven't explained that yet, have I," I replied. "If you borrow money, you are a debtor – you are in debt to the one who loaned you the money. In England, if you couldn't pay it back, you could be put in a prison – debtors' prison."

"Put in prison because you owed money?" Hannah exclaimed. "That's crazy!"

"How so?" I asked.

"Prison is for criminals. How is owing money a crime?"

"I agree, but that's what their law was."

"And besides," she continued. "How could they pay it back if they were in prison? That makes no sense."

"No, it doesn't," I said. "And there were a lot of debtors in prison. The English economy wasn't very good then, and there were many poor people who had to borrow money to live, but couldn't pay it back.

"That's where Oglethorpe came in. He saw how crazy it was to put debtors in prison, and he also saw that the debtors' prisons were overflowing. He knew that these people were not criminals, but he didn't have enough clout with the King to get him to change the law.

"So, Oglethorpe went to the King with a different idea. He would start a new colony as a place where the poor and those in debtors' prison could go for a fresh start. And the King agreed.

"In 1732, the King gave Oglethorpe and his group a Charter for a colony in Georgia. Their motto was, 'Not for ourselves, but for others.' And the Charter included a provision for religious freedom as well.

"After Oglethorpe got things set up, the poor and the debtors were sent over. Soon other people heard about the religious freedom being offered there, and they came, too. Before long, Huguenots, Scotch-Irish, Moravians, Jews, and people of all faiths flooded in."

"Did they have slaves, too?" asked Carter.

"What a great question, Carter," I replied. "Oglethorpe's idea really was different, because they adopted a policy that said no slavery."

"Yay!" they both exclaimed.

"Don't celebrate too soon," I said. "Farmers from Carolina began settling there, and they insisted on having slaves for their plantations. Seventeen years later, in 1749, the Colony reversed the policy, and slavery was allowed."

"Boo," the children called.

"In the meantime, in 1742, the Spanish attacked, trying to catch Oglethorpe off guard. This began a short war that was called The War of Jenkins' Ear."

Both kids laughed uncontrollably. "You were serious about that last week?" Hannah finally asked when she had gotten control of herself.

♧

"The War of Jenkins' Ear," I repeated. And they laughed some more.

"It began when the Spanish started attacking British merchant ships and stealing their cargo."

"What's a merchant ship, Gomps?" Hannah asked.

"A merchant ship is a ship that just carries cargo for trade and isn't in war," I answered. "By international rules of the sea, merchant ships are supposed to be safe from warships, since they carry no weapons. All seafaring countries pretty much agree to this rule.

"But in this case, the Spanish wanted to cripple the English colonies, so they violated the rule. Unfortunately, since the King and Parliament couldn't afford to get into another war with Spain, they pretended that Spain wasn't attacking the merchant ships and did nothing. With no opposition, of course, the Spanish kept right on attacking.

"Now, the captain of one of the English merchant ships was Robert Jenkins. His ship was attacked, and one of the Spanish sailors hacked off his ear with a saber. He was so mad at Parliament for not protecting him and the other merchant ships that he sailed back to England himself, marched into Parliament, and showed them his ear. Because of what Jenkins did, the English had to admit what was going on and declared war. So, the war became known as The War of Jenkins' Ear."

"That's a riot," Hannah exclaimed. "Even I liked that war story. What happened then?"

"Well, to make a long story short, The War of Jenkins' Ear became the start of a big war that spread throughout Europe. It was called The War of the Austrian Succession and it lasted for six more years until a treaty was signed to bring about peace."

"The War of Jenkins' Ear. I can't get over it. But what happened to the Spanish?" Carter asked.

"In the treaty, they gave up all claims to land north of Florida," I replied. "So the war ended up well for the colonies. But we've got to get back to Georgia now.

"As in New York and New Jersey, there were disagreements among the many groups that had flooded into Georgia. These disagreements led to conflict among them. Oglethorpe and the other leaders couldn't keep the peace, and in 1752, just 20 years after he founded it, Oglethorpe gave up and turned Georgia back to the King. The King now owned another colony."

"Is that it for the colonies?" Carter asked.

"How do you mean, Carter?" I replied.

"Was Georgia the last of the colonies?" he said.

"No, it wasn't," I said, "but it's the last one for tonight. I'll bet you guys have homework and maybe a chore or two to do. Next time I'll tell you the stories of the Quaker, the outcast, and the last colony. So, off you go."

"Mom, do we have to?" Carter begged.

"Yup," Mandy said.

"Dad, weren't you going to show me how to . . ." Carter began.

"Nice try, pal," Mark interrupted. "You obey your Mom."

"Okaaay," Carter whined. "G'night, Gomps."

17

THE QUAKER, THE OUTCAST, AND THE LAST COLONY

"How many original colonies were there, do you know?" It was the following Wednesday, the night before Thanksgiving, in fact, and I took up right where I had left off.

"I think it's 13," Carter said, "but I'm not sure."

"You're right, Carter," I said. "There were 13 original colonies. We've covered ten of them, so there are only Pennsylvania, Rhode Island and New Hampshire to go. Let's start with Pennsylvania.

"Pennsylvania is the area that starts on the west side of the Delaware River, across from New Jersey. It extends west to the Ohio River with Maryland to the south and New York to the north. It's a big place.

"Before it was Pennsylvania, it was part of our old friend New Netherland."

"The Dutch?" Hannah asked.

"That's right," I replied. "The Dutch claimed a wide area after Henry Hudson's explorations. Pennsylvania was the last part of their claims.

"Now, remember that when New Netherland was settled, people from all over Europe flooded in and started spreading out as soon as they did. Pennsylvania was one of the areas they spread to, especially Germans and Dutch.

"Do you remember what happened to New Netherland?" I asked.

"Didn't the English take it?" Carter responded.

"That's right," I replied. "And who was the English leader?"

"The Duke of York!" Hannah shouted.

"And they changed the name of New Netherland to . . . ?"

"New York!" they both chimed.

"Exactly right," I said. "Then Delaware and New Jersey were split off. That left what is now Pennsylvania as still a part of New York.

"Doesn't sound like a very good arrangement, does it? Having to go across New Jersey to get to another part of your own colony?"

"I guess not," said Carter.

"Well, the King didn't think so, either," I said. "And, just about that time, in 1681, along came a guy named William Penn. He was the son of a rich admiral who had loaned the King some money.

"Penn knew that the King had money trouble, so he asked for land in the New World instead of repayment of the loan.

"Well, this was a no-brainer to the King. Here was this piece of land sticking way off in the middle of nowhere, hard to get to and full of Dutch and Germans. So he took Penn's deal and gave him a Charter for the land.

"The King wanted to name the place Penn, after William's father. William wanted to name it Sylvania, which means 'wooded land' in Latin. And that's how it got its name – Pennsylvania - Penn's Woods.

"Now, William had two special plans for his colony and he had the King put them in the Charter. First, the Charter allowed Penn to divide up the colony into smaller areas called counties, and the people in each one elected their own local government – the first County Commissions. Then, he wanted the colony to have true religious freedom, so he insisted that the King write that into the Charter, too."

"Was he a Puritan, Gomps?" asked Carter.

"Another great question, Carter," I replied. "No, he was a Quaker."

"What's a Quaker?" Carter continued. "That's a funny name."

"The official name is the Religious Society of Friends. It has elements of Christianity."

"Why are they called Quakers, then?" Carter continued.

"Quaker is a term that was first used to criticize them. Quakers warned nonbelievers that they would end up 'trembling' at the sight of God, or 'quaking.'"

"Like an earthquake?" asked Hannah.

"Something like that," I replied.

"So why were they criticized, really?" she continued.

"They were pacifists," I answered.

"What's a pacifist?" Carter asked.

"A pacifist is someone who does not believe in war and refuses to fight in wars," I replied. "To them it is a matter of basic religious belief."

"What would happen if they were, like, forced into it?" Carter asked.

"They would refuse to do it," I replied.

"Wouldn't they get into trouble?" he continued.

"Oh, yes," I said. "Quakers were persecuted for these beliefs."

"Persecuted how, Gomps?" Hannah asked.

"Well," I said. "I was hoping I wouldn't have to go into detail about it, but I can see that I have to. They were beaten and put in prison and banished."

"This was in England?" Hannah asked.

"Yes, in England," I replied, "and just about everywhere in Europe, and then here. They were even driven out of New Netherland and the Massachusetts Bay Colony," I replied.

Suddenly, I saw a look of understanding come over Hannah's face.

"The Quakers were a pain to the King, weren't they," she said.

"Yes, they were," I replied.

"So he could kill two birds with one stone, couldn't he," she continued.

"Yes, he could," I said, smiling.

"What do you mean, Hannah?" Carter asked.

"The King could pay back his loan to Admiral Penn with land that wasn't worth much to him," she said, "that's one bird. And it would be a place for Quakers to go, that's the second bird. He must have known that William Penn was a Quaker and saw a chance for religious freedom. The King could get out from under the trouble that the Quakers were causing him."

"Wow, is that right, Gomps?" Carter asked.

"That's about how I figure it," I replied. "Hannah, that was pretty good thinking."

"It just seemed obvious," she said matter-of-factly.

"So, there we have Pennsylvania," I concluded. "It wasn't long before the Pennsylvania settlers discovered that a place not far from the mouth of the Delaware River was an excellent harbor, and they soon made a port there. And that is where they set up the city of Philadelphia. Needless to say, people of many religions settled in Pennsylvania, and it became an important part of our story."

"Two to go," Carter said.

"I'm sorry, Carter," I said. "Two to go, what?"

"Two colonies to go," he said.

"Oh, yes," I said. It occurred to me that he was pushing me to get on with the story.

❦

"Two colonies to go – Rhode Island and New Hampshire.

"Let's start with Rhode Island. For that, we have to go back to the Massachusetts Bay Colony. The Puritans believed that each church congregation should run its own affairs. They were very suspicious of church higher-ups from their experience with the Church of England.

"This practice had a good side and a bad side. People could practice their religion without being told what to do, but there were no church officials to help them make tough decisions about their religious practices. As a result, it was easier for a stranger to lead a congregation away from their beliefs.

"When this happened, it usually took the congregation a while to figure out what the stranger was up to. This happened in Jamestown and in Plymouth, and it would happen again, more than once, in the Boston area. One person in particular, Roger Williams, was preaching what to people then were unusual ideas.

"Roger Williams was a Baptist and Separatist who believed in pure religious freedom. To him, as long as you believed in God, it didn't matter what your religion was - you should be able to worship that way, Christian or not.

"In addition, Williams believed there should be no established religion; that any one religion, if officially adopted by a colony, would become corrupt just as the Church of England had become in England.

"Neither of his beliefs sat well with the colonists, who by now were insisting that people obey the Puritan way.

"Williams was first banished from the Bay Colony and then from Plymouth for his beliefs. From Plymouth, he traveled west and a little bit south to what is now called Narragansett Bay. There he found few settlers from the Bay Colony or Plymouth at that time, and the Indians there were the Narragansetts and the Wampanoags, both friendly tribes.

"So Williams set up another settlement that came to be known as Rhode Island Colony. And he was able to establish rules that prevented any one religion being made the official religion of the Colony.

"Needless to say, once word got out, people of various faiths went there, and soon the city of Providence was set up on Narragansett Bay and a harbor was built.

"Two religious groups came there in large numbers - Baptists and Quakers - both of whom had been suffering religious discrimination in other colonies. Williams welcomed them with open arms, as he did other faiths.

"Williams' rule against an established church of Rhode Island worked well, and it led to his writing about it. He wrote that he had set up a high wall of separation between 'the Garden of Christ' and 'the Wilderness of the World.' Remember that phrase because it became an important part of our country to this day.

"So, under Roger Williams's leadership, Rhode Island was up and running as a colony and as a center of religious freedom.

"Now, let's quickly cover the last colony – New Hampshire.

"Remember at the beginning I said that English fishermen had been fishing off the coast of New England and landing north of Boston from time to time?"

"Yup," they both said.

"Well, a few of those fishermen decided to settle there just three years after the Plymouth voyage arrived," I said. "And where do you think they settled?"

"Is this a trick question, Gomps?" Carter asked.

"Nope," I replied.

"New Hampshire?" they shrugged.

"Yup," I said. "And, six years later, in 1629, the King carved them a grant of land out of his claim to everything north of Boston.

"Then, just ten years after the New Hampshire grant, the Massachusetts Bay Colony tried to claim New Hampshire as theirs, but the King said no. They tried it again in 1686, and the King said no again. Finally, in 1741 the King made New Hampshire an official colony."

"So he shut up the Bay Colony?" she continued.

"That's how it looks to me," I said. "Now, before we stop for tonight, I'd like to know if there's anything you'd like me to talk about next time."

"Well, we don't know what comes next," Carter said, "so how would we know?"

"I thought you might be curious about something we just touched on, or skipped over," I replied. "Maybe you have a question you haven't asked."

"I do," Hannah said. "What was life like, back then?"

"How do you mean?" I replied.

"Well, when you told us how the Pilgrims lived, it sounded pretty bad," she said. "Was life any better in these other places?"

"That's a good question, Hannah," I said. "That's where we'll begin next time. Now, I'll see you tomorrow for Thanksgiving dinner!"

18

LIFE IN THE COLONIES, AND DANIEL BOONE LEADS THEM WEST

"Last week, Hannah, you asked about life in the colonies," I said. "Are you still interested?"

"Yes," she replied, "I want to know how they lived."

"It depends who you're talking about," I said. "But, generally speaking, living conditions got better as the colonies grew.

"The wealthy, of course, brought their money with them and a few earned large amounts after they got here. But now, a middle class was forming. These were people who figured out what the population needed – food or clothing or shelter or transportation – and started businesses to provide it. As these businesses made a profit, their owners could afford to buy nice things, and other businesses sprang up to supply them.

"So high earners and the middle class were able to create a reasonably comfortable lifestyle. They built houses that were very similar to those of today, and many still exist, some as museums. There were still no modern conveniences, but there were kitchens, living and dining rooms, and upstairs bedrooms.

"Everyone who wanted to eat and have shelter had to work for it. There was no government of the sort that could give money to the poor."

"What happened to people who couldn't work?" Carter asked.

"Well, there were far fewer of them than there are now, for one thing," I replied. "But for those who were truly in need, there were two main sources of charity: churches and individual people. Help of this kind was all voluntary, and no one had a right to it."

"Tough," said Carter.

"Really?" I said. "Think about it the other way. Look what happened in Jamestown and Plymouth when they started out with a communal system. A third of the people stopped working when they found out they could get things for free.

"To me, by giving a person what they could earn for themselves, you are telling them that they can't take care of themselves. That's a kind of insult. It's amazing what people can do in the face of starvation."

"I see what you're saying," he said.

"What about children, Gomps?" asked Hannah. "What was their life like?"

"For one thing, Hannah," I answered, "there were a lot of them. Nearly everyone had big families — four, five, ten children. Even more.

"Because there were so few comforts of home as we know them, there was a lot more to do to keep things going, and children did a lot of the work. They cleaned, cooked, fetched water, fed the horses, milked cows, picked crops, and even did manual labor in their fathers' businesses.

"They got up early in the morning and did their chores, then went to school, if there was one, then more chores when they were done with school, then schoolwork, then prayers, and off to bed. Six days a week."

"Not seven?" Carter asked.

"Nooooo," I replied. "Sunday was the Sabbath Day, and they had to wash up, dress up and go to church with the family."

"You said they had big families, Gomps," said Hannah. "Why was that?"

"There were a lot of things to do," I replied, "and children provided the cheapest source of labor."

"Ooooh," said Hannah.

"How much would they get paid?" Carter asked.

"Not much, if anything," I replied. "Some parents thought the children should help the family make ends meet as soon as they could.

"Sadly, there was another reason for big families. Life was not as healthy in those days, so more people died young than today. If you had eight children, say, only four might survive to old age. And if it looked like you were going to live a long life, you would want to have children around to take care of you.

"On top of all that, the birth rate was just much higher then. Parents just had a lot more children."

"Was that harder on the wives?" Hannah asked.

"Yes, it was, Hannah," I replied. "Because there wasn't the cleanliness and modern medicine of today, there was a much higher rate of mothers' death in childbirth. Men became widowers much more often, and second and even third marriages were common among men."

"What was school like?" asked Carter.

"Schools as we know them only existed in cities and towns where there were enough people to afford them. Often, there were one-room schoolhouses where the kids of all ages went. All the neighbors got together and paid for a teacher. Some of a teacher's pay would be in food or cloth from those families who didn't have money to spare.

"In families that could afford it, the children had tutors. Where there weren't enough people for a school, mothers taught the children at home."

"Like homeschooling?" Hannah asked.

"Exactly like homeschooling," I replied.

"How did the people get around?" Hannah asked.

"On horseback or by horse and wagon," I said. "If they couldn't afford a horse, they walked."

"How about the kids?" Hannah continued.

"If the family could afford it, they had ponies for the kids," I said. "Otherwise, the kids rode in the wagon or walked."

"What did kids do for fun?" Carter asked.

"There wasn't much time for fun, but when there was, they would play outside with simple toys that their dads might have made in the barn or woodshop. The boys might have toy wagons, and the girls might have dolls made from straw or wood."

"Sounds like a pretty rough life to me," said Carter.

"For sure," Hannah said. "I'm glad our ancestors survived it, because I'm not sure I could have."

"Yes, we do have to be thankful to them," I said. "Now, it wasn't as hard for the wealthy. They had to live without modern conveniences, too, but they had servants and, in many cases, slaves to do a lot of the work for them.

"As for laborers, indentured servants and slaves, it was worse. Their houses were crude shelters, more like the Pilgrims'. They had fewer clothes and of poorer quality. Some had shoes; some went barefoot. They were hungry much of the time, unless they were farmers. Because they needed the children to work, many of the poor didn't want to send them to school.

"Does that give you an idea of how people lived?" I asked. "Any other questions?"

"Nope, we got the picture," said Hannah and Carter nodded.

"OK," I said. "We've got our 13 original colonies. Let's see what happened next."

❧

"In fact, lots of things happened at the same time. More people came to the New World, more were being born here, and to some people, it was getting too crowded."

"Too crowded?" Carter exclaimed. "How many people were there?"

"Well, Boston had about 10,000, New York probably 20,000, Philadelphia maybe 8,000, and the main southern cities maybe 5,000 apiece."

"Ha, ha," they both laughed. "That's nothing. What were they complaining about?"

"A lot of these people had come here to get away from crowded places," I said. "They had had enough of crowding in the cities in England and Europe. Others came to the colonies from rural areas, so unless they were shopkeepers or merchants, being in a city didn't do them much good.

"Also, they wanted their own land," I continued. "They knew that the New World stretched way beyond the Atlantic coast and that the land out to the west was there just for the taking, or so they thought. Farmers were probably the first to go, and then the barrel makers, carpenters, trappers, and even shopkeepers followed them right out.

"It wasn't easy because there were no roads to the west, just forests and mountains. There were mountain ranges from New Hampshire to Georgia. In fact, once they decided to go west, the first thing they had to do was figure out how to get over the mountains."

"How did they do it?" Carter asked.

"With mountain guides," I answered. "The first people to get across the mountains were mountain men. These were hunters and trappers who were at ease in the forest — it was where they worked every day. They knew that there must be good hunting and trapping territory on the other side of the mountains, so they kept looking until they found the secret."

"What secret, Gomps?" they exclaimed.

"Gaps," I answered.

"Gaps?" they asked. "Isn't that the name of a store?"

"Different thing," I replied. "Gaps were places in the mountains that were lower than the mountain peaks. It was easier to go through the gaps than it was to climb over the peaks. And the mountain men found them."

"Oh," said Hannah. "You said gaps. There was more than one?"

"There were several gaps, scattered here and there among the ranges. That meant that people at different places along the coast had a gap that they could go through without having to go too far north or south.

"The most famous gap is probably the Cumberland Gap. It starts in Virginia and comes out where the states of Tennessee, Virginia and Kentucky come together.

"Why was it famous?" Carter interrupted.

"Carrrrterrrr," Hannah said. "You interrupted Gomps again."

"You do it, too," he said. "Besides, I get it. Let's just hear about this one so we can get on with the story."

"OhhhhKaaaay," I said. "I got the picture.

"Cumberland Gap was famous because it was the best gap and was used the most. It was only 1,600 feet high and the peaks on either side were 5,000 feet or higher. Once it was discovered, people poured through it, heading west."

"Who discovered it, Gomps?" Carter asked.

"Daniel Boone," I replied. "Have you heard of him?"

"Nope," said Carter.

"Me, neither," seconded Hannah.

"Hmm," I muttered. "Daniel Boone was among the first of the mountain guides. When he was very young, his family moved to western Pennsylvania and set up a lumber mill. He grew up with his dad and brothers in the woods among the Indians, but he wanted more out of life than to work the mill."

"Indians?" Carter asked. "There were Indians there, too?"

"Oh, yes," I replied. "There were Indians just about everywhere in the New World."

"Did they fight?" Carter continued.

"There you go again," sighed Hannah.

"Hey, it's a good question," said Carter, standing up for himself.

"It is a good question," I replied.

"See?" Carter interrupted, turning toward his sister. Hannah stuck out her tongue at him and he raised a fist in mock anger.

"You wouldn't dare," Hannah said, making sure he understood who still had the upper hand.

"Hey!" I exclaimed. "Cut it out. If you two don't knock off this kind of stuff, I'll stop right now."

"OK," said Carter calmly. "But we were just sparring."

Sparring? I thought. I wondered how long this balance of power would last in its current form. Carter was starting to show more understanding than I'd imagined.

"So, back to Daniel Boone and Indians," I continued. "Yes, there were Indians on the west side of the mountains, too. And, just as on the east side, not all tribes were the same. Some were warlike and others peaceful. Some stayed in one place and others wandered. Their languages differed to some degree. And some welcomed the settlers and others did not.

"Growing up among them, Daniel Boone learned the ways of the various tribes and how to deal with them. So he was the perfect guide.

"The first thing he did was to explore the area south of his home. He traveled through what is now West Virginia, Kentucky and Tennessee, and he came upon the Cumberland Gap.

"It didn't take him long to figure out how he could turn it to his advantage. When he came back out of the Gap on the east side of the mountains, he saw that there were settlements close by. Talking with the settlers, he learned that there were many who wanted to find less crowded places. He must have thought something like, 'Who better than me to take them there?'

"Most of these settlers were new to the woods, and leading them would be tough. He needed a long-range plan for his business. He thought, 'What will they need to be able to travel to the west? A road. How do you make a road through the woods? Cut down the trees. Who cuts down trees? Lumbermen.'

"So off he went and found a lumber company who wanted to spread out into new territory, too. He made them a deal. He would lead them into the woods and they would cut the trees to make a road. They would then saw the trees into lumber and use the road to carry the lumber back east for sale.

"He kept scouting out the best direction for the road, and they kept cutting and clearing the way. Before long, they were through the Cumberland Gap and forging ahead into what is now Kentucky and Tennessee.

"Boone called it the 'Wilderness Road.' He now had the route by which he could lead the settlers."

"What kind of road was it?" Hannah asked.

"You mean what was it made of?" I asked.

"Yeah."

"Well, it wasn't much of a road by our standards," I replied. "It was just a dirt path with roots and ruts and mud and dust. The wagons lurched along, tossing the settlers around, but it was good enough if they took their time.

"Boone was now in business. He went from settlement to settlement on the eastern side, looking for settlers who wanted to move west. For a price, he guided them along the Wilderness Road until they found places where they could settle down. Then he went back for more settlers.

"Boone became famous. A town in Kentucky was named after him, and he was elected to political office. There was even a television series about him back when I was a boy."

"Gomps, if there were Indians all around these places, weren't there fights?" Hannah asked.

"Yes, there sure were," I replied, "especially where the Indians were warlike. Many settlers were killed. Some families adopted the Indians' ways and lived among them, and others were made slaves and their livestock was taken."

"Slaves? The settlers?" Carter asked.

"Yes," I replied, "and some wished they had been killed instead of taken."

"Why did they go out there, then, if it was so dangerous?" Hannah broke in.

"These were people who really, really didn't like to live among people. And they didn't like to have other people tell them what to do. They were willing to risk everything to try to live the way they wanted."

"Wow," said Carter. "They must have been brave."

"And tough," I concluded.

"What kinds of houses did they have?" Hannah asked.

"Well, they didn't have much time or taste for niceties," I answered. "So they built basic shelters. A lot of them built log cabins."

"Where did they get the logs, from that lumber company?" Carter asked.

"No, they cut the trees themselves to clear their fields and they used the logs from those trees to make their cabins."

"Wow," said Hannah. "That was hard."

"Women and children, too," I said. "The whole family would have to pitch in."

"Were there towns or schools or anything?" Hannah asked.

"Not at first," I replied. "Remember the subsistence farmers I talked about in New England and Carolina?"

"You mean the ones who just farmed for their own food?" Hannah asked.

"Yup," I replied. "Same thing here. They started out just trying to provide for themselves. Then, as more people came, the more ambitious farmers expanded and produced enough food for themselves and for sale to the newcomers.

"So we've got settlers spreading out all . . ."

"Uh, Dad," Mandy interrupted.

"Yes, Mandy," I replied.

"It sounds like you're at a good stopping point, and these two have a lot of homework that they've been putting off. I'm afraid I'm going to have to end the story here for tonight. Will you be in town next week?"

"I sure will," I replied. "Next time, I'll tell you about how the King had his cake and ate it, too. OK, you guys, give me a hug and off to your homework."

19

THE KING HAS HIS CAKE AND EATS IT, TOO

"Let me start this week's story with a question," I said. "Who owned the colonies?"

"I thought the people owned them," Carter said.

"Not yet," I said. "It took a big war for that to happen, and that was a ways off. Hannah?"

"The investors?"

"Why do you think that?"

"They paid for them?"

"That's close," I replied. "Each colony was started by a leader, like Lord Berkeley or Lord Baltimore, who got a charter from the King."

"Oh, yeah," they both chimed.

"These charters gave the colonial leaders the right to run their colonies, as long as they obeyed English law and followed the rules in the charters," I continued. "The Virginia Charter was a good example. It said, 'Each of the said Colonies shall have a Council, which shall govern and order all Matters-and Causes, which shall arise, grow, or happen, to or within the same several Colonies, according to such Laws, Ordinances, and Instructions, as shall be, in that behalf, given and signed with Our Hand.'

"But as the colonies began to grow and make money, the King noticed that things weren't going as he expected.

"First, he saw that the colonies weren't paying their own way. He had expenses in protecting and running them and he wasn't getting much in return.

"Second, he saw that the colonies were starting to get out from under his control. They were making their own laws and running their own lives."

"What do you mean 'running their own lives,' Gomps?" asked Carter.

"Well," I said, "the colonial Assemblies were passing laws beyond what he wanted and the colonists were forming militias and town councils. They were even electing their council members."

"I see," he said, "like their own governments."

"Like their own governments," I confirmed. "Little by little, they were going off on their own.

"Now, not all of the colonies ran smoothly," I said. "Remember that Maryland, New Jersey, and Georgia didn't work out, and their leaders gave their charters back to the King. They called them Royal Colonies then."

"Oh, yeah," said Hannah. "Their leaders got tired of the grief."

"That's right," I replied. "For those colonies, the King had his cake and ate it, too. He hadn't had to take the risk and expense of settling them, yet he got control of them anyway."

"Do you think he planned that all along?" Hannah asked.

"Planned what?" I asked.

"Near the beginning of the story," Hannah continued, "Carter asked why the King gave charters to the investors to start colonies when he could have done it himself. You said that it would cost him money he didn't have and that the colonies might fail."

"Yes, I did say that," I said.

"So, do you think the King knew back then that some of the colonies would fail and that he would be able to get them for free, anyway?"

"Well, by this time there was a different King," I replied, "but most kings understood this kind of business and had advisors who certainly did. The King probably figured that sooner or later, this would happen.

"Then, in the case of one colony the King just took it. Remember the Duke of York?"

"Yeah," replied Carter. "He ran the New York colony."

"Right," I said. "And he got the rights to it from his older brother, who was King at the time. Well, the Duke's brother, the King, died without any heirs, and the Duke of York became King. With that, in 1685 he took over New York, made it a Royal Colony, and cancelled their Constitution.

"Verrrry interesting," Carter said as he rubbed his chin in mock wisdom. "The King got some colonies without paying for them."

"That's the point," I said, "although in the case of York, it didn't do him much good. He was overthrown just four years later, and two years after that the New York Constitution was reenacted."

"I see what you mean about just calling them all 'the King,'" Hannah said. "What a pain it would be to try to keep track of them all. Thank you.

"But if the colonies were all getting out from under his control, even if they were his," she continued, "what could he do?"

"Well, Hannah, you can probably answer that for yourself," I said. "Tell you what, let's play 20 Questions. I'll name something and you two tell me how the King handled it. OK?"

"OK!" they chimed.

"The King wanted more control over the colonies, right?"

"Yup."

"Did he want to run them himself?"

"Ah, no," Carter said.

"But he picked his own guys to run them," Hannah concluded.

"Right," I said. "He called them governors, and he hand-picked most of them.

"Next, control of the people. How did the governors keep the peace?"

"The army!" Carter exclaimed. "He sent in the army!"

"You beat me on that one," Hannah said. "I was gonna say that, too."

"Exactly," I said. "British troops showed up in every colony, reporting to each governor.

"Next, money. Did the King want to make money from the deal?" I asked.

"Oh, yes!" they both exclaimed.

"Of course," I said, "and how did he do that?"

"Taxes!" they both yelled, really getting into it.

"And tariffs from trade," Hannah added.

"Collected by the army!" Carter exclaimed.

"I knew you guys were smart," I said. "Although, in reality, the taxes were collected by tax collectors. The army enforced the collection if someone wouldn't pay.

"How about religion?" I asked.

"Hmm," said Carter.

"Church of England?" Hannah said uncertainly.

"That's right," I replied. "Most Kings hoped to set up the Church of England in all the colonies and make it the established religion, just like in England. Although the Duke of York had become a Catholic before he became King, but that was part of the reason why he didn't last long as King."

"But what about freedom of religion?" Hannah asked. "Isn't that why the people left England in the first place? Not to have to worship in the Church of England?"

"Yes, they did," I said. "Although by this time, many of the people who came over were loyal to the King. They were called Loyalists. They just wanted freedom to seek a better life. For them, making the Church of England the official religion was a good thing."

"How about the colonies that didn't want to?" Carter asked.

"They still allowed the Church of England," I answered. "They just didn't make it the established religion. Remember, just about

every settler was religious. Most just didn't want to be forced to worship in a church they didn't choose.

"Now, how did the colonists feel about the King taking over?" I
asked.

"Hmm," Carter pondered, "they couldn't have been too happy."

"Why not?" I continued.

"They were trying to get out from under him and now he was
back in charge."

"I think you're right," I said. "So, what did they do about it?"

"War?" Carter said.

"Not yet," I replied. "Loyalist or not, they still felt connected to
England to some extent. Hannah, do you have any ideas?"

"Well, if he got more power over them," she said, "did they try to
keep him from doing it?"

"I think you're on the right track," I replied. "Let's start with a
basic question. The colonists came here for freedom, right?"

"Right," they said.

"They didn't want the King to control how they lived, right?"

"Right."

"They wanted to control their own lives, right?"

"Right."

"So they took a page from England's own book," I said. "England
had Parliament. Parliament made the laws and the English people
elected their representatives to it, right?"

"Right."

"So the colonists did the same thing," I continued.

"They elected their own people to represent them in making laws. These representatives gathered in what were called Assemblies or Houses of Burgesses or Councils, and they became permanent parts of the government of each colony. In fact, each colonial charter granted by the King *required* the colonies to set up a House of some kind. The Connecticut colony even had two Houses — one to pass laws and the other to elect representatives to do it.

"Massachusetts was the first colony to have an elected Assembly. The people there had their first election in 1634. Then, five years later Massachusetts passed a law that created two houses in their Assembly, like our House of Representatives and Senate of today.

"The last colony to form an Assembly was New York in 1683, although Georgia's came much later, in 1750."

"Why do you say that New York was the last when Georgia was?" Hannah asked.

"Good question, Hannah," I replied. "Remember that Georgia was carved from the Carolina colony land, so the early settlers were covered by the Carolina colony until then, and the Carolina Assembly started in 1663."

"I get it," Hannah said.

"Gomps?" Carter asked. "Can I ask one of the 20 questions?"

"Sure."

"How did the King feel about the Assemblies?"

"Good question. How do you think?" I asked.

"I don't think he liked them," Carter answered.

"Why not?" I asked.

"He couldn't tell them what to do," Carter continued.

"Do you think he tried?" I asked.

"Sure," he replied.

"Carter, you're right," I said. "He probably thought his Loyalists would all be elected and would vote in his favor. Then he saw how independent the Assemblies were acting, and that's when he put his governors into action."

"He wanted the governors to control the Assemblies?" Hannah asked.

"Yes, he did," I replied.

"And the governors had the army?" Carter continued.

"You're catching on fast," I said.

"Sounds like trouble," Hannah said.

"Trouble was a-brewin'," I said. "But that's going to have to do it for tonight. Next time, I'm going to tell you about the slave who gained her freedom in court."

"Sounds impossible, Gomps," Hannah said.

"Well, she did," I said, "so prepare yourself."

"OK," she said. "Good night, Gomps."

"Good night, all," I said. "See you next week."

20

THE SLAVE WHO GAINED HER FREEDOM IN COURT

"This time, I'm going to talk more about slavery," I said. "We're going to have to face up to it, and now's the time to start."

"Gomps, this is so hard to hear about." Hannah said.

"Yeah, we get it," said Carter.

"I'm afraid you don't get it," I said, "at least not all of it. So far, we've started the story, but now we are going to go deeper. And toward the end, I'll tell you about Elizabeth Key, the slave who gained her freedom in an unbelievable way."

"OK," they said.

"As we have said, slavery became a key question in the growth of the colonies, especially in the southern colonies.

"As the years went by, farmers in the south needed plenty of labor. There were white indentured servants from England, Scotland, and Ireland, but there weren't enough of them. So the farmers brought in more and more black slaves from Africa.

"Now, we're not talking only about the South. The northern colonies didn't have land that was good for big farms, but as I've told you, they still owned slaves for household help and for small farms and factories."

"Slavery is horrible," Hannah said. "Wasn't there anyone against it?"

"There were some, but we don't know how many," I replied. "A few were outspoken about it and published pamphlets. Some northern ministers preached against it. And from time to time a few slave owners, mostly in the North, set their slaves free. They all came to be known as Abolitionists, because they wanted to abolish slavery.

"But they were up against some powerful forces. Slavery was too good at providing cheap labor. As the southern plantations grew and became more profitable, more and more slaves were brought from Africa. Within a hundred years or so, there were about 600,000 slaves in the colonies."

"Wowww," Hannah breathed. The kids fell quiet for a moment, contemplating that number.

"How did it work?" Carter broke the silence.

"Carter, do we really have to know?" Hannah pleaded.

"I want to know," Carter said firmly.

"What do you think, Gomps?" Hannah asked, hoping for support from me.

"I think Carter's right," I answered. "You really need to know in order to understand the rest of the story."

"OhhKayyy," Hannah sighed.

"Once slave owners bought slaves, they had to make a profit from them. To do that, they had to manage their slaves at a low-enough cost."

"What do you mean 'manage' them?" Hannah asked.

"One thing they did was to hire people who would organize and supervise the slaves to keep them working hard," I replied. "They were called slave masters or overseers. Plus, the owners had to feed the slaves, provide clothing, shelter, and so on. They wanted to do this as cheaply as possible so they could get more profit."

"Gomps, I'm starting not to like the sound of this," Hannah said.

"Slavery was an evil practice – we can't condemn it strongly enough," I replied, "but you might as well know the truth. Owners would provide their slaves with only as much as they needed to keep them working."

"If I were a slave, I would have run away!" Carter declared.

"You wouldn't have gotten far," I said. "Slave owners hired men to hunt down runaway slaves and bring them back."

"How did the owners keep the slaves from just running away again?" he continued.

"This is where it gets worse," I said. "Are you sure you're up for it?"

"I guess," Carter replied.

"We might as well know now," Hannah sighed.

"The slaves were often beaten and many times put in chains to keep them from running," I replied.

Both kids shivered. Hannah looked ill. Carter stared off into space.

"I had no idea it was that bad," Hannah said.

"Me either," seconded Carter.

"I'm with you," I said. "But there are other parts to the slave story, because it's important to get the whole picture. I said that there were a lot of slaves in the colonies in the next hundred years, but not all of them came from slave traders."

"Where else did they come from?" Carter asked.

"From being born here," I replied. "In spite of the horrible conditions that they were kept in, slave men and women formed families and had children. So the slave population grew not just from bringing more slaves from Africa, but also from the birth of children to slave mothers and fathers."

"So . . . children were slaves?" Carter asked.

"Yes, they were," I answered, "although not in one case. In 1656 in Virginia, up stepped Elizabeth Key."

❧

"Who was she?" Hannah asked. "I never heard of her."

"Me either," Carter added.

"Few people have," I replied. "Elizabeth Key was the daughter of an African slave woman and a white English man. She had been declared by her owner, who was probably her father, to be of 'negro' race and, therefore, a slave. But she didn't like that at all, and she decided to fight it."

"How could she fight her owner?" Hannah asked. "Wouldn't he just beat her and put her in chains?"

"No, she knew she couldn't come to blows with him," I said. "Instead, believe it or not, she sued him!"

"Ha, ha," they both shouted. "She sued him? How did she do that?"

"That's right," I said. "She sued him in a Virginia court of law. And guess what?"

"No way," Hannah exclaimed. "You're not going to tell us that she won, are you?"

"That's exactly what I'm going to tell you," I replied. "She won her case, and the court set her free."

"Holy cow!" Carter shouted.

"But you said slavery got bigger, didn't you?" Hannah asked. "Didn't other slaves take their owners to court, then?"

"Well, right after that," I said, "the plantation owners figured that if they didn't do something, that's exactly what would happen. So, six years later, Virginia passed a law that any child of a slave was also a slave, and that was the end of that."

"That's too bad that more slaves couldn't do what she did," Hannah said.

"Yes, it is," I agreed. "Unfortunately, that meant that slaves ended up being treated as property rather than as people, both in day-to-day business and in the courts. Slaves were bought and sold both privately and in public auctions. Slaves had market value to their owners — they were assets of the plantation or household and were treated as such. So, if slavery were abolished, the owners would be losing a lot of money in the value of their slaves, and their plantations or factories would go out of business. They would lose everything."

"Is that why it was so hard to get rid of slavery?" Hannah asked.

"I think that was one of the biggest reasons," I replied. "But it didn't stop the Abolitionists from trying.

"In 1652, four years before Elizabeth Key went to court, the Rhode Island Colony passed a law abolishing slavery. Unfortunately, it was ignored, for the most part, but it was a start. Then, in 1700, a man named Samuel Sewell, seeing how the law was ignored, wrote and published a protest against slavery. It was a story he called 'The Selling of Joseph,' about the treatment and conditions of a slave named Joseph."

"Did it do anything?" asked Carter.

"It didn't change the laws," I replied. "But at least it opened people's eyes. And it added to the Abolition movement."

"Was he the only one who came out against slavery?" Carter continued.

"No, twelve years before, in 1688, the Quakers came out against slavery," I said. "They met in Germantown, Pennsylvania, and published a pamphlet called the Petition Against Slavery. That got all Quakers thinking about it, and in 1776, less than 100 years later, the Quakers passed a rule that no member of their religion could practice slavery. And just four years after that, in 1780, the State of Pennsylvania passed a law banning slavery."

"Gomps, you make it sound like the Quakers abolished slavery right after they passed the Petition, but then you said it took a hundred years," Hannah said. "That was really a long time."

"Yes, it was," I replied, "but I think it goes to show just how strong slavery was. Here you have a northern religious group that despises slavery, and still, it took that long.

"Then, there was the colony of Georgia. Remember that they started out prohibiting slavery, and yet 30 years later, Oglethorpe and his fellow founders had to give in to the plantation owners.

"Here's another example of how widespread slavery was: even some Indians and free black people owned slaves."

"Black people owned slaves??" Carter asked.

"Apparently they did," I replied. "There are letters and diaries that describe it. And don't forget that slavery among African tribes was common."

"Gomps, this is so horrible." Hannah said. "How could the slaves stand it?"

"That's a good question," I answered. "I'm not sure I could have."

"Me either," they both agreed.

"I think one reason is that they were tough," I said. "They had come from places where food was scarce and had to be hunted or grown in poor soil. Water was not always good there, or easy to find, and it often had to be carried long distances. Their homes were not much better than what they were given in slavery, if at all. And transportation was often by foot. So they were used to hard living.

"I think that being together helped the slaves through the ordeal, too. To the extent that they could help one another, they didn't have to suffer alone, and that may have given them strength.

"And there's one other thing," I said.

"What's that, Gomps?" asked Carter.

"Believe it or not, Christianity," I replied.

Carter looked surprised. "Slaves were Christians?"

"Yes, I think the majority were," I said.

"But, Gomps, how could that be?" Hannah asked. "Did the owners convert them?"

"I think a small minority of owners probably did," I replied. "Don't forget, the Jamestown Charter included the goal of converting Indians to Christianity. It's not too much of a stretch to think that some of the owners were devout Christians and that they converted Africans, too.

"On the other hand, converting them would have meant that they'd have had to teach their slaves to read and write, and most owners didn't want that."

"Why not, Gomps?" Carter asked. "Wouldn't they be able to do more for their owners if they could read?"

"You would think so," I replied, "but that would make it possible for slaves to become educated and fend for themselves."

"You mean, if they ran away and didn't get caught," Carter continued.

"Right," I said. "The owners believed that they could keep better control of their slaves if they kept them ignorant. Nonetheless, it is known that some slave owners did teach some of their slaves to read and write. And those owners that did suffered criticism, and sometimes worse, from other owners who did not share their beliefs."

"Worse how, Gomps?" Carter asked.

"Slave owners who taught their slaves to read could be fined, imprisoned or even beaten," I replied. "And, slaves who were found to be literate could be beaten and even have their fingers or toes cut off."

"Oh, this is so gross," Hannah groaned.

"Yeah," Carter agreed.

"I'm sickened by it, too," I said, "and I think everyone is. So we were talking about how Christianity came into the slaves' lives to help them.

"We said a few likely were converted by their owners, but there may be one other explanation for the slaves' adoption of Christianity, and it came from within their midst," I said.

"What are you talking about?" asked Hannah. "Do you mean that some were already Christians?"

"That's exactly what I mean," I said. "The main source of slaves was West Africa. For years before the slave trade began, European Catholic missionaries, probably Portuguese, had converted some African tribes to Christianity."

"Amazing," exclaimed Hannah. "Makes sense."

"Yeah," agreed Carter. "It does."

"Now, there's still a lot more to the slavery story, but that will have to wait until we get closer to the formation of our nation. We'll stop for tonight so you guys can do what you have to do. Next time, I'll tell you about the King and the cat-and-mouse game."

21

THE KING AND THE
CAT-AND-MOUSE GAME

After two weeks of being away on business, I had gotten back from the airport just in time to drive directly to the kids' house for dinner. After we ate, everyone gathered round and I began.

"A few weeks ago, I talked about how the King started to take more power over the colonies," I said. "Do you remember?"

"Yes," said Hannah. "They were doing things their own way."

"That's right," I said. "And he started thinking about how he could profit from them."

"We remember," said Carter.

"Great," I said. "So, here we have this huge new place – the colonies. They were growing and getting more and more prosperous.

"The King thought he owned them in one way or another, and he expected to profit from them. But he had to set up a way to do it."

"Didn't you say he used taxes?" Hannah interrupted.

"Yes, I did, Hannah," I said. "And now is the time when we see how he taxed the colonies. And we see why the taxes created such a problem for him, in the end."

"This sounds like it's going to be dull," Hannah said. "Couldn't we skip this part?"

"Yeah, and go right to the war," Carter added.

"That's tempting," I said. "And I hope I can make it exciting for you. But if you don't know what upset the colonists so much, you won't know what drove them to war and why they fought so hard."

"OK," they both chimed.

"So, it started in 1651, less than 50 years after the Jamestown settlers arrived," I said. "The King got the English Parliament to pass laws that made the colonies use only English ships for anything they shipped to and from anywhere in the world. Even if they were shipping something to Sweden or buying from the Netherlands, they had to use an English ship. These laws were called the Navigation Acts."

"So what?" said Carter. "The colonists were English, weren't they?"

"Yes, for the most part," I replied, "but they were also seeking freedom, and that included the freedom to choose the ships they wanted to use."

"Why would it matter to them which ships they used?" Carter asked.

"Let me answer that with a question," I said. "If you were an English sea captain, what would you do to your prices once the Navigation Acts had been passed?"

Both kids fell silent, thinking.

"I'm not sure," Hannah said. Carter kept quiet.

"Give us a hint," she said.

"OK," I said, "you know from the Navigation Acts that businesses in the colonies had to use you to get things shipped to them or to ship things to other countries. They couldn't go to the ships of any other country. Do you have an advantage?"

"Sure," said Carter.

"What kind of advantage?" I asked.

"You have guaranteed business," Hannah replied.

"That's right," I said. "Do you want to make as much money as possible?"

"Sure," said Carter.

"So, I can raise my prices because the colonies can't use anyone else!" Hannah exclaimed.

"That's exactly right," I said. "And how did the colonists react to that?"

"They couldn't have been happy about it," Hannah reasoned.

"You got it," I said with a wink. "Carter, do you see how that works?"

"Oh, yeah," he replied. "The English captains could rip off the colonies."

"Right you are," I concluded, with a wink to him.

"Now, do you think these colonial businesses gave in to these laws?" I continued.

"No, I don't think so," said Carter.

"Why not?" I asked.

"They didn't go through all that trouble to settle the colonies just to give in to the King," Carter replied.

"You're a smart boy," I said. "They were already paying tariffs on goods coming in and going out. They weren't about to put up with this if they could help it."

"But, Gomps, how did they avoid it?" Hannah asked.

"Well, in some cases, they just ignored the law and used the lowest-priced ships they could find," I replied.

"But wouldn't the King send in the navy?" Carter asked.

"He would if he could catch them at it," I replied.

"Wouldn't he just put his ships outside the harbors?" Carter continued.

"He did that, Carter," I replied, "but the colonists smuggled things right past them."

"What's smuggling?" Hannah asked.

"That's when you secretly move things past the lookouts," I said. "The colonists used their own small boats to carry goods to and from foreign ships that were waiting in other harbors or offshore. They often did it at night or in rough weather.

"Now, did the King find out about this?" I asked.

"Must have," Hannah replied.

"So what did he do?" I asked.

"Sent in the army!" Carter shouted.

"Close," I said, "but remember that this was on the ocean, not land."

"Oh, yeah – the navy!" he exclaimed again. "He sent more ships."

"That's right," I said. "And so started a cat-and-mouse game between the colonial traders and the English Navy that lasted at least 150 years. Every time the traders tried to sneak goods in or out, the English Navy would try to catch them."

"Neat," said Carter.

"OK, one more question about this," I said. "Was the King happy that the colonies were getting around his law?"

"No," they both chimed. "He couldn't have been."

"Why not?" I continued.

"They were disobeying him," Carter replied.

"Right, and . . . ?" I continued.

"They weren't paying as much tariff?" Hannah offered.

"You're both right, but there's one more reason," I replied. "It was costing him money to enforce the law."

"Oh, of course," Hannah said.

"Because he had to use the navy for this instead of for something else," Carter said.

"Now we're cookin'," I said. "After 50 years of this, the King still needed more money, so Parliament passed another law that made the Navigation Acts small by comparison."

"What was that, Gomps?" Carter asked.

"In 1699, Parliament passed the Trade Laws. These were a series of laws that made the colonies buy and sell only with English companies. Another of the laws made it illegal for the colonies to even make certain things like iron, woolen cloth, and hats."

"Holy cow!" Carter exclaimed. "The King really put the screws to us, didn't he?"

"But, Gomps, why did he try to keep iron and cloth from being made here?" Hannah asked. "Wouldn't that cut down on the taxes and tariffs?"

"Great question," I said. "It turns out that the iron and cloth being made in the colonies were better quality and cheaper than what was being made in England, even with tariffs. The colonies were putting some English companies out of business.

"So, what did those English business owners do when they realized this? They went to their representatives in Parliament and demanded that they pass a law protecting them. And that's how that part of the Trade Laws came to be."

"Did it work?" she asked.

"Did the colonists go through all that trouble to settle the colonies just to give in?" I asked.

"I get it," Hannah replied. "Of course not. But how did the colonists get around it?"

"They went underground," I said. "They set up secret factories and warehouses."

"And the King found out about it anyway," Hannah said. "We can guess what he did."

"Yeah, sent in the army," Carter shouted, certain that his answer was correct.

"Yes, he did, Carter," I said. "He sent the army to enforce the Trade Laws."

"And this was costing him more money, too," concluded Hannah.

"We're all on the same page," I said. "So this went on for another 50 years, until the colonies were becoming more unruly and the King needed still more money.

"During this time, some of the colonies had begun to print their own money. This meant that they could do business among themselves without the King knowing about it.

"Again, the King found out, and in 1751, Parliament passed the Banking Laws. One of these laws kept the colonies from printing their own money."

"So what did they use, Gomps?" Carter asked.

"The Banking Laws made them use English money. These laws also allowed English courts to seize colonists' property if they couldn't pay their debts."

"What kind of property?" Carter asked.

"Everything, really," I replied, "including land, buildings, and even slaves."

"Wow!" exclaimed Hannah. "The English were getting everything they could."

"Yes, but believe it or not, this wasn't the worst of it," I said. "The Banking Laws repealed all banking laws passed by the colonial Assemblies."

"What's repealed mean, Gomps?" Carter asked.

"To repeal means to pass a law that cancels another law," I replied.

"Got it," he said.

"I knew you would," I said. "So the colonies kept trying to run themselves independent of the King. In the middle of it all, the colonial governors, who were loyal to . . . ?"

"The King!" they both shouted together.

". . . and the Assemblies, who were loyal to . . . ?"

"The people!" they shouted again.

". . . were having constant arguments over land ownership, local taxes, and business laws. To make matters worse, investors in England didn't have to pay the taxes that the investors in the colonies had to pay. So things were not going well."

"You mean if an investor in the colonies lived in England, he didn't have to pay, but if he lived in the colonies, he did?" Hannah asked.

"That's right," I replied.

"That wasn't fair," Hannah concluded. "Why did the colonists put up with it?"

"Well, as much as England was squeezing money from them and trying to control them, the colonists were also getting something out of the deal," I replied.

"What could they possibly have gotten that was worth all that grief?" she continued.

"Protection," I said. "England was protecting them from being taken over by the French or the Spanish. You see, all during this time, France and Spain had been trying to take over the New World.

"The French had established some settlements in Canada, and Spain was still occupying what is now Florida. The French were trying to move south and the Spanish were trying to move north. The King didn't want either country to take over, and neither did the colonies."

"Why not?" asked Carter. "What could have been worse?"

"It could have been much worse." I replied. "The Spanish ran their colonies by brute force, including brutal capture and treatment of slaves. And, since France was a continual enemy of England, the colonies didn't want to get caught in the middle. So they put up with the King's demands until some years later, when it just became too much."

"Did we have a war?" Carter asked, hopefully.

"Yes, we did, but that comes a little later," I answered. "In the meantime, there was a war in Europe."

"Great!" said Carter.

"I knew you would say that," said Hannah to Carter. "But who cares about a war in Europe?"

"You'll find out," I said. "But I got in late today and I'm tired. Next time I'm going to introduce you to some new friends – the Super Six."

22

THE SUPER SIX, THE CHERRY TREE, AND THE SILVER DOLLAR

The next Wednesday I no sooner got in the door than the kids began to pester me.

"Who are the Super Six, Gomps?" Carter asked. "We've been racking our brains all week."

"Yeah, Gomps, can you start now?" Hannah said. "We can't wait to find out."

"Sorry, kids," I said. "Dinner first, but I'll make you a deal. I'll start right after that and then you can have dessert. OK?"

"OK," Carter said. "We'll eat fast."

"Dad, that's OK," said Mandy, "but dessert will be mixed fruit. No sweets."

Ulp, I realized I had overstepped our deal. "Sorry," I said to Mandy.

"That's OK," she said. "Just this one time."

As soon as dinner was over, I picked up the story.

"Last time, I promised to introduce you to some new friends – the Super Six."

"Yeah, we're so curious," Hannah said. "We've never heard of that before. Sounds like comic-book characters."

"It's just a name I made up to help me remember them," I said. "These were the six most important men in the building of our nation.

"Have you heard of the Founding Fathers?" I asked.

They both nodded.

"Who were they?" I continued.

"Weren't they the ones who set up our country?" Hannah asked.

"That's a good way to put it," I replied. "How many were there?"

"Six?" Carter replied.

"Hannah?" I asked.

"I thought there were more than that, but I don't know," she answered.

"Well, there were quite a few, maybe into the hundreds, depending on how much credit you want to give to each one.

"That's why I came up with the idea for the Super Six. These were the six most important men among the Founding Fathers. Each of them played a big part."

"Who were they?" Carter asked.

"The Super Six are George Washington, Benjamin Franklin, Thomas Jefferson, John Adams, Alexander Hamilton, and James Madison," I replied. "Have you heard of any of them?"

"I've heard of Washington, Franklin and Jefferson," Carter replied, "and maybe Adams, but not the others."

"Hannah, how about you?" I asked.

"I've heard of all of them, but I'm not sure what they did," she replied.

"Well, each one played a different part," I said. "They were the designers, the leaders, the diplomats, the early Presidents, and the defenders. Our country could not have been started without all of them."

"Did they work as a team?" Carter asked.

"Not often," I replied. "The parts they played were so different that they often worked by themselves, but they got together during big meetings and wrote letters to each other when they were apart. On some things, they were on the opposite sides of the fence from one another."

"I thought they would have agreed on everything," Hannah said.

"Not on everything," I said, "and, I'm not sure that would have been a good thing. Part of designing a good system is to look at things from all sides and talk them out in debate."

"Hmm," she said, "never thought of that."

"So, tell us about them, Gomps," Carter said.

"Not all at once," I said. "If I did that, they would be too hard to keep track of. Instead, I'll introduce you to each one as we go.

⌒

"Let's start with a question," I said. "Who is called the Father of our Country?"

"George Washington," Hannah said.

"That's right!" I said. "How did you know?"

"They taught us that in school," she replied.

"That's great," I said. "What else did they teach you about him?"

"That he was the General in the Revolutionary War and then our first President," she answered.

"Anything else?" I asked.

"That's about it, as far as I can remember," she added.

"Did he really throw a silver dollar across a river when he was a boy?" Carter chimed in.

"Yeah," said Hannah, "and did he chop down a cherry tree and confess to his father?"

"Well, you two have been hearing quite a lot about Washington, haven't you," I replied. "No, he didn't do either of those things. Both stories were made up."

"Why would anyone make them up, Gomps?" Carter asked.

"I think to show what kind of a person he was," I answered. "Let's take the cherry tree story. I think that this story was told as an example of how truthful he was. He was said to be so honest that he told the truth knowing that he was in for punishment from his father."

"What about the silver dollar?" Carter asked.

"The silver dollar story is told for a different reason," I said. "Washington grew up to be a big man, probably six-four, with the strength to match. So I think that story was told to show that he was big and strong.

"Washington grew up on his family's plantation in Virginia. They called it Mount Vernon. His grandfather had come over from a little village in England and had begun farming. He expanded the farm and passed it along to his son, Augustus — George's father. Augustus expanded it still further into a plantation. "As was common in farm areas, George worked on the plantation as a child and received very little formal education. He only attended school for two years, but . . ."

"Two years?!" blurted Hannah. "That's all?"

"Apparently," I said. "The records of his school days are spotty, but it looks like he only went to a school for two years. Then he had another four to six years being taught by a tutor and by family members."

"Gee, it sounds like he wasn't very well educated," she continued. "How did he get so far?"

"Oh, I wouldn't confuse formal schooling with education," I cautioned. "By all reports, he was very smart and read everything he could get his hands on.

"He soon learned that he was good at math, and by the age of 13 or so, he had taught himself geometry and trigonometry, and that led to his becoming a land surveyor.

"His father had surveyed their farmlands, and George helped him. By the age of 15, George had his own surveying crew and was doing surveys all over Virginia."

"At 15?" Carter asked, wide-eyed.

"That's right," I replied. "In fact, at the age of 17 he was made the official surveyor for Culpepper County, Virginia."

"Wow," he remarked.

"He made good money," I continued, "and eventually went as far as western Pennsylvania to survey wild forest land.

"Now, one of the main investors in the Virginia Company was Lord Fairfax. Washington had done surveying jobs for him, including the western Pennsylvania job, and Fairfax had been impressed with him. George's older brother, Lawrence, had worked for Lord Fairfax in the Virginia militia, so Fairfax knew George's family, too.

"Lawrence performed well, but he died suddenly at the age of 34. So Fairfax turned to George to replace Lawrence, and at 20 years of age, George was sworn in as a Major in the Virginia militia."

"He was only 20 and already a Major?" Carter exclaimed.

"That's right," I replied. "And it's funny you should say that, because that's the reaction that a lot of other Virginians had. When asked about it, Lord Fairfax just said, 'All Washingtons are born old.'"

"What did he mean by that?" Hannah asked.

"He meant that the Washington family was, by nature, mature and responsible beyond their years," I replied.

"Now you know how George Washington started out. The next part of the story will be a pretty long one, so I'm going to stop here."

"Is that the war?" Carter asked.

"Yes, it is, Carter," I said, "but it's the European war I mentioned last time. Our war with England came after that. In the meantime, there's a bowl of fruit over there that is calling to me."

23

WAR, BUT NOT THE ONE YOU THINK

"Last time I promised I would tell you about a war," I began. This week I was working from home, so I was feeling refreshed. A good dinner and dessert hadn't hurt, either.

"But it isn't the war you think. This was a European war that spilled over into the New World, and the colonies got pulled into it.

"It was called the Seven Years' War. Can you guess why?" I asked.

"Because it lasted seven years?" Carter offered.

"That's right," I said, "although there were skirmishes for two years leading up to it."

"Huh," said Hannah.

"The Seven Years' War began in Europe in 1754," I continued. "It was the first truly worldwide war. There were several countries involved, but the countries we care about were England, France, and Spain."

"What were they fighting about?" Carter asked.

"Oh, the usual," I replied, "land, money, and power. All three countries had colonies around the world by this time, and they were fighting over which of them owned what land and who could trade with whom."

"Sounds complicated," Carter said.

"Yes, it was," I replied. "In fact, there were several wars within the Seven Years' War. The one we care about was called the French and Indian War."

"So, England fought the French?" Hannah asked.

"That's right," I replied. "The French and Indian War was fought in the New World. As I said a couple of weeks ago, France had set up some settlements in Canada, and from those, they tried to move south into New England, New York, and Pennsylvania."

"What about the Indian part?" Carter asked.

"What Indian part?" I replied.

"You said the war was called the French and Indian War," he said. "What was the Indian part?"

"Ah, yes," I replied. "Just as in the English colonies, there were Indian tribes where the French had settled. So, the French made deals with these tribes to help them fight the English."

"Why would the Indians agree to that?" Hannah asked.

"For the same reason that the French fought against the English," I replied. "The tribes had been at war with one another off and on for years before we ever got here. The northern tribes tried to take territory in the south, and the southern tribes tried to go north."

"Didn't that give the French an advantage, to have Indians on their side?" Hannah asked.

"It would have if the English had done nothing," I said. "But the English set up deals with some of the tribes in the colonies, and that pretty much balanced things out.

"So the French and their Indian allies came south into northern New York and western Pennsylvania and set up forts. And the fighting began."

"What's this got to do with anything, Gomps?" Hannah interrupted.

"Two things," I replied.

"First, the invasion by the French and Indians forced the colonies to join forces to help the English. This was the first time that the colonies had gotten together to defend themselves since the Pequot War.

"And second, this war was costing the King a lot of money, and he had to find a way to pay for it."

❧

"So here we are in 1753 at the start of the French and Indian War. The French set up forts in Pennsylvania right where George Washington had done land surveying.

"The Virginia Governor wanted to send a formal message to the French that this was English land and to give up their takeover of it. He talked with Lord Fairfax, and guess who they chose to deliver the message?"

"George Washington!" they both shouted.

"Major George Washington," I said. "He knew the territory, had proven himself reliable in the wilderness, and was now a military officer. Who better — at age 21, no less?

"Washington left Virginia in October with a small group and reached the French fort in December. He delivered the message to the French General and waited for a reply. Four days later, the General gave Washington the French reply, and Washington left for Virginia.

"The weather grew bitter cold, and all of Washington's team quit the journey along the way. Washington continued through snow, ice, and freezing rivers for two more weeks, by himself, across the mountains and on to Williamsburg, where he delivered the message to the Governor.

"Washington's report on the journey was published, and overnight, he became a celebrity."

"What was the answer from the French, Gomps?" Carter asked.

"Refusal, on all counts," I answered.

"So that whole trip was for nothing?" Hannah asked.

"No, a lot of good came out of it," I replied. "For one thing, Washington saw the French forces and passed that information along. And the Governor and others now knew that Washington was a brave and reliable leader.

"Soon after, Virginia organized a counterattack. Washington was promoted to Lieutenant Colonel and commanding officer of the attack. He recruited a force of 100 men and trained them over the next month. Unfortunately, the Governor had not given him enough guns and supplies, so he was faced with having to make do.

"Nonetheless, by April, Washington and his men began their march to fight the French. It took them almost two months to get there, and they immediately came upon a French scouting party of about 50 men. There was a small battle, and Washington's forces won."

"Yay," they both exclaimed.

"Don't be too quick to celebrate," I said. "They marched on to the French fort, where they were vastly outnumbered and soundly beaten. In fact, Washington had to surrender."

"Oh, no," they both lamented. "How did he get out of it?"

"The French General agreed to let him go if he and his men gave up the ground they had gained in the first battle and returned to Virginia," I said.

"Why would the French guy do that?" Carter asked.

"War had not yet been declared," I replied, "so this battle meant little to the French. Also, the General may not have taken Washington seriously, since he was only 22 years old."

"What happened next, Gomps?" Carter asked.

"Later that year, the British sent a British Army General — Major General Edward Braddock — and about 2,000 soldiers to take back the land. Since everyone knew of Washington's experience there, Braddock made him one of his four assistants.

"After some time to recruit some Virginia militia and to train, the whole force started across the mountains, headed for the French forts. Not long after, though, Washington came down with a severe fever, probably smallpox, and he was carried a good part of the way in a surgeon's wagon.

"Once they got close to the French, General Braddock attacked right away, but his soldiers had no experience fighting in the forest, and many were killed or wounded by the French and Indian sharpshooters. In fact, Braddock himself was badly wounded and later died.

"Seeing this, Washington demanded that he be given a horse so that he could take over the lead. Despite his illness, he had his men strap him into the saddle, and off he galloped to the front lines. There he rode back and forth, trying to rally the troops, but the British, in their confusion, dropped their guns and ran away.

"By the time it was over, Washington had had two horses shot out from under him and had a bullet go through his hat and three more through his coat, but he was never hit."

"Holy cow!" Carter exclaimed. "Is that really true, about the bullets?"

"Yes, Carter," I said. "There are several written reports by soldiers who were there, and years later an Indian chief who had been in the battle on the French side also reported it. Washington himself later showed his hat and coat to others who asked him about it."

"How did he keep from getting hit?" Carter continued.

"Many thought he must have supernatural powers," I replied. "But Washington, in his humble way, denied that. Later, he wrote in a letter to a friend that he was spared only 'by the miraculous care of Providence that protected me beyond all human expectation.'"

"Providence?" Hannah asked. "What did he mean by Providence?"

"It's a word he often used to refer to God," I replied. "Washington was a religious man and frequently prayed. He believed that God had kept him safe."

"What do you think, Gomps?" Carter asked.

"Who am I to argue with George Washington?" I said.

"What about the Indian chief?" Hannah asked.

"What Indian chief?" I asked.

"The one who witnessed the battle," she continued. "You said he reported it. How did he do that?"

"Ah, yes," I said. "The story of the Indian Prophecy comes next, but that's enough for tonight."

"Oh, no, Gomps," Hannah whined. "You can't leave us hanging like that."

"I'm afraid I'm going to have to," I said. "Your Dad is giving me the high sign that you have chores to do."

24

THE INDIAN PROPHECY
AND THE END OF A WAR

"Last week, I promised to tell you the story of the Indian Prophecy," I began the following Wednesday evening.

"What's a prophecy?" Carter asked.

"Carter, you know what that is," said Hannah. "It's when someone predicts the future. Like a prophet."

"Oh, yeah," said Carter.

"So," I said, "during the battle with the French, this chief had seen Washington rallying his troops from horseback with bullets whizzing all around him. About 15 years later, he met with Washington and a group of colonists who were trying to settle an argument over the ownership of land in that area. The chief had a council fire one night to talk with the colonists about the tribe's views of the matter. Suddenly, he stood up and gave a speech.

"The chief said that he had been the one in charge of the Indians who had fought the English in that battle and that he had gotten all his sharpshooters to aim at Washington. But none could hit him. He said, 'A power mightier than we shielded him from harm. He cannot die in battle.'

"Then he said that he himself was going to die soon, but he wanted to say something '. . . in the voice of prophecy.' 'The Great Spirit protects that man [pointing to Washington] and guides his destinies – he will become the chief of nations, and a people yet unborn will hail him as the founder of a mighty empire!'"

"No way!" exclaimed Hannah. "How do you know he said that?"

"Well, Washington made no mention of it himself," I said. "That shouldn't surprise us because of his humility. But others who were there wrote it down in letters and reports and told the story frequently after that. So that's the Indian Prophecy. What do you think?"

"Sounds iffy to me," said Hannah.

"It coulda happened," Carter said.

"In any event, after losing that battle, Washington and the remainder of his forces dragged themselves back to Virginia. News of the events reached home before he did, and he was showered with praise."

"Even though they lost?" Hannah asked.

"Even though they lost," I replied. "The colonists saw this as a British loss, not a Virginia loss. The commander had been a British General, and most of the troops were British."

"What happened next?" asked Carter.

"Two things," I answered. "First, the British kept losing, and as a result, the Prime Minister in England was replaced by a man named William Pitt. Pitt saw that they had to send lots more troops. Once they did, the British were able to hold back the French.

"Second, Indian tribes in western Virginia began attacking colonial settlements, killing the settlers and taking their stuff. The Governor of Virginia needed someone who could put together a defense force to protect the settlers."

"Here comes George Washington!" Hannah exclaimed. "I just know he was the one."

"You're absolutely right, Hannah," I said. "Washington was made a Colonel in charge of the Virginia Regiment. He spent the next three years on the Virginia frontier protecting the settlements there.

"Despite his efforts, though, the French and Indians were once again gaining the upper hand. Washington knew that his forces by themselves were not enough to stop them. To bolster his forces, he convinced Pennsylvania and Maryland to give him troops.

"Meanwhile, back in England, the King sent 3,000 British troops to join up with Washington. This would add to the enormous costs of the war, but the King felt he had no choice. The French were winning.

"So, this new force of 6,000 troops battled the French and Indians for months. Finally, in November 1758, they were a day away from the main French fort when they saw smoke in the sky. Scouts rushed forward to see what was happening. When they got back, they reported that the French had set fire to the fort and were gone!"

"Yay," shouted the kids.

"Yay is right," I said. "The French had seen that they couldn't stand up to Washington and the British, and rather than get wiped out, they destroyed everything and retreated into Canada. And that started to turn the war in England's favor."

"Gomps, you said that the war was costing the English a lot of money," said Hannah, "but how much could it have cost them to send 3,000 troops?"

"Great question," I replied. "The English were fighting the French and the Spanish all over the New World and in Europe. So the fighting in Virginia was just one part of it. England was broke, and so, for that matter, were France and Spain."

"How did the war end, Gomps?" Carter asked.

"I think they just got tired of fighting," I replied. "Each had captured some territories and lost some. The English saw that they could end the expense and maybe come out ahead in the peace talks. So they called for peace.

"In 1763, all the countries met in Paris, France and worked out an arrangement to end the war. The deal resulted in a treaty – the Treaty of Paris."

"*Did* England come out ahead?" Hannah asked.

"I think so," I replied. "Here's how it ended up. France gave Canada to England in return for some Caribbean islands. France also gave the eastern half of Louisiana to England."

"Whoa, wait a second, Gomps," Hannah said. "You're going too fast. What did France get for Louisiana?"

"Nothing," I replied, "except a temporary peace and an end to the cost of the war."

"That's all?" she continued.

"Doesn't seem like a big deal to me," Carter interjected. "Half of Louisiana isn't very much in the first place."

"I think you're jumping to conclusions, Carter," I said. "You're thinking of the State of Louisiana as it is today, right?"

"Well, yeah," he replied.

"That's what I thought," I said. "Back then, Louisiana went from the west side of the Appalachian Mountains in the east all the way to the Rocky Mountains. It was about half the size of the whole New World."

"Holy cow," he said, his eyes wide in wonder. "So the eastern half of Louisiana in those days *was* a big deal."

"It sure was, and there was more to the deal," I continued. "Spain gave Florida to England in return for Cuba and the Philippine Islands. And France gave to Spain the western half of Louisiana."

"Wow!" Hannah exclaimed. "How come France gave up so much? Did they know how much land that was?"

"I think they knew," I replied. "There had been French explorers all over the New World for 150 years. But they were facing the enormous costs of defending it."

"I think they miscalculated," Hannah concluded. "Look at what it became."

"Easy to say now," I said, "but no one expected that we would end up getting it instead of England."

"Well, sure," she said, "if you put it that way. Still, it looks like England did get the best of the deal."

"Yeah," said Carter.

"So the French and Indian War was over," I went on, "and now it was time for the King of England to face the costs. But before we see what he did, I'm going to end the story for tonight. This is a good stopping place and I want another piece of cake. How about you?"

"Me, too," said Carter. "Chocolate's my favorite."

"OK," said Hannah.

And we went back to the dining room table despite the look of disapproval on Mandy's face.

25

THE KING TURNS THE SCREWS ON THE COLONIES

My company didn't send me out of town the next week, so I was back that Wednesday to continue the story. "The King of England was broke from the French and Indian War," I said. "What were his choices, do you think?"

"Did he charge it?" Carter asked.

"Yeah, he whipped out his credit card!" Hannah exclaimed, as they both laughed.

"Well, in fact, that's exactly what he did," I said.

"Ha ha!" said Hannah. "You're funny, Gomps."

"No, really," I said. "Of course, there were no credit cards back then, but what he did amounted to the same thing. He went out and borrowed the money."

"Who from?" Carter asked.

"Mostly from other countries and from his nobles," I said. "But now he had big loans to pay back."

"How did he pay them?" Hannah asked.

"I'll let you answer that one," I said. "How had he gotten extra money before?"

"Taxes!" they shouted together.

"You got it!" I said. "And guess where was the first place he looked?"

"The colonies?" said Hannah, knowing she was right. "That wasn't fair."

"Let's look at it from the King's point of view," I said. "Did the colonies want to be ruled by the French?"

"I guess not," Carter replied.

"So, without England, would the colonies have been able to hold off the French?" I continued.

"No," Hannah said reluctantly.

"As far as the King was concerned," I said, "he was just asking them to pay for the protection he had provided to them. He felt he had every right to go ahead and tax them."

"I guess if you put it that way . . ." Hannah sighed.

"Of course, the colonies didn't see it that way," I said. "They understood the part that England played, but they had done a lot of the fighting themselves. They felt that they should at least be consulted about the taxes, just like the English people were."

"He asked the English people about taxes?" Hannah asked.

"Yes, he did, in a way," I replied. "Parliament had a long-standing rule, 'No taxation without representation.' Meaning that the English people, through their elected representatives in Parliament, got a say in any new taxes. But that right didn't extend to the colonies."

"That wasn't fair," Hannah said.

"Nonetheless," I said, "the King went ahead with more taxes."

"What was left to tax?" Hannah asked. "Hadn't he taxed everything already?"

"Oh, he was just getting started," I replied. "First was the Sugar Act of 1764. This was a tax on sugar cane. Then, taxes on other farm products were added. But these taxes still didn't bring in enough money.

"Up to this time, the taxes had been charged against only parts of the colonies — the Navigation Acts taxed only importers and exporters. The Trade laws taxed warehouse owners. The Banking laws applied mainly to the rich and to bankers. The Sugar Act taxed sugar cane growers and other farmers, mainly in the South."

"Didn't the colonies get mad at all these taxes?" Carter asked.

"Yes, they did," I replied, "but no tax hit everyone, so no big segment of the colonists got mad at any one tax.

"Of course, that meant that each tax was only a small part of what the King needed, and even added together, they fell far short.

"Seeing this, the King decided that the best way to bring in more money was a tax that would be paid by every colonist. And what he came up with was the Stamp Act, passed by Parliament in 1765."

"How would buying stamps raise all that money?" Carter asked.

"Yeah," Hannah agreed.

"Oh, this wasn't about buying postage stamps," I said. "The Stamp Act charged a tax on every single thing that was printed on paper. Every time a colonist signed a loan, a tax was due. Every time a colonist wrote a contract, a tax was due. The Stamp Act taxed every sale of a newspaper or calendar, every deed and mortgage on the sale of property, every college diploma, every gambling bet, all records of goods held in warehouses for sale, every license granted, every advertisement published."

"Oh my God," Hannah exclaimed. "How could they do that?"

"Well, I hear two questions," I replied. "First, how could they justify the Stamp Act? And second, how could they collect? Right?"

"Yeah," replied Hannah and Carter together.

"Let's take the first question," I continued. "Parliament and the King figured that the colonists were the King's subjects, and therefore had to obey whatever laws they passed. The King had protected them from the French, and he needed the money for having done so. Parliament passed the laws, so pay up."

"Yeah, but this sounds like they taxed everything!" Carter said. "Didn't it hurt the colonies?"

"It was going to hurt them big time," I replied. "But, the King felt he had the power to do it, so he did. And this is where Hannah's second question comes in.

"That was, how could they collect the Stamp Act taxes?" I said.

"The King sent tax collectors into every colonial city and town. Every time the colonists did anything that was covered by the Stamp Act, they had to go to a tax collector, pay the tax, and he would stamp the papers with the King's seal of approval."

"Ah, so that's why they called it the Stamp Act," Carter said. "The papers had to have the tax collector's stamp on it."

"You got it," I said. "Now, I have a question for you. If you were a colonist, would you pay the tax?"

"Not if we could help it!" they both exclaimed.

"Why not?" I continued.

"I'd be going to the tax collector a hundred times a day!" Carter answered.

"And, I'd be broke!" Hannah added.

"You're both absolutely right," I said. "And that's just how the colonists saw it. So they just ignored the Stamp Act and went about their business."

"What did the King do?" Hannah asked.

"Sent in the army!" yelled Carter. "Yes, yes, yes, I knew it!"

"Oh, Carter," Hannah scolded. "That's always your answer."

"Hannah, don't be too quick to judge," I said. "That's just what he did."

"See?" said Carter, turning to his sister.

"Whatever," Hannah replied in mock derision.

"All right, you two," I said. "Calm down.

"Up to now, there had been only the occasional need for British troops in the colonies, so there hadn't been too many of them. The Stamp Act was a different story. Colonists everywhere were ignoring the law, so the King needed to send troops to every place there was a tax collector."

"But I thought that the King didn't have the money for something like this," Hannah concluded. "Wasn't the cost of the army what got him into this in the first place?"

"That's a smart insight," I said. "He didn't have the money, but his advisors had an idea."

"What was that, Gomps?" Carter asked.

"Make the colonies pay for it," I replied.

"You're kidding!" Hannah exclaimed. "How did he think he could get away with that? They were already resisting the taxes."

"He thought he could get away with it because he was the . . . ?"

"King!" they both shouted.

"Right!" I said. "He believed that he had the right and the power to do pretty much whatever he wanted. So, Parliament passed what was called the Quartering Act in late 1765. This Act forced the colonists to house and feed the British troops who were there to enforce the tax collection."

"That's ridiculous!" Hannah exclaimed.

"Yeah," echoed Carter.

"So what do you think happened?" I asked.

"The people hated the British troops." Carter said.

"Right." I said. "And, they hated the . . . ?"

"King?" Carter asked.

"They were beginning to," I said, "even though they had been loyal to him. But, they also hated the . . . ?"

"Tax collectors!" Hannah exclaimed.

"Riiight," I said. "So, what do you think the colonists did to solve their problem?"

"Fight the troops?" Carter asked. Hannah sighed.

"Why did you sigh at Carter's answer, Hannah?" I asked.

"The troops would have killed them," she replied. "Besides, some of the people were still loyal to the King."

"How do you know?" her brother said, challenging her directly for the first time.

"In the first place, the colonists didn't have an army," she retorted. "And Gomps himself said that some were loyal – the Loyalists."

"They had militia, didn't they, Gomps?" Carter asked, turning to me.

"They did, Carter," I said, "but I don't think they thought they were strong enough to beat the British. Not yet, anyway."

"But they could have, couldn't they?" he continued.

"We'll soon find out," I said.

"See?" Carter said, facing Hannah and not yet willing to give up his point.

"What about the Loyalists, Carter?" I asked. "Didn't Hannah make a good point there?"

"All of them?" he asked. "Were all of the colonists still loyal?"

"What do you think?" I continued.

"I wouldn't have been," he replied. "Not anymore."

"So what would you have done, if you didn't fight?" I asked.

"Tried to get around it," he said. "Paying those horrible taxes, I mean."

"Any ideas how?" I asked. Carter paused.

"Hannah, how about you?" I asked. "Any ideas on how to get around it?"

"Didn't you say that they did things in secret to get around some of the other laws?" she asked.

"I did," I replied.

"Then I think the colonists went into secret again," she said.

"Carter? You buy that?" I asked.

"Sure," he said. "That's what I would do."

"Well, you're right," I said. "They operated in secret, made things in secret, conducted business in secret, smuggled things. They tried to do everything in secret."

"Cool," Hannah said.

"Now, what happened the last time the colonists tried that?" I asked.

"The army tried to catch them," Carter answered.

"Right," I said. "Any reason why they wouldn't try again this time?"

"Nope," said Hannah.

"Right again," I said. "Only this time, the King came down on the colonies with both feet. He had the colonial governors, who were loyal to . . .?"

"Him!" they yelled.

". . . issue search warrants to the troops. And the troops used the search warrants to search factories, shops, warehouses, ships, and even individual homes for evidence that the laws had been broken.

"He had the English Navy patrol the coastline to stop smuggling. And he had the governors recruit spies and informers to help report the lawbreakers."

"What did the troops do when they caught them?" Carter asked.

"The troops took their money to pay the tax," I replied, "and if they didn't have it, took their property."

"How could they take their property, Gomps?" Carter asked.

"As if the King needed a reason, but remember the Banking Laws?" I asked. "One of them made it legal to take property to pay off a debt. So the King was good to go."

"Oh, yeah," he replied. "I guess they had all the angles covered, didn't they."

"All that they could think of," I confirmed. "But they didn't have any experience with what the colonists came up with next."

"What was that, Gomps?" Hannah asked.

"The Sons of Liberty!" I said. "And that's all for tonight."

"Aw, Gomps, can't we hear it now?" Carter begged.

"No, Carter, I've got some things to do back home, but I'll give you a little preview.

"The Sons of Liberty were the first protesters in the colonies," I said. "They carried out a raid against the English. And that's all I'm going to say until next week. Sleep tight."

26

THE SONS OF LIBERTY PROTEST IN THE STREETS

"The Sons of Liberty tonight, right, Gomps?" Carter blurted as we settled in the living room after dessert.

"We've been looking forward to this all week," Hannah added.

"That's right," I confirmed. "Tonight we meet the Sons of Liberty, but to understand them we have to go back a few years to the French and Indian War.

"Remember that some colonial militias fought alongside the British troops?"

"Oh, yeah," Carter said.

"Where do you think they got the food, clothing, guns, wagons, and all that they needed? England?"

"I don't think so," Hannah replied. "The King didn't even have enough to send to his own troops."

"Right," I said. "So where did the stuff for the militia come from?"

"Had to be the colonies, right?" she continued.

"Yup," I said. "Colonial factories made the stuff, and colonial farms produced the food. Was business good for them during the war?"

"Had to be," Carter replied.

"Why's that?" I challenged.

"The militias couldn't work and fight at the same time, so the rest of the people had to provide for themselves and the militias," he continued.

"You hit the nail right on the head," I said as he beamed. "There was plenty of business for everyone, and that meant plenty of jobs. You with me?"

"Yup," they both nodded.

"But now the war was over," I said. "Were all the supplies for the militias needed?"

"No."

"Why not?" I asked.

"'Cause those guys went home and could get their own," Carter replied.

"Right again," I said. "So what happened to business?"

Hannah gave two thumbs down.

"Right," I continued. "And, what happened to all those jobs?"

"People got laid off?" Carter replied.

"That's exactly right," I said. "Lots of people lost their jobs or businesses, and the colonial economy slowed down.

"They had to go on unemployment," Carter wisecracked.

"Seriously, what about the taxes, then?" Hannah asked.

"Well, the taxes didn't go down," I said. "Any money they might have had to keep their businesses afloat was being eaten up by the taxes. The colonists became desperate and began looking for someone to blame. Who do you think they blamed?"

"The King?" Carter replied.

"Who else?" I said.

"The tax collectors," Hannah added.

"And the army," Carter added.

"Anyone else?" I asked.

"The spies!" Carter shouted.

"Right on all counts," I said. "The people started to revolt in the streets. The British troops were harassed, and people who were suspected of being spies were shunned or even run out of town.

"In Boston, a man named Samuel Adams, the son of a malthouse operator and church deacon, got together a secret group of businessmen and jobless people. They called themselves the 'Sons of Liberty.'"

"Gomps, we're not supposed to notice, but Dad sometimes drinks Sam Adams beer," Hannah said. "Is that the same guy?"

"Ha, ha," I laughed. "In fact, it is, although the beer is just named after him. Sam Adams had tried to become a maltster in his father's malt house, but that didn't work out."

"What's a maltster?" Carter asked.

"It's someone who makes the malt for brewing beer," I replied.

"Why is he important?" asked Hannah.

"Even though he wasn't good at business or at making malt, he was good at politics," I replied. "And he organized a number of protests that led up to the Revolutionary War, like the Sons of Liberty.

"Soon, Sons of Liberty groups sprouted up in cities and towns all around the colonies. And they were what some called rabble-rousers."

"What did they do?" Carter asked.

"Well, they went into the streets and demonstrated. Some rioted and broke into tax collectors' offices and burned Stamp Act documents.

"They also organized a boycott of goods from England. The boycott spread throughout the colonies and caused quite a reaction in London, as we'll see later.

"Through the various Sons of Liberty chapters, Sam Adams set up a meeting of colonial representatives in New York City and called it the Stamp Act Congress.

"Nine of the 13 colonies sent representatives to the Congress. They met in October 1765, and issued a proclamation called 'The Declaration of Rights and Grievances.' Among other complaints, this Declaration insisted that there could be no taxation without representation."

"Just like the English," Carter said.

"Just like them," I said.

"I thought every colony had an elected Assembly that passed the laws," Hannah said.

"The colonial assemblies could only pass local laws. The big taxes were passed by the English Parliament, remember?" I said. "The colonies had no representatives there. Parliament passed all these taxes by themselves and forced them on the colonies."

"Oh, yeah," she said. "I get it now. I got the colonial assemblies mixed up with Parliament."

"Glad you straightened that out," I said. "Carter, do you see what we're talking about?"

"I think so," he replied. "Parliament didn't care whether we liked the taxes or not."

"That's about it," I said. "They saw the colonies as not being equal to them.

"So what happened to the Declaration, Gomps?" Carter asked.

"Of Rights and Grievances?" I asked.

"Yeah."

"The Stamp Act Congress sent it to London, but the English just ignored it," I said. "If it didn't suit their purposes to face up to something, they just pretended it wasn't happening."

"Like the War of Jenkins' Ear?" Hannah asked.

"Just like that," I replied.

"Did the colonies start the Revolutionary War when they heard about that?" Carter asked.

"Not right away," I replied. "The colonies were still trying to work things out with England. And that leads us to the second of our Super Six – Benjamin Franklin. His is a pretty long story, so you're going to have to wait till next time to hear about him."

"OK, Gomps," said Carter. "We've got homework, anyway."

"Well, that works for everyone, then," I said. "Give me a hug and I'll be on my way."

27

SUPER BENJAMIN FRANKLIN

This week the kids beat me to the sofa for story time.

"You promised to tell us about Benjamin Franklin," Carter said. "We're ready."

"OK," I said. "In 1757, Benjamin Franklin had been sent to London by the Pennsylvania Colony to work out various disputes between the colony and their investors. By this time, Franklin was already a famous man.

"Franklin was born in Boston in 1706, the son of a . . ."

"Candlemaker," Hannah interrupted.

"What, Hannah?" I asked.

"A candlemaker," she said. "Franklin was the son of a candlemaker. His father sent him to Boston Grammar School, but after two years they couldn't afford it and they pulled him out. He had two more years with a tutor, but they couldn't afford that either, so that was it for school."

"What is going on?" I asked.

"I studied up!" Hannah said proudly. "I was curious about him and decided to see what I could find out."

I looked at Carter, Mandy and Mark. They shrugged as if to say, "News to me."

"OK," I said to Hannah. "What else did you learn about Franklin?"

"Oh, lots," she said, glancing down at notes she had taken. "His father put him to work in his candle factory when he was ten and . . . "

"Ten?" Carter exclaimed.

"Carter!" she said. "You're interrupting."

"Sorry," Carter said, "but how could he go to work at ten?"

"Remember?" she said. "Gomps told us that kids went to work much younger than today, especially in family businesses."

"Oh, yeah," Carter confirmed.

"So, to continue the story before I was so rudely interrupted . . . " she continued.

"Now, now, Hannah," I said. "No point in rubbing it in."

"OK, sorry," she said. "Anyway, Franklin worked in his father's candle factory for two years, but he didn't like it.

"While this was going on, his older brother, James, had started a print shop. Their father could see that Franklin didn't like making candles, so he gave him a choice: make candles or go to work for his brother. Benjamin chose the print shop."

"Didn't he have to know how to read to work there?" Carter asked.

"Oh, yes," Hannah answered.

"But he had only two years of school." Carter continued.

"The books say that he read everything he could find," she said. "Like George Washington, I guess. Right, Gomps?"

"Apparently," I said. "Franklin said in his autobiography that he could not remember a time when he could not read, so he must have learned at a very early age."

"What's an autobiography, Gomps?" Carter asked.

"That's when you write the story of your own life," I said.

"Got it, but if he didn't go to school for very long, how did he learn?" Carter continued.

"He taught himself," I replied. "He also taught himself to read Latin, French, and German, and to play at least three musical instruments. And he invented one he called the armonica."

"It looks like Franklin was very, very smart," Hannah said, "as you'll soon see. So, at twelve, Franklin became an apprentice in the print shop. He worked the printing presses and he began to write.

"After a while, James started a newspaper called the *New England Courant*, and over the next two years, Franklin wrote a bunch of letters to the editor under the name of Silence Dogood, a pretend widow he dreamed up so no one would know it was him."

"What did he write about?" I asked.

Hannah looked down at her notes, and then said, "I'm not sure, Gomps."

"Well, if I can add to your story, he wrote about a lot of things," I added. "Sometimes he poked fun at politicians and criticized customs of the day, like public drunkenness and hoop skirts.

"But he wrote about some serious subjects, too," I continued. "In one of the letters he said that people must be free to say what is on their minds."

"You mean freedom of speech?" Hannah asked.

"That's right," I replied. "He wrote that freedom of speech 'is the right of every man as long as he does not hurt or control the right of another.' See, Hannah, I've been studying up, too." And, with that, I gave a wink to Carter.

"Ha, ha," Hannah laughed. "You got me there, Gomps."

"And," I continued, "in that letter he also said that freedom of speech was vital to an honest government."

"Why?" Carter asked.

"He felt that if you are not free to criticize your government, it will be too easy for politicians to do what's good for them and not necessarily good for the people."

"How would criticizing them make them honest?" he continued.

"Well, it might not make them honest," I replied, "but at least if they tried to pull something, they could be found out and forced out."

"I see," he said. "What happened next?"

"Let's see what else Hannah has learned," I said, turning to her.

"James found out what his brother was doing and got really mad," she continued.

"Why did he get mad?" Carter asked.

"I think his little brother was showing him up," Hannah replied. "Benjamin was only 16."

"Sixteen?" Carter said.

"Yup," Hannah confirmed. "Pretty embarrassing, huh?"

"I guess," replied Carter, "but if he was smart, he was smart. It's not like Benjamin was keeping his brother from doing something cool himself."

Hmmm, I thought. Out of the mouths of babes . . .

"Anyway," Hannah continued, "they started having arguments, so at 17 Benjamin ran away to Philadelphia and got a job with a printer there. Then, a year later, he went to England and got a job with an important printing company in London."

"Why were they important?" Carter asked.

Hannah looked at her notes and again said, "I'm not sure. Gomps?"

"The company did printing for many authors and scientists, as well as for the King," I continued. "This put Franklin in contact with important people and gave him the chance to make friends with them."

Picking up the story again, Hannah said, "But he wanted to go back to Philadelphia, so after two years in London, he went back and worked for his old printer, where he was made the manager.

"Then, at 22, he left and started his own print shop. A year after that, he started his own newspaper, the *Pennsylvania Gazette*. And then he started something called *Poor Richard's Almanack*."

"What's an Almanack?" Carter asked.

"I think it's kind of a magazine," she replied. "It had information about weather, recipes, and jokes and things. Right, Gomps?"

"That's about right," I said. "Did you find out anything in particular about *Poor Richard's*?"

"Yeah," she said. "It looks like Franklin also put in the same kind of stuff that he wrote as Silence Dogood – sayings, manners, and his ideas on things."

"Did you come across any of the sayings?" I asked.

"The one I liked best was, 'Fish and visitors smell in three days.'"

We all laughed at that. "Any others?" I asked.

"Yeah," Hannah replied. "Early to bed and early to rise makes a man healthy, wealthy and wise."

"That's a good one," I said.

"Anyway," said Hannah, "the Almanack sold like crazy and made him famous.

"Then, that helped him get more business. Pretty soon, everyone knew about him, even though he was still in his twenties."

"What kind of business did he get?" I asked.

"He printed books. He printed other newspapers. He printed documents. He even printed the money for the colony of New Jersey," she said.

"As he met people, he often formed other businesses with them," she continued. "So, before long he had print shops in other colonies.

"And that's just the beginning!"

"Benjamin Franklin was also a scientist and an inventor. He invented a wood stove; he invented batteries, the lightning rod, and bifocal eyeglasses.

"He proved that lightning was electricity," Hannah said.

"I heard that he flew a kite in a thunderstorm," Carter asked. "Did he really do that?"

"I think so," Hannah replied. "Gomps, do you know for sure?"

"Yes, he did," I confirmed. "But I want to tell you something very, very important about that. You must never do that yourselves. Never.

Franklin was lucky that he didn't kill himself. Seriously. So, promise me you won't ever fly a kite in a thunderstorm."

"I promise," Hannah said.

"Me, too," Carter added. "I didn't know if that story was like George Washington throwing a silver dollar across a river."

"No, Carter," I said, "Franklin really did. But, Hannah, I may be horning in on your story. Looks like you have some more to tell us about him."

"Sure do," she said. "He was named the clerk of the Pennsylvania Assembly at the age of 30 and the Postmaster for Philadelphia at 31."

"What's a Postmaster?" Carter interrupted.

"Carter! I was talking," she said.

"Hey, I wanna know," he protested.

"Easy does it, kids," I said. "Carter, a Postmaster is the person who runs the post offices. But, in this case, a post office system hadn't yet been set up, so Franklin had to do that first. He became so good at it that he later was made the Postmaster for other colonies. He was probably the first to use horses and riders to deliver the mail quickly over long distances."

"Like the Pony Express?" Hannah asked.

"Like the Pony Express," I confirmed. "I take it there's more, Hannah?"

"Oh, yes," Hannah said. "At 41, he organized the Pennsylvania colonial militia — the first colony to have one. Before that, each city or town had their own militia, but he was the first to put them all together. He later became the commander of it.

"He also created the first public library, the first hospital, the first fire department, and the first fire insurance company. And he started the University of Pennsylvania."

"No way," Carter said. "No one could have done all that."

"Yes, he did," Hannah said. "And more."

"Where did he get the time?" Carter asked, astonished.

"Well, for one thing," I interjected, "he put in long hours. He started his work day every morning at 6."

"Started at 6?" Carter asked. "Don't you mean he got up at 6?"

"No, Carter," I replied. "He started work at 6.

"Sorry, if I interrupted, Hannah."

"That's OK, Gomps, I'm just about done," she said. "The only other thing is that he was elected to the Pennsylvania Assembly, and they sent him to England on business deals. When other colonies heard what a good job he was doing there, they got him to represent them, too. I think that's about where you started, Gomps."

She paused, looking at her notes. "Now I'm done."

"Well, thank you for a great report, Hannah," I said. "You did a wonderful job.

"There's just one other thing I want to mention about Franklin, and it has to do with the English shooting themselves in the foot."

"Shooting themselves in the foot?" Carter laughed. "Why would they shoot themselves in the foot?"

"That's just a figure of speech, Carter," I replied. "It means that they did something against their own interests without realizing it.

Instead of shooting what you're aiming at, you shoot yourself in the foot by mistake."

"Oh, I get it," Carter said.

"What did they do?" Hannah asked.

"You'll find out next time," I said. "Just know that Ben Franklin was in the middle of it. But, that's enough for tonight. The report on him is plenty for us to digest - that and your Mom's apple tarts. They were delicious.

"That report was a wonderful surprise, Hannah," I continued. "Thank you."

"No problem, Gomps," she replied. "I had fun doing it."

And, after hugs all around, I bid them a good night.

28

THE ENGLISH SHOOT THEMSELVES IN THE FOOT AND GET US GOING

The next Wednesday was here in no time. As usual, we gathered around the living room.

"Last time, I promised to tell you how the English shot themselves in the foot," I started. "But to understand that, we have to go back to the French and Indian War again.

"Remember that the English wanted the colonies to help with the fighting, but they knew that individual militias wouldn't be able to do the job. They wanted the militias to work together.

"So in 1754, the English Prime Minister called for a meeting of all the colonies to work out a plan. As instructed, representatives of the colonies met in Albany, New York, to join forces and coordinate their militias. They called it the Albany Congress of 1754."

"Sounds like a good idea to me," Carter observed.

"So did the British," I said, "but they didn't think about what else could happen. By making the colonies fight together, the English planted a seed of wider cooperation that would doom them in the end."

"Gomps, I thought you were going to tell us something else about Benjamin Franklin," Hannah asked.

"Hannah, you're just in time," I replied, "because Franklin was a representative of the Pennsylvania Colony to the Albany Congress. By that time, he had already been thinking that the colonies needed to work together. So he drew up a plan for the colonies to unite completely, not just for war, and he presented it to the Albany Congress.

"The Congress thought it was a good idea and they sent it to England, but the English rejected it flat out. Nonetheless, Franklin had gotten started the idea of a 'united states,' and the English had forced him into it, in a way."

"So that's how they shot themselves in the foot, Gomps," said Carter, "by forcing the colonies to start to work together?"

"That's exactly right, Carter," I said. "It's hard to imagine that the British could expect the colonies to limit themselves just to a discussion of military cooperation. But I guess they were used to having their orders obeyed to the letter.

"So, back to our story. It was 1767 and Franklin was already in England trying to get the English to remove the Stamp Act, when . . ."

"Gomps?" Carter interrupted.

"Yes, Carter?" I replied.

"Can I do a report, too?" he asked.

"Sure," I said. "Did you have anything particular in mind?"

"One of the other Super Six, maybe?" he suggested.

"Well, that's a little ambitious for your first report," I said. "How about a battle?"

"Oh, yeah!" he said. "Which one?"

"Well," I replied, "what I have in mind is a kind of battle, but not really."

"What do you mean, Gomps?" he said, hesitantly. "What is it?"

"The Boston Tea Party," I replied.

"A tea party?" he exclaimed. "I don't want to report on a tea party! I thought you said you were going to give me a battle."

"This wasn't your normal tea party," I said. "It was like a battle, but that's all I'm going to say. Trust me. You'll like it."

"OK, Gomps," he said. "How soon do you need me to report?"

"We'll need it for next time," I said. "If you get started in the next day or two, you should be ready."

"OK," Carter said. "I'll do it, but this better not be about ladies sitting around drinking tea."

"Don't worry," I laughed, "it won't be. I guarantee it.

"Back to our story again. Franklin was already in London when he heard about Parliament's plan to pass the Stamp Act. So he met with representatives of the King and of Parliament to talk them out of it, but it didn't work. Then, after it passed, he tried to get it repealed.

"By this time, the boycott of English goods by the Sons of Liberty was doing some good. English factories, merchants, and shippers saw their businesses go down, and they complained to Parliament.

"So Parliament was forced to find out what was wrong. They asked some experts on the colonies to give their opinions. The last of them was Franklin. He stood in front of them for hours, answering one question after another. They could not overcome his arguments, and eight days later, Parliament repealed the Stamp Act.

"Franklin's arguments were written down and published back in the colonies, and he became a hero overnight."

"Yay!" they both shouted. "He backed them down."

"Yes," I said, "but not without side effects for both Franklin and Parliament."

"Up to this point, Franklin had been a loyal British subject. In spite of the disagreements, he believed that things could be worked out and that the colonies could remain under English rule. But Parliament's refusal to face up to the colonies' problems changed his mind. Shortly after he left, he wrote to a friend in England that these disputes would lead to complete separation of the colonies from England.

"At the same time, Parliament could not afford to have a single colonist make them look bad, and Franklin had done that, especially after warning them beforehand that this would happen. So in 1767, just two years after the Stamp Act, they passed the Townshend Acts. These laws required taxes on a number of things that the colonies bought."

"Holy cow!" Hannah exclaimed. "Didn't they get it?"

"Yeah," said Carter, "that had to make things even worse. What did Franklin do?"

"Well, as you might imagine, Franklin tried to get the Townshend Acts repealed also," I replied, "but Parliament wouldn't listen."

"Why not?" Hannah asked. "Wasn't it obvious?"

"Remember the War of Jenkins' Ear?" I replied. "When Parliament didn't want something to be true, they pretended not to hear."

"Aha," she said, "so there is a pattern here."

"Yes, there is," I said.

"What did the colonies do?" Carter asked.

"What do you think?" I asked.

"Probably the same thing they did before," Carter replied.

"Which was?" I continued.

"Boycotts, riots, attacking the tax collectors?" he responded.

"Exactly right." I said. "The colonies saw the Townshend Acts as the latest in a long line of heavy taxes.

"Did that start the war?" Carter asked. I looked over at Hannah, and she just rolled her eyes.

"Not just yet, Carter," I said, "but you can see it coming, can't you?"

"Yeah, I'm surprised the colonies took it as long as they did," Carter said. "Why did they?"

"Well, there are probably a few reasons," I said. "For one thing, like Franklin, the colonists still considered themselves English subjects, and England was providing them protection from the French and Spanish.

"For another thing, England was a major military force, and the colonists didn't think they had the power to go up against them. In addition, there were a number of English officials in the colonies, like the governors, and they were supported by lots of people – the Loyalists."

"I see what you mean, Gomps," Carter conceded. "But we did have a war, didn't we?"

"Yes, we did, Carter," I said. "But it didn't start overnight. Like many wars, this one was the result of many things over a long period of time."

"Like how the French and Indian War started?" Hannah asked.

"Exactly," I replied. "George Washington alone was in, what, three battles before that war was even declared? The same thing was happening now.

"So the colonies rebelled against the Townshend Acts in the same way that they had rebelled against the Stamp Act. But this time, it took three years before Parliament got the message. All the while, Franklin was in England, still arguing for repeal.

"Back in the colonies, the rebellions got even worse. Tax collectors' offices were burned, their houses were burned, and they were attacked. Goods that had been seized by the British troops were retaken by mobs. Spies were chased out of town, or worse."

"What do you mean 'worse,' Gomps?" Carter asked.

"Many were beaten, a few were killed, and some were tarred and feathered," I replied.

"What's 'tarred and feathered?'" Hannah asked. "Doesn't sound too good."

"No, it wasn't," I answered. "A mob would take off the person's shirt, spread hot tar on him, roll him in a pile of feathers, and parade him around town to shame him."

"Eeeww," the kids yelled. "Time to get out of the tax collection business," Hannah said.

"Or, out of town," I said. "Now, it wasn't long before the British troops themselves were jeered and ridiculed, by adults and children alike. Children had taken to throwing sticks, stones, and snowballs at them.

"Then, in March 1770, a mob stood up to a platoon of British soldiers outside the Customs House in Boston. The rioters began throwing sticks and stones at the soldiers, who then fired their guns. When the smoke cleared, five colonists were dead and eleven were injured. They called it The Boston Massacre."

"They didn't have a chance!" Hannah exclaimed.

"What happened to the soldiers?" Carter asked.

"There was a trial a few years later," I replied. "The two soldiers who shot directly into the crowd were convicted of manslaughter, and the other six were found not guilty."

"Not guilty?" Hannah said. "The colonists were unarmed!"

"I think the reason was self-defense," I said. "The soldiers felt like their lives were in danger. And, they had a very good lawyer."

"Who was that?" Carter asked. "An English guy?"

"No, they were defended by a colonist," I replied. "A man by the name of John Adams, who, if you remember, is another one of our Super Six."

"He doesn't sound so super to me, if he defended the English," Carter proclaimed.

"Well, afterward he wrote in his diary that, while he was worried about his own safety, his defense of the soldiers was 'one of the best Pieces of Service I ever rendered my country.' Adams believed that they deserved a fair trial."

"Was he related to Sam Adams?" Hannah asked.

"Good question, Hannah, especially since they are sometimes referred to as the Adams brothers," I said. "But they were only second cousins, and were not close. We'll talk more about John Adams in a little while. We still have to finish the part about Ben Franklin and the Townshend Acts.

"Franklin finally got his reward for all his work against the Townshend Acts," I continued. "One month after the Boston Massacre, Parliament repealed all of the Townshend Acts, except for the tax on tea. Carter, does this tell you anything about how soon we will need your report?"

He nodded vigorously.

"And that will do it for this week," I said. "I have to fly out on business Sunday afternoon, but I'll be back in time for Wednesday night. I look forward to your report on the Boston Tea Party, Carter. And now I've got to go do my homework for the trip. How about a hug before I go?"

29

THE BOSTON TEA PARTY
AND SUPER JOHN ADAMS

"How was your trip, Gomps?" Hannah asked as we settled into the living room.

"Fine," I replied. "I flew back from Cleveland this afternoon, and boy, are my arms tired."

The kids groaned.

"What?" I said, "That's not funny?"

"Gomps," Hannah said, "we may be young, but we're not babies. We've heard that one a hundred times."

"Oh, OK," I conceded.

"Can we start with a question?" Hannah asked.

"Sure," I said.

"Last time, you said that Parliament repealed all the Townshend Acts except the one on tea. Why didn't they repeal that one?" Hannah asked.

"I think Parliament was determined to show the colonies who was boss," I said. "If they had repealed everything, it would have looked like they backed down completely."

"Egos," Hannah muttered.

"What, Hannah?" I asked.

"Egos," she said, "They did something stupid because of how they would have looked."

"You have a point," I said, "but at the same time, England was still deeply in debt, and they were desperate to find sources of money. There's no doubt, though, that they were worried about their power slipping away.

"Seeing that Parliament had kept the Townshend Act on tea, Franklin seemed to have given up any hope of the English seeing the light. From England, he wrote to Sam Adams that the Parliament had 'sown the seeds of total disunion of the two countries.' Notice that he now thought of the colonies as a country!"

"Did he lead us to war, then?" Carter asked.

"That's actually a very good question, Carter," I replied. "He didn't. While he gave up on the two sides ever patching things up, he believed that the separation could be done peacefully, through negotiations. And for the next three years he stayed in England, trying to work out a solution."

"But he couldn't, could he," Hannah said.

"No, he couldn't," I confirmed. "And believe it or not, Parliament was not done. The East India Tea Company, an English company which harvested tea in India, was about to go bankrupt. They appealed to Parliament to bail them out, and that's just what Parliament did.

"In 1773, Parliament passed the Tea Act. This law allowed the Company to sell tea directly in the colonies without tariffs or taxes, bypassing the colonial warehouses and shops entirely. This meant that they could sell at a lower price and put the colonial tea companies out of business."

"Why would Parliament do that?" Hannah asked. "If the colonial companies went out of business, wouldn't that have meant less taxes and tariffs back to England?"

"Here's where the power of privilege comes in, Hannah," I replied. "Many members of Parliament and nobility had big investments in the East India Tea Company. If the Company went bankrupt, they would lose everything."

"Ooooh," both kids said.

"So, they were looking out for their own skins by passing that law, weren't they," Hannah concluded.

"Looks like it," I said.

"Now, here is where you come in, Carter. Can tell us about the Boston Tea Party now?"

"Oh, yeah!" Carter said. "I'm ready. This was way cool.

"You were right, Gomps. This wasn't a tea party at all. They just called it that."

"What was it, then?" Hannah asked.

"The book called it an act of rebellion," he replied. "The people were mad about the tea coming in, and they did something about it.

"That Tea Company sent a big load of tea into Boston Harbor on three ships. When the ships came in, the Sons of Liberty got together in the Old South Church to talk about what to do."

"You said they were mad, Carter," I said. "What were they mad about?"

"That England was forcing another law on them," he replied, "and it was going to put some of them out of business."

"Any other reason?" I asked.

Carter thought for a moment. "I think they were afraid that England was going to take over completely," he replied.

"Very good," I said. "What happened next?"

"They decided to throw the tea in the water," he continued. "They went to the harbor that night disguised as Indians. Then, they went on the ships, grabbed all the tea and threw it into the Harbor."

"When did this happen?" I asked.

"Oh . . . yeah, it was in December 1773," he replied, looking down at his notes.

"Did this really happen?" Hannah asked, "or was it another throwing a dollar across the river?"

"No, it really happened," Carter said.

"What happened to the guys who did it?" Hannah asked.

"Nothing, I guess," he replied, "the book didn't say they even got caught. I bet they had a big party after they got home, though!"

"Ha, ha," we all laughed.

"Anything else, Carter?" I asked.

"No, that's all they said," he replied, looking at his notes again. "Was there something more?"

"No, you covered it very well," I said. "That's about all there was to it, but it was a big deal."

"Why is that, Gomps?" Carter asked.

"This was the second direct act against England," I said. "The first was the Boston Massacre. Here the colonials stood up to England again.

"What did England do?" Hannah asked. "The King couldn't have been happy."

"No, neither the King nor Parliament was happy," I replied. "Within a few months, Parliament passed the Intolerable Acts. The Intolerable Acts shut down the port of Boston and took away some powers of the Massachusetts colonial government."

"Uh oh," said Hannah. "Now Massachusetts was unhappy."

"Exactly," I said, "but not only Massachusetts. The other colonies heard about it and figured that the same laws could be passed against them, too."

"What did they do then?" Carter asked.

"Well, there was more rebellion, as you probably would guess," I replied, "and the Loyalists came under more abuse by the rebels. But the colonial Assemblies also took action."

❧

"In almost every colony, committees formed in the Assemblies to decide what to do. After much debate, they did two things.

"First, the other colonies sent supplies to Boston to make up for the things that the British ships were blocking. That broke the blockade, and the British were forced to give it up.

"Second, the Assemblies voted to form the First Continental Congress."

"Was that like our Congress today, Gomps?" Hannah asked.

"Not exactly," I replied. "Our Congress passes laws. This Congress didn't pass laws. Instead, the representatives of the colonies worked out ways that they could act as a united front.

"So, on September 5, 1774, the First Continental Congress met in Philadelphia," I said. "There were 56 representatives there, including Sam Adams, John Adams, and the Father of our Country . . . ?"

"George Washington?" they both shouted.

"George Washington," I confirmed. "He was one of the representatives of the Virginia colony. Now, Washington and Sam Adams you already know, but . . ."

"Gomps?" Carter interrupted.

"Yes, Carter," I said.

"How about Benjamin Franklin?" he asked. "Was he there, too?"

"Good thinking, Carter," I said, "He wasn't. He was still in England, trying to get those thick-headed Englishmen to see what they were doing to us.

"Oh, too bad," Carter continued. "He might have been able to come up with some good ideas."

"I think you're right," I said, "but there was plenty of brainpower at the Congress as it was. You already know Washington and Sam Adams, but I haven't told you about John Adams yet, except to say that he had defended the British soldiers after the Boston Massacre. This is a good time to introduce him.

"John Adams is one of our Super Six Founding Fathers. But he started out in a very ordinary way. He was born in 1735, the oldest of three children, in a rural area south of Boston. His father was a farmer and a deacon in the local Congregational Church.

"His family didn't have much money, but they were active in their church, and his father served as a lieutenant in the local militia as well as a town councilman on their town governing board.

"John himself was a hard-working boy who had a deep Christian faith. He was drawn to the Puritan idea that people have the right to freedom. That idea stayed with him his whole life.

"He went through a local school and, at 16, he went to Harvard. His father encouraged him to become a minister, but after early religious studies, John turned to the study of the political philosophers of Greece, Rome and Europe.

"John graduated without a good sense of what he wanted to do. He started by teaching school for two years, and during that time, he realized that he wanted to be a lawyer. So he studied law and passed the Bar in 1758, at the age of 23. He set up a law practice in his hometown and became good at speaking in court and writing opinions. He was also made a circuit court judge."

"What's that, Gomps?" Hannah asked.

"In many rural towns, there were not enough cases or money for a full-time court. Instead, a judge would ride from one town to the next in a circuit to hold court for a day in each. So, John Adams rode all over eastern Massachusetts to hear cases. In the course of doing that a lot of people got to know him.

"At the same time, he was concerned about the power that the King and Parliament were wielding against the colonies. He was strongly opposed to the Stamp Act, and he wrote a letter about it to his representative in the Massachusetts colonial Assembly.

"In Adams's letter, he said that rights guaranteed to Englishmen were being denied to colonists, most importantly, no taxation without representation, and trial by a jury of one's equals. He argued that those rights came from basic Puritan and Christian principles.

"The letter was widely copied and sent to all Massachusetts representatives, and this started John on his career as a respected constitutional scholar and thinker.

"Later, as I said before, he defended the British soldiers who had shot the people in the Boston Massacre. In his arguments, he made the famous statement that 'facts are stubborn things.'"

"What did he mean, Gomps?" Hannah asked.

"He meant that whatever we may wish to be true does not change a fact or a piece of evidence," I said. "After the trial, even his critics had to admit that he was brave and that he had done the right thing.

"In 1770, he was elected to the Massachusetts Assembly. Two years later, the Massachusetts Governor announced that he would accept pay only from Parliament. The colonists objected, and John wrote a letter to the Governor in which he said that the Massachusetts Bay charter had been with the King, not with Parliament. If Parliament insisted that they governed the colonies and not the King, the colonies would be forced to choose independence."

"Wow," exclaimed Hannah. "So he saw it even back then!"

"Yes, he did," I said.

"Over the next few years, he was often asked for his opinion on how to structure a new government. This led him in 1776 to write his ideas about it in a pamphlet. He called it 'Thoughts on Government.' In it, he stated that government should be based on laws and not on the wishes of whoever was in power at the time. He also insisted that only a republican form of government could result in good government."

"What does that mean, exactly, Gomps — a republican form of government?" Hannah asked. "What about a democracy?"

"One of the best questions of all!" I said. "There is a difference. Let me try to explain it."

⁂

"A democracy is a government in which the people have the direct say in all the laws. If a law is to be passed, everyone votes on it and the majority wins."

"Isn't that what we have?" Carter asked.

"No, Carter," I replied, "as a matter of fact, it isn't.

"We have a republic. In a republic, the people elect other people to represent them. It is these representatives who discuss the ideas and pass the laws. Like our Congressmen and Senators of today."

"Why wouldn't a democracy be better?" he persisted.

"Well, with majority rule, the rights of the minority could be ignored. A majority of people could gang up on the minority and dictate to them. Kind of like mob rule."

"You mean like racial minorities?" Hannah asked.

"Yes, racial minorities, religious minorities, political minorities, any kind of minority, really," I said. "But the Founders were thinking of even more basic minorities, such as people practicing a certain profession or owning land in a certain area, people loyal to the King, or British soldiers who were defending themselves, even."

The kids paused, thinking.

"So why is a republic better?" Carter asked, finally.

"Adams and others said that it was because the representatives could discuss things away from the pressures of public opinion," I replied. "They could take public opinion into account, but they didn't always have to follow it. The majority isn't always right."

"But if that's what the majority wants, shouldn't they get it?" Carter continued.

"What if the facts say different?" I replied. "Facts are stubborn things."

"I'm getting the idea," Carter said.

"Good," I said. "Now, here are some other things that Adams said in his 'Thoughts on Government.' He said that there should be two separate elected groups that have to agree before an idea can become law. Like our Senate and House of Representatives. He thought it would be too easy for the majority of representatives to take over in a government with only one lawmaking group. With two groups, the majorities in both would have to agree.

"He also said that there should be definite separation of powers among the different parts of government. So, the lawmakers couldn't run government or try court cases; the executive – that's our President and departments - couldn't pass laws or try court cases; and the courts couldn't make laws or run the government.

"And, finally, Adams said that the government should have only those powers that are spelled out beforehand. By that, he meant that the people should decide before creating it what the government has the power to do. They would write that down in a constitution. And if the constitution doesn't say that the government has a certain power, it can't use that power."

"So, who would have the powers that are not given in a constitution, Gomps?" Hannah asked.

"Adams insisted that the people had those powers, through their freedoms," I replied. "The people might choose to create state or city governments to use some of those powers, but it would be up to the people to decide whether or not to create them and what powers to give to them."

"So if the constitution doesn't say the government can do something, it can't do it?" Hannah asked.

"That's right, Hannah," I replied. "It's called the enumeration of powers — the power has to be spelled out in the constitution before the government can use it."

"And, if the constitution doesn't spell it out, the government can't use it," Hannah confirmed.

"That's right," I said.

"This is going to take a little thinking about, but I think I'm getting the idea," Hannah said. "One thing's for sure, you're right about Adams. He may not have been as well known as Washington and Franklin, but he was really, really smart."

"That's right, Hannah," I confirmed, "and a lot of other people thought so too. His 'Thoughts on Government' was used throughout the colonies to structure state governments, and, of course, it became the foundation for our national constitution and government.

"So, here we are in the First Continental Congress with John Adams right in there among all the other representatives. Since it was 1774, he had not yet written his 'Thoughts on Government,' but we can be sure that he was thinking them.

"They met for about seven weeks, and in the end, they agreed on three actions. First, they approved a boycott of all English goods.

The boycott was set up in all the colonies except New York, which voted against it."

"Why didn't New York vote for it?" Carter asked.

"New York was the biggest port in the colonies, and the boycott would have hurt their shipping businesses," I replied. "Also, New York had a lot of Loyalists."

"Oh," Carter said, "but wouldn't New York have hurt the boycott?"

"Good thinking, Carter," I replied. "Yes, it would, but I think the other colonies decided that they didn't want to turn New Yorkers against them by forcing them into it. New York was a powerful colony and would be needed for other things.

"The second thing this Congress did was to write a letter to the King with a list of their complaints. It was called a petition."

"Did it work?" Hannah asked.

"Not in the least," I replied. "In fact, the King may have just ignored it."

"That must have made the colonists mad," Hannah continued.

"I don't think so," I said, "I think they expected it."

"Why do you think that, Gomps?" Hannah asked.

"Because the third thing the First Congress did was to plan the Second Continental Congress, assuming the petition wouldn't work," I replied.

"They even set the date — May 10, 1775," I added. "I don't think they expected any of these actions would do any good, but they felt like they had to try everything."

"So, did the boycott work?" Carter asked.

"It sure did," I replied. "English exports to the colonies were cut in half."

"Wow," Carter exclaimed, "that's amazing. What happened next?"

"What do you think?" I asked.

"War?" he asked, excitedly.

"You're going to have to wait until next week to find out," I said. "I'm ready to go home and get some sleep."

"OK, Gomps," said Carter, "but waiting won't be easy."

"We'll be here," said Hannah.

30

THE GENERAL'S WIFE SPILLS THE BEANS, AND THE SHOT HEARD 'ROUND THE WORLD

"Carter, last week you asked if the boycott of English goods meant war," I began right where we'd left off. "Well, we're finally going to get our war, but as with other wars, some things happened before war was declared.

"The Massachusetts militias around Boston had begun stocking up on guns and ammunition. They stashed a lot of it in storehouses in the town of Concord, just 17 miles west of Boston.

"Through spies, the British found out about it and decided to take the guns away. So about 700 British troops in Boston got ready to march to Concord. But word leaked back to the militias about the plan."

"Did we have spies, too?" Carter asked.

"The source of the leak was never proven," I said, "but it looks like the wife of the British General was the one who spilled the beans!"

"No way!" both shouted.

"Way," I said. "She had been born in New Jersey, not England, and she was known to be opposed to the actions against the colonies. She had become friends with Joseph Warren, a Boston doctor who was working with the rebels. Many think she told him."

"Holy cow," Hannah whistled.

"However they found out," I continued, "the rebels quickly moved the guns and ammo away from Concord. Then they got ready to deal with the British troops.

"First, they made a plan to warn the militias when the British left Boston. One of those in the plan was Paul Revere. Have you heard of him?"

"Nope," they both said.

"Revere was a silversmith in Boston and a supporter of independence," I continued. "He and his father made fine tableware and jewelry for both colonists and the English. And, he was friends with Joseph Warren.

"Once the British started out for Concord, they would either have to go the long way over land or they would have to cross the Charles River on boats. When Dr. Warren found out which route they were taking, the plan was for him to tell Paul Revere.

"Now, the Old North Church in Boston had a steeple that could be seen for miles around. So, Revere told the Church janitor to go up in the steeple at his signal and hold up one lantern, if the British were going the overland route, or two lanterns, if they were starting out over the river. Then Revere passed the word to the militias so they would know what the signals would mean.

"On the evening of April 18, 1775, the British started out on boats. Dr. Warren passed the word to Revere. Revere told the janitor, and the janitor went up in the steeple and held up two lanterns. Then Revere and another man, William Dawes, got on their horses and rode toward Concord to warn all the settlers along the way. Revere went one way and Dawes went the other, so the word would still get out if one of them got caught. Meanwhile, those who saw the lanterns spread the word as well. The British were coming.

"Are you guys with me?" I asked.

"Oh, yeah," Carter said.

"This is exciting," Hannah exclaimed.

"By sunrise the next day, the British troops were out of the boats and were marching down the road. Now, just before you get to Concord, there is another town called Lexington. Lexington was known as a rebel stronghold. By the time the British got there, the Lexington militia was waiting for them on the town green.

"We're not sure what happened next. The British troops said the rebels fired first and the rebels said the British did. It's not even clear if the militia were carrying their guns at the time. In either event, the first shot was fired and the militia was driven back. It only lasted a few minutes, but when the smoke cleared, eight militiamen were dead and several were wounded. Only one British soldier was wounded, and only slightly. The Battle of Lexington was over."

"Was that it?" Carter asked.

"Yes and no," I replied. "The Battle of Lexington was over, but the war was just beginning. Years later, a famous poet called that first shot 'The Shot Heard 'Round the World.'"

"Why did he call it that, Gomps?" Carter asked.

"Because this was the beginning of a war that resulted in a form of government that had never been tried before, anywhere," I said. "And, it worked so well that people all over the world heard about it and were inspired by it.

❧

"The British then marched on to Concord, arriving later that same morning. While the British were marching, the rebel leaders were assembling the local militias. When they saw how big the British force was, they kept out of sight and let the troops search the town.

"Of course, the British found little, but by the time they had finished, so many militias had gathered that they outnumbered the British! In fact, the militias arrived so quickly from so many places that people called them the Minutemen, and the name stuck.

"In the course of their searches, the British troops hadn't noticed that they were in a place that left them open to attack. Seeing this, the militia leaders placed their forces in good positions all around the British.

"Then the shooting started. The British maneuvered as best they could, but it was no use. They were beaten badly and began a retreat back to Boston. By noon, the Battle of Concord was over."

"Yay!" the kids shouted.

"The militias couldn't believe it," I continued. "They had beaten part of the world's best army, but they took no time to celebrate. As the British marched back, the militias followed them on either side, continuing to fire.

"The remainder of the British force got back to Boston the next day. They broke through the barricades and crossed into Charlestown and relative safety.

"But their safety was only temporary. By this time, Minutemen from everywhere had joined the fight. They now numbered over 15,000, and they closed off every escape route from Boston. The British were trapped, and the Siege of Boston was underway."

"Wow, Gomps, I'm exhausted just hearing about it," Hannah said.

"Me, too!" Carter exclaimed. "But what's a siege?"

"A siege is when the soldiers corner the enemy and starve them into giving up," I replied. "In the Siege of Boston, the British were cornered on two islands - Charlestown and Boston. Only a narrow strip of land connected each with the mainland, and the militias had both of those covered. So the colonials set up to starve the British out."

"But, Gomps," Hannah interjected, "couldn't their ships bring them more food?"

"Sure," I replied, "but it would take time. At the very least, the Siege kept the British Army from doing any more damage to the towns on the mainland."

"I see," said Hannah.

"Carter, get it?" I asked.

"Got it, thanks," Carter said. "Were there any more battles?"

"Yes, there were," I replied. "The next one was between the British and Ethan Allen and his Green Mountain Boys in northern New York, at Fort Ticonderoga."

"The Green Mountain Boys?" asked Carter. "That's a cool name. Who were they?"

"The Green Mountain Boys were a militia from what is now Vermont — which comes from the French for 'Green Mountain.' Ethan Allen was their commander."

"Cool," said Carter.

"Ticonderoga was a British fort at the south end of Lake Champlain," I continued. "Champlain is a long, narrow lake that stretches for 125 miles from the Canadian border south to the northern end of Lake George in New York. It was like an interstate highway of water that bypassed the mountains and forest. The British controlled it at Fort Ticonderoga.

"In May 1775, Ethan Allen and the Green Mountain Boys swooped in on Ticonderoga and took the fort from the British. They captured cannons, rifles, and ammunition and broke the British lines of communication between New York and Canada.

"Now, the victory at Fort Ticonderoga is a good stopping place for tonight. Next, we'll see how the Continental Army was formed. And I'll leave you to guess who commanded it."

"I bet I know," blurted Hannah. "It was . . ."

"Now, now," I interrupted. "You are going to have to save it for next week."

31

SUPER GEORGE
WASHINGTON

I had been called out of town unexpectedly the next week, so it was now two weeks since we had met last.

"Glad to be back," I said. "Sorry we had to miss last week.

"Last time, I told you about the victory at Fort Ticonderoga by Ethan Allen and the Green Mountain Boys.

"News of the victory came just as the representatives were arriving in Philadelphia for the Second Continental Congress. This was the second victory in the last two months, and the representatives were very encouraged.

"But it was clear that this would not be the end of the fighting, and the representatives knew it. So they turned to a man who had played almost no role in the First Continental Congress, but whose military knowledge and experience now became vital."

"Here comes George Washington, again!" Hannah shouted.

"That's right, Hannah," I said.

"On June 14, 1775, the Congress created a joint army of the colonies. They called it the Continental Army, and Washington was named its General."

"Did he give a speech?" Hannah asked.

"Ha, quite the opposite," I said. "In his usual humble way, he had left the room so that they could talk about him freely. He didn't come back until after they had chosen him — two days later.

"His first job was to take command at the Siege of Boston. But just before he left for Boston, bad news came from the north. On June 17, British forces tried to break the Boston siege, and they defeated the militias in a bloody battle at Bunker Hill. Both sides had big losses, with over 1,500 killed. The British had captured the Hill, but they couldn't break the siege."

"So we won, right?" Carter asked.

"Not exactly," I replied. "We still lost the battle, and a lot of Minutemen were killed.

"Once he got there, Washington sized up his troops, and his worst fears proved true. These were brave men, but most had no military training or experience at all. They ranged from city dwellers to frontiersmen. They had guns of every sort, each having brought his own. Their clothing was just as haphazard. And they had no reliable sources of food.

"Washington got right to work to set up training and supply lines. But he met with frustration at every turn, so much so that he went off every day by himself to pray.

"Despite these difficulties, the Siege of Boston held, if only because the British were not aware of the sorry state of the rebel troops. Washington took every step he could to make sure that they never found out.

"In September, he wrote a letter to the Continental Congress begging for supplies and for money to pay his men. But he heard nothing from them."

"That's terrible," Hannah announced. "Didn't they promise to support the Army?"

"They did, Hannah, and I'm sure they meant to," I said. "But each colony was like a separate country, and there was nothing that required the colonies to do anything. Their governors were opposed to the rebellion. The colonial assemblies were being prevented by the King and governors from collecting local taxes, so there was no money to send. Colonial businesses were being hurt by Parliament's taxes. And there were Loyalists in every colony who opposed any support."

"Did Washington get any help at all?" Carter asked.

"He got some, but only from time to time," I replied. "His sources were the pockets of sympathizers who could afford it, and, eventually, foreign loans.

"And on occasion, he had a little luck. Remember the guns that the Green Mountain Boys captured at Fort Ticonderoga? In November 1775, Washington appointed a Boston bookseller named Henry Knox to be chief of the artillery corps, and . . . "

"A bookseller?" Hannah interrupted. "What did a bookseller know about artillery?"

"Washington found out that he had read up on it," I replied.

"That's it?" Carter asked.

"Yup," I said. "That made him the man who knew the most about it. It was Washington's only option at the time.

"So Knox's first assignment was to go to Fort Ticonderoga and bring back the captured cannons and guns. Knox put together a team, and off they went, in the middle of winter.

"They got back at the end of January, exhausted, with 60 cannons and some guns and ammo, but they'd had to suffer horrible winter conditions the whole way, including frostbite, injury, starvation, and death. Can you imagine having to haul those cannons through forests and over rivers in the freezing cold?"

"Holy cow!" Carter exclaimed. "Couldn't they have waited until spring?"

"I think Knox knew how desperate the situation was," I replied. "In another three months, the British might have figured out how badly off the Americans really were and mounted an all-out attack.

"So Washington now had the cannons that he needed, and here's where some luck came in. While Knox was on his way back with the cannons, another militia had captured a British gunpowder warehouse in Rhode Island and brought the gunpowder back to Boston. With enough artillery and supplies at hand, Washington took the next month to work out his plan of action, and on the night of March 2, his forces got to work.

"Washington had chosen Dorchester Heights as the place. This was high ground overlooking Boston from the south with a part of Boston Harbor in between. After dark, they brought in wagon after wagon of logs and set up small forts on the heights. Then they put the cannons on top. By sunrise, they were ready.

"When the British woke up the next morning, they saw forts that had not been there the day before. And these forts had cannons – 60 of them. A British engineering officer said afterward that the work must have been done by 'the genie from Aladdin's wonderful lamp.'

"The British decided they had to attack, but as they set out in their boats, a terrible windstorm arose, and they saw the impossibility of the task. They retreated to Boston, and over the next few days, they packed up and left Boston by ship. Washington's rebel army had won the Battle of Dorchester Heights without firing a single shot."

"That's great," observed Hannah. "But that didn't end the war, did it?"

"Not at all," I replied. "This was just the beginning, but before we get into more about it, I have to fill you in on things that were happening in Philadelphia at the same time."

"By this time, Ben Franklin had given up any hope of persuading the English to treat the colonies fairly. So he sailed back home and arrived in Philadelphia in May 1775, just days before the start of the Second Continental Congress. The next day the Pennsylvania Assembly appointed him as a representative to the Congress, and he got right to work.

"Franklin served on a number of committees in the Congress. At the same time, he worked on his own plan for a union of the colonies. He called it 'Articles of Confederation and Perpetual Union,' and it was based on the plan he had drawn up for the Albany Congress in 1754. He presented it to the Congress on July 21, 1775, just two months later.

"Franklin's plan contained 13 articles, or paragraphs, that outlined a structure for a united government. He called it 'The United Colonies of North America.' The plan did not pass the Congress, but it did provide a starting point for discussion when the time came a year later.

"At the same time, Franklin and four others began negotiations for support with a secret agent from France. This agent told them that if the colonies would openly declare their independence from England, France would at least begin foreign trade with them.

"In February of the next year, 1776, Franklin made a motion in Congress to declare independence from England and to open the colonial ports to trade with other countries. The vote came out against his motion, but . . ."

"Why did they vote against it, Gomps?" Hannah asked. "Isn't that what the Declaration of Independence did?"

"Yes, just five months later, but at this time the Congress was not quite ready," I replied. "This would be a huge step, and some feared the British would send their whole army and navy at them. Still, they voted to send a representative to Europe to set up trade arrangements."

"Was that Franklin?" Carter asked.

"No," I replied. "Franklin was not ready to go back so soon, so they sent a man named Silas Deane instead. Deane tried hard to get a treaty, but without a formal declaration of independence, the French resisted.

"In the meantime, an essay written by a man named Thomas Paine was firing up the colonies. Paine was an English newspaper reporter, and Franklin had met him while he was in London. Franklin was so impressed by Paine's writing that he urged him to move to the colonies, which he did in 1774.

"Paine was a fiery writer and strong believer in freedom. He was able to make the ideas favoring colonial independence easily understood. The result was a pamphlet that he called *Common Sense*. He published it in January 1776, and it quickly sold thousands of copies throughout the colonies.

"Paine's writing whipped up the anti-British feelings to such a degree that the colonial legislatures quickly sent instructions to their members of Congress to take action. This was all Congress needed to begin the process of a formal declaration of independence from England.

"On June 7, 1776, Congress set two more actions in motion. They started setting up for a united government; and they named a committee to write a declaration of independence.

"Next time, I'll tell you . . . "

"Oh no, Gomps, don't stop now!" Hannah protested.

"A story is like food - better when you're hungry for it," I said. "I'm glad you guys have an appetite. Next week you'll be hearing about another very important one of our Super Six."

32

SUPER THOMAS JEFFERSON WRITES THE DECLARATION OF INDEPENDENCE

I started right in the following Wednesday. "It was June 7, 1776, and the Continental Congress had just named a committee to write a declaration of independence. The committee had five members, including Franklin, John Adams, and someone we haven't talked very much about yet: Thomas Jefferson."

"Gomps, didn't you say that Jefferson was one of the Super Six?" Hannah asked.

"That's the guy," I said. "Good memory. More about him in a minute. First, let's see what happened in that committee.

"Over the next week, the committee tried to decide what the declaration would say, but they couldn't agree on actual wording. So they asked Jefferson to write a draft for them to review and revise. And that's just what he did.

"Thomas Jefferson had been born in Virginia in 1743, so he was only 32 years old by the time of his appointment to the Congress. He grew up on Monticello, his father's plantation in the Virginia hills.

His mother came from a very powerful family in Virginia – the Randolphs.

"Jefferson was a shy kid who loved to read. He went to a local school taught by a Scottish Presbyterian minister, and starting at the age of nine he began studying Greek, Latin, and French."

"Nine?" Carter exclaimed.

"Nine," I confirmed.

"His father died when Jefferson was 14, and he inherited Monticello. A year later, he left it to be run by the plantation manager and went to a boarding school in another part of Virginia.

"At 16, he entered the College of William and Mary in Williamsburg, Virginia, where he studied philosophy and law. He graduated with highest honors two years later. He then studied to be a lawyer and was admitted to the Virginia Bar in 1767, at 23 years of age.

"Jefferson returned home and immediately set up a law practice. He was best at writing opinions for presentation to the court. Being shy, he was a weak public speaker and did not do well arguing before judges or juries. Nonetheless, he quickly became very successful and had many well-known clients, including the Randolphs.

"Jefferson was elected to the Virginia colonial legislature in 1769, and then was named to the Second Continental Congress.

"When the English Parliament passed the Intolerable Acts in 1774, he wrote a detailed argument against the Acts that he submitted to the Congress. He called it 'A Summary View of the Rights of British America.' In it, he listed the complaints that the colonies had against the King and insisted that the colonists had the natural right to govern themselves."

"What did he mean by 'natural right,' Gomps?" Hannah asked.

"He meant that God, not governments or other humans, gives basic rights to all human beings, including the right to self-government. Therefore, other humans cannot take those rights away, not even a king.

"Jefferson's Summary View was published and widely read. While his idea of natural rights was considered radical at the time, his Summary View made him known as a clear thinker and skilled writer.

"The Declaration Committee had been impressed by Jefferson's Summary View, and they asked him to write the draft.

"So in June 1776, off Jefferson went to write the Declaration. In addition to his Summary View, he also put in parts of the Virginia Constitution (which he had helped to write), parts of a draft of the Virginia Declaration of Rights — written by a friend, George Mason — and some ideas from philosophers he had read, especially the Englishman John Locke.

"After several days of writing, Jefferson returned to the committee with the draft. The committee made a few changes, and on June 28, they gave it to the Congress. After four days of debate, the Congress made a few more changes, including one major one.

"The major change had to do with the slave trade. Jefferson had spoken out against it in the past, and he had included it in the Declaration as one of the reasons that the colonies were separating from England. But the southern colonies wanted the slave trade to continue, and therefore they insisted that section be taken out.

"Jefferson was furious when he heard this, but it became clear that the southern colonies would not go along with the Declaration as long as the slave trade statement was in it. In the end, the slave trade statement was removed from the document, and on July 4, 1776, the Congress approved it. Later, the 56 representatives signed it."

"Yay," they both shouted. "Time for fireworks!"

"Gomps?" Hannah interrupted.

"Yes, Hannah?"

"Did you say that they took out the part that criticized the slave trade?" Hannah continued.

"Yes, they did," I replied.

"So Jefferson was against slavery?"

"That's what he wrote," I replied.

"But you said that he owned a plantation, didn't you?"

"Yes."

"In Virginia?"

"Yes."

"Wouldn't he have had slaves, then?"

"Yes, he did. Quite a lot of them."

"If he was against slavery, why didn't he set them free?" Hannah persisted.

"That, my dear, is a question that no one has been able to answer to everyone's satisfaction," I replied. "Jefferson was a man of many opposites. This appeared to be one of them."

"That's not much of an answer," she said.

"I suppose not," I said. "This part of his story has caused people to line up on one side or the other."

"What about the Congress?" she continued. "Were they in favor of slavery?"

"Some were and some weren't," I replied. "Most of those in favor were from the South, and most who opposed it were from the North."

"But those northerners owned slaves, too, didn't they?" she asked.

"At least some of them, yes," I replied.

"Then they were just as bad as Jefferson," she concluded. "I would have settled it right then and there."

"OK, but if you did," I asked, "suppose all the representatives from the South walked out. Would you have given up on forming the country? Would you have given up on the principles of freedom? Suppose the southerners broke away from the North and formed their own country. Would either country have had a chance in a war against England?"

Hannah paused, a frustrated look on her face. "Couldn't there have been another way?" she asked.

"I don't know," I replied. "But I do know that the representatives thought they had agreement among the members that a new country could be formed with all 13 colonies. They were sure that they could not solve the slavery question, country or no country. They took the new country option, with the hope that the slavery problem could be solved at a later date."

"As soon as it was published, the Declaration became an instant sensation. And I think it is fair to say that it is one of the most famous, respected, and even loved political statements in history. Have you read it or heard any of it?"

"No, I haven't," Hannah said.

"Me either," said Carter.

❧

"Well, I just so happen to have it with me," I said, pulling a rolled-up scroll of paper out of my pocket with a flourish. "It's long, so I won't read the whole thing, but I think you should hear a few parts of it.

"It's titled, 'The unanimous Declaration of the thirteen united States of America.' So they were saying upfront that they were all together on this.

"The first paragraph starts, 'When in the course of human events . . .' and goes on to say that if one country is going to break away from another country, they need to explain why they are doing it. What comes next is our explanation.

"The explanation starts: 'We hold these truths to be self-evident, that all Men are created equal, that they are endowed by their Creator with certain unalienable Rights, that among these are Life, Liberty, and the Pursuit of Happiness . . .'

"This means that God created human beings to be equal to one another and to have the right to life, freedom and the pursuit of happiness — not the right to happiness, but the right to work toward being happy — and that these rights cannot be taken away by other people or governments.

"Then, it goes on to say, '— That to secure these Rights, Governments are instituted among Men, deriving their just Powers from the Consent of the Governed . . .'

"This means that people can form governments to protect these rights, but the government can only have powers that are granted by the people. Does this ring a bell from the things that were already written by some of our Super Six?"

"Didn't Adams say that a government couldn't use powers that weren't listed in the constitution?" Carter asked.

"Excellent memory, Carter!" I shouted. "You got it."

"How about taxation without representation?" Hannah asked. "Didn't Franklin say that you can't pass a tax unless the people being taxed have a say in it?"

"Absolutely!" I said. "You're both right on the money."

"So, Gomps," Hannah said, "this wasn't something that Jefferson just dreamed up, then, was it?"

"No, it wasn't, Hannah," I said. "I'm happy to see that you're getting that. In fact, Jefferson admitted in a letter to a friend that he did not think all this up; rather, he pulled the ideas together from a number of sources and rewrote them in a way that could be understood by all.

"Now, there's a little more I want to say about the Declaration.

"After saying that we were breaking away from England, the Declaration goes on to describe a long list of reasons for doing it – all of them tyrannical actions of England's King. The biggies were: dissolving colonial Assemblies and canceling their laws; taxation without representation; forcing his governors, army, and tax collectors on us; preventing us from trading with other countries; and giving himself powers to make laws, run the colonies, and decide court cases.

"But I do want to read to you a part that is rarely read – the end of the Declaration," I said. "I'll read just a little of that. It says, 'We, therefore, the Representatives of the united States of America, in General Congress, Assembled, appealing to the Supreme Judge of the world for the rectitude of our intentions, do, in the Name, and by Authority of the good People of these Colonies, solemnly Publish and Declare, That these United Colonies are, and of Right ought to be, FREE AND INDEPENDENT STATES . . . '"

"So this said we're a country?" Carter interrupted.

"Ah," I said. "No, we weren't a country yet, even though he used the words 'united States of America.' This wasn't our Constitution. The Declaration just said that the colonies had banded together as united States and become independent of England. The Constitution took the Declaration and formed the country from it."

"Oh," Carter said. "So, we hadn't formed our country yet; we just divorced England."

"I couldn't have said it better," I said.

"Now, let's skip to the last sentence. It says, 'And for the support of this Declaration, with a firm Reliance on the Protection of divine Providence, we mutually pledge to each other our Lives, our Fortunes, and our sacred Honor.'

"This means that they thought that this was about the most serious thing they could do. They were relying on God's help to do it. It means that they knew they were risking their lives: there was a chance that they could be caught by the British and killed. It means that they expected that they were going to have to put their own money into it, but they were swearing an oath to God to do everything in their power to make it work.

"As soon as they finished the Declaration, the Continental Congress began to design a plan of government for the united colonies. They called it the Articles of Confederation."

"What does 'confederation' mean, Gomps?" Carter asked.

"Well, that was a fancy word that they used to mean working together," I replied. "The Articles were the description of the various ways the colonies would work together.

"Now, when they started to write the Articles, they decided they needed a starting plan that they could work with. Guess what they used."

Both kids thought for a moment, but could come up with nothing.

"Give us a hint," Hannah said.

"That is a tough one," I replied. "Ben Franklin."

"Oh, yeah," Hannah remarked. "The plan he gave to them at the start of Congress."

"That's right," I said. "The Articles of Confederation and Perpetual Union. It was the one he based on his Albany Plan of 1754. And, now, that was the plan that the Continental Congress used as a starting point for the final plan that they called the Articles of Confederation."

"Is this how the English shot themselves in the foot?" Hannah continued.

"You're so smart," I said. "They didn't realize it at the time, but the seed of cooperation that they themselves had required the colonies to plant in Albany now sprouted, 22 years later.

"Over the next year and a half, the Continental Congress debated and expanded Franklin's original plan. They signed it in November 1777, and sent it off for approval by the colonies. And that's when the name 'the United States of America' was officially adopted."

"We were a country then?" Carter asked.

"We were a country then," I replied. "The Declaration said, 'We're no longer a part of you.' And the Articles of Confederation said, 'This is who we are.'"

"Yay," the kids both shouted.

"In the meantime," I said, "we're fighting a war — next time, that is. I'll end here for tonight."

33

WAR

"OK," I began. "Last time we met, the British had hightailed it out of Boston, leaving the region to the Continental Army. Soon after, Washington returned to Philadelphia to meet with the Congress.

"Congress was thrilled with his successes, but Washington was not. He knew that a militia force he had sent to capture Montreal was not doing well. He knew that the British were planning attacks on New York and on Charleston to the south. And he knew that he had nowhere near enough troops or supplies to do the job.

"The Congress ordered him to finish the taking of Montreal and to defend New York at all costs. In return, Washington asked for a regular, paid army. Congress refused, and thus began a long string of military defeats.

"Carter, I'm going to have to disappoint you here, because I am not going to describe every battle. I'm just going to tell you about the main ones so you can get the idea of what Washington was up against, and what a smart and determined leader he was."

Carter scowled, while Hannah looked relieved.

"Let's start with Washington's war strategy," I said. "He knew that he could not stand up to the British in a direct battle. The British had full-time soldiers who outnumbered him and had far better guns, supplies, and experience. The Congress gave him an army in name only. His soldiers came and went with the seasons and there was never enough money for anything.

"Washington's strategy, therefore, was to avoid facing the British head on, but instead to pester them and wait for them to make mistakes. When they did, he would try to isolate small groups of them and gain an advantage. Still, there would be more defeats than victories.

"Second, Washington knew that the Continental Congress would be no more supportive of him than the colonies had been during the French and Indian War. They praised him. They promised him. They prodded him. But these were some of the same men who had been unable to give him support before. He had experience in running a bare-bones army, and he knew he was going to have to use it."

"Why wouldn't they at least make a full-time army?" Carter asked.

"Good question, Carter," I said. "I think there were two reasons. First, a practical one – they didn't know how they would pay a full-time army. But second, and more importantly, the colonists were afraid of what a full-time army could do to civilians. They had seen what the King had done to abuse the colonies with full-time British troops. The colonial leaders were afraid that even a leader of our own could maintain power with a similar army."

"But this would have been our own people in the army, wouldn't it?" Carter persisted.

"I think that the colonists were that afraid that it could happen again," I replied. "Have you ever heard the expression 'gun-shy'?"

"No," Carter replied.

"Well, 'gun-shy' refers to a hunting dog that hears gunfire for the first time and is afraid of it," I said. "From that time on, the dog always shies away from the hunt at the first shot."

"But the leader would be our guy!" Carter continued.

"Yes, but the Founders had seen what political power in the hands of one person could do," I cautioned. "Someone once said, 'Power tends to corrupt, and absolute power corrupts absolutely.'"

"What does that mean, Gomps?" Carter asked.

"It means that having power tempts a person to use it in the wrong way," I said. "And the more power they have, the more likely they are to give in to that temptation. They may resist the temptation, but it will always be there. Got it?"

"I think I understand," Carter replied, "but if you believe that, then doesn't it mean that just about everyone has a bad side?"

"In a way it does, I guess," I replied, "but I think of it more as meaning that we have to accept that no one is perfect. The Founders believed that and tried to design our government to make it as hard as they could for anyone to get too much power and use it in the wrong way."

"OK, we got it," Hannah said impatiently. "So how did he do it?"

"How did who do what?" I asked.

"Washington," she said. "How did he run an army without support?"

"Out of desperation," I said, "he came up with five ways."

"First, the troops foraged and scavenged for food, clothing, and ammunition wherever they were. Occasionally, local patriots gave them what they could.

"Second, they tried to use colonial paper money to pay for things. Unfortunately, the money was only a promise to pay later. So the paper money was largely worthless, and once people found that out, few would accept it.

"Third, they took what they could from the British. When we won a battle, or whenever the British troops left anything behind, the Continentals scooped it up for their own use. Remember the cannons from Ticonderoga and the gunpowder from Rhode Island?"

"Oh, yeah," they both replied.

"Fourth, his Continental Army was to be paid something, but the rule was that they would not get their pay until the end of their enlistment. Now, because of the poor supplies, there were many deserters. While that hurt the size of the Army, it meant that those soldiers didn't get any pay, even though they had fought at least a part of the time. That saved some money."

"Why did they leave, Gomps?" Hannah asked. "What kind of patriots were they?"

"Well," I said, "we really haven't gotten into the worst of the conditions they were in. Once we do, you'll have the answer to that one."

"OK," she said.

"The fifth and biggest way that Washington managed to keep the Army going was through loans," I continued, "both from other countries, mostly France and the Netherlands, and from within the colonies."

"I thought you said that France wouldn't give us anything unless we declared our independence," Hannah said.

"I did say that, Hannah," I replied, "but that was the French *government* that refused.

"Silas Deane was able to set up a secret system of unofficial supply shipments to us. And that started the French support that Washington needed.

"Then, after the Declaration was signed, Deane tried again for a treaty, but the French government had heard that things were not going well for us and delayed some more.

"It wasn't until we won a key battle that the French finally agreed to the treaty."

"Which battle was that, Gomps?" Carter asked.

"Saratoga," I replied, "but you're going to have to wait to hear about that one.

"So here you have Washington's strategy. Basically, it was do the best you can with what you have. Now, back to the Revolutionary War."

❧

"Once the British left Boston, Washington had to get to New York as soon as possible. He found out that the British were planning to invade there. Starting in March of 1776, he and part of the Continental Army moved down to New York. They arrived in late June, 1776, and Washington began to plan its defense right away."

"Uh, Gomps, did you say June, 1776?" Carter interrupted.

"Yes, I did," I replied.

"So the Declaration wasn't signed yet?" he continued.

"That's right," I replied.

"But it sounds like the War had already started," he said.

"Oh, I see what you're getting at," I said. "There were already battles before we declared our independence, is that what you're asking?"

"Yeah," he replied.

"That's how it happened," I said. "Remember how there were battles before the French and Indian War was declared?"

"Oh, yeah," he said.

"Same thing here," I said. "The fighting began before war was declared.

"So Washington was in New York in June. He had, by that time, about 23,000 troops, and he split them into thirds: one-third to the north in Harlem Heights, overlooking the Hudson River; one third at the Battery in the southern end of Manhattan; and one third on Long Island where Brooklyn now stands.

"It wasn't long before the British fleet showed up. They had 100 ships of all sizes and 32,000 troops. The question in Washington's mind was where they would land. The British waited in the harbor, sizing up the situation.

"Finally, on August 27, the British put ashore – on Long Island. Washington had had forts built there, but they were not enough. His troops were pushed back by overwhelming superiority of numbers.

"That night, in a daring move, Washington evacuated all his troops by small boats across the East River to Manhattan. When the British awoke the next morning, the Continental Army was gone.

"So the British stayed right where they were. In their slow way, they took another three weeks to unload their supplies onto the shore and to set up their attack. Then, on September 15, they crossed the East River onto Manhattan Island and marched to the Battery.

"Once the British arrived at the Battery, they faced a combined force of the troops that Washington had stationed there and the ones who had escaped from Long Island. But those troops still weren't enough, and after fierce fighting, the Continentals retreated north to join the Harlem Heights group.

"The British would have captured them all, though, had it not been for a brave new character and his artillery company. His name was Alexander Hamilton, and he is the fifth of our Super Six. Had you heard his name before?"

"Not until you told us, Gomps," Hannah replied.

"Me either," chimed Carter.

"You're not alone," I said. "I think most people know him only from his face on the ten-dollar bill. What they don't know is that he saved the Continental Army. And you will hear about that next time."

34

ALEXANDER HAMILTON SAVES THE CONTINENTAL ARMY

"Tonight, I'm going to introduce you to our fifth member of the Super Six – Alexander Hamilton," I began. "His is probably the most unusual story of all.

"Hamilton was born on the Caribbean island of Nevis in either 1755 or 1757, depending on which records you accept. His mother, Rachel, had been separated from her first husband, and it is unclear whether they were ever divorced.

"Rachel moved to the island of St. Kitts, where she met James Hamilton, a descendant of Scottish royalty. They moved back to Nevis and started a family. Alexander was the second of two sons born to them.

"Shortly after Alexander was born, James abandoned the family. When Alexander was about twelve years old, Rachel came down with a fever and died. Hamilton was an orphan. All he had left were his schoolbooks.

"What happened next would determine the course of young Hamilton's life. A kindly man, probably an uncle, took pity on him and arranged for an apprenticeship in the office of an import/export company on the island of St. Thomas.

"Hamilton, still twelve years old, worked there as a clerk and saw purchases and sales of every kind from all over the world, including our 13 colonies. He soon learned how economics, international trade, and banking worked. He also continued his studies and began to write. He read a lot about our colonies, and the more he learned, the more he wanted to go there.

"In 1772, at just 15, he wrote a story describing the damage that a severe hurricane had done to one of the Caribbean cities. The story was published in the local newspaper, and it was so well received that the townspeople put together a fund that allowed Alexander to go to the colonies to further his education.

"The next year, he moved to the New Jersey Colony and took up his studies there. In less than a year, he was accepted into Columbia University in New York City. In addition to his studies, he also began to write essays in favor of colonial independence. By the end of his first year, he had published four of his pieces under his name and had 14 more published anonymously."

"What's anonymously?" Carter asked.

"That means without your name attached," I replied. "People can't tell who wrote it."

"Why wouldn't he want people to know he wrote something?" he continued.

"Maybe because he was only 18 years old, and they might have dismissed his writings as the ramblings of a boy," I replied.

"Aha," Carter said.

"In addition to his being smart, he was also brave," I continued. "The President of Columbia University was Myles Cooper, a Loyalist. On May 10, 1775, an angry mob of rebels stormed the

University in search of Cooper. They wanted to run him out of town. Even though Hamilton opposed what Cooper stood for, he also opposed mob rule, so he stood in front of the mob and gave a long speech. That gave Cooper enough time to escape.

"Hamilton was fascinated by military history and tactics, as well. In 1775, he joined a New York City militia called the Hearts of Oak and soon rose to the level of Lieutenant. On March 14, 1776, he was promoted to Captain of the Artillery on the condition that he recruit 30 men for his unit. He recruited 68.

"On August 23, 1776, as part of the British invasion of Long Island, a British warship sailed right near an installation of 24 Hearts of Oak cannons at the Battery. Seeing that their cannons were at risk of being taken by the British or blown to bits, Hamilton assembled 15 of his fellow militia, and, under bombardment by the British ship, they moved the cannons to safety.

"Six days later, George Washington and the Long Island detachment of troops made their midnight escape from Brooklyn Heights to the Battery, and Hamilton was ready. His artillery company was made part of the defense force. When the British crossed the East River on September 15, Hamilton's artillery unit was in the thick of the fighting.

"The Continental Army was overpowered by the British and began their retreat north to Harlem Heights. Hamilton positioned his artillery at the rear of the retreat and continued firing and retreating to protect the main force from capture.

"Hamilton and his unit were the last to arrive at Harlem Heights. They had only two cannons left, but they had given Washington the time he needed to get his troops there.

"Unfortunately, the British were hot on their heels, and Washington had only one choice. After trying without success to get away by marching north, he finally ordered the entire Army to retreat across the Hudson River to New Jersey. Thus began a series of military defeats during the rest of 1776, as the British chased them from north of New York City across New Jersey, and then across the Delaware River to the Pennsylvania side.

"By this time, it was December and winter was setting in. The British, thinking that Washington would settle down for the winter, settled down themselves. Leaving companies of troops at key places in New Jersey for the winter, the main British force went back to New York City and its comforts.

"One of those key places was Trenton, New Jersey, not far from the Delaware River. There, a force of German mercenaries . . . "

"What are mercenaries, Gomps?" Hannah interrupted.

"Mercenaries are soldiers who fight for pay – professional soldiers for hire," I replied. "In this case, they were Hessians – Germans that the British had hired to help them."

"Didn't the British have enough troops?" she continued.

"As it turns out, no," I replied. "The British army was undersupplied and underpaid by this time, having been stretched thin by all the wars. So the King just hired what he needed."

"I see," Hannah said.

"So, the Hessians were in Trenton for the winter. They thought, as did the British, that the Continentals would bed down for the winter, too, but Washington had other ideas.

"On Christmas night, Washington and over 2,000 Continental troops were rowed in small boats across the Delaware River to the

New Jersey side. There was a terrible snowstorm with temperatures below zero and ice floes all around, but the boatmen were experienced Massachusetts fishermen and they were quite at home in that weather.

"By four in the morning, Washington's entire force was on the New Jersey side, including an artillery regiment, led by . . .?"

"Alexander Hamilton?" Carter ventured.

"None other than," I replied. "And, his artillery commander . . .?"

"Don't know that one," Hannah replied.

"That's a tough one, but he's one you've heard of," I said. "Henry Knox."

"Was he the book guy that brought the cannons back to Boston?" Hannah said.

"He's the one," I replied.

"Well, that makes sense," she concluded. "And he just continued on with the Army, then?"

"Yup," I said. "Washington trusted him and kept him with the artillery from then on.

"So, they marched nine miles in the early morning hours and attacked the Hessians at daylight. The Hessians had been partying the night before and were caught completely unawares. Without losing a single soldier, the Continentals killed and captured over 1,000 Hessians. The rest of the Hessians ran away, and the Continentals seized needed clothing, supplies, and weapons.

"The British organized a counterattack as soon as they heard. A force of 5,000 British troops marched immediately from Princeton, only a few miles away.

"Washington, having been told of the move, set up a bold plan. He left 400 troops in Trenton with instructions to keep the campfires burning, dig fortifications, and make as much noise as they could. Meanwhile, he led his main force out of Trenton and marched overnight to Princeton by a different route.

"Once again, surprise gave Washington the upper hand. In a battle lasting only 15 minutes, the Continentals defeated the British who had been left behind. And, once again, the Continentals were able to get still more supplies and weapons.

"All this time, Washington was looking for an able, trustworthy assistant. Several officers had applied for the job. One was Aaron Burr, a New York lawyer who had been looking for assignments behind the lines where he could stay out of danger and be noticed by his superior officers. Washington, however, didn't trust him, and didn't want an assistant who had no fighting experience. He refused to promote Burr.

"Instead, Washington chose Alexander Hamilton. He had seen Hamilton's ability and bravery firsthand. And, he perhaps had read some of Hamilton's publications. In one of them, written a year before the start of the war, Hamilton described the strategy that could win a war against the superior British army. He wrote, 'It will be better policy to harass and exhaust the soldiery by frequent skirmishes and incursions than to take the open field with them.' This, as we know, was Washington's strategy to a T."

"No wonder Washington chose him," Hannah said.

"Hamilton became a major advisor to Washington," I said, "but as you might imagine, Aaron Burr was resentful and jealous. This would lead to fatal consequences for Hamilton some years later.

"On the gloomy side, Washington was not able to take advantage of his victories. It was the end of the year and the enlistments of most of his troops were up. They just went back home. The rest were in no condition to fight further.

"Washington took his remaining troops and set up winter camp in a protected area outside Morristown, New Jersey. With that, the British set up their own winter camp to the south.

"And so we'll set up camp for tonight. Next week's story will be tough to withstand. Washington and the Continental Army will suffer through icy winters, bitter defeats, and shortages of everything.

"See you next Wednesday."

"G'night, Gomps," they said in unison.

35

BLOODY FOOTPRINTS IN THE SNOW

It was snowy and very cold for early April. That didn't bother Hannah and Carter, who loved to go out and play in the snow for as long as they could. That's where they were when Peach and I arrived for a visit while their mom and dad took care of some household errands. Suddenly the kids burst through the door, cheeks rosy red, noses running, laughing joyfully.

"Hi, Peach. Hi, Gomps," said Hannah. "It got too cold out, even for us."

"How long have you been out there?" asked Peach.

"Oh, I don't know," answered Carter. "We went out after breakfast."

"That was over an hour ago," observed Peach. "You must be frozen!"

"Not really, but we would like to get warm before we go out again," said Hannah.

"How about some hot cocoa?" Peach asked.

"That would be great!" they chimed. "We were hoping you'd say that."

"Coming right up," said Peach.

"So, Gomps," asked Carter, "When can we hear more about the Colonies?"

"Well, I thought maybe it was boring. So I've been waiting for you to ask."

"Boring?! No way," said Hannah.

"This a good time?"

"Yeah!" they both chimed.

"Last time we met, I told you how the Continental Army was suffering from shortages of all kinds. The winter conditions of 1776 to 1777 made that painfully clear, especially when troops just walked away.

"Tired of the troops coming and going at will, Washington wrote to Congress, begging for funds for a paid army. Finally, Congress agreed to his recruiting sixteen regiments of regular troops, or about 4,000 men. Each man who enlisted would get $20 and 100 acres of land."

"That's not much," said Carter. "Did anybody sign up?"

"Not many," I replied. "Most reacted as you did. The $20 was in worthless paper money, and Congress never said where the land would be. So Washington still faced a shortage of soldiers.

"He also continued to face a shortage of shelter, clothing, and food in the Morristown winter quarters. His men suffered brutal conditions. Many had no boots; those who didn't wrapped their feet in rags. Many had only tents. They were completely unprepared for what turned out to be one of the coldest winters anyone could remember. Everywhere he looked, Washington saw bloody footprints in the snow. And, every day, he went off by himself and prayed.

"By late winter, only 800 were left. On top of starvation, frostbite, and desertion, Washington's camp had been infected with smallpox. He ordered all troops to get inoculated, but it was of little use.

"Then, by April 1777, the Continental Army was back up to about 4,000 men."

"The money from Congress worked, then?" Hannah asked.

"Only to a small degree," I answered. "Most of the newcomers were farmers. After they finished planting their crops, they joined the Army to fight. Then, in August or September, they left again for harvest. They were called 'Summer Soldiers.'"

"By this time, of course, the British were out of their winter quarters, too, gearing up for a new year of battle. Washington was afraid that sometime during the summer the main British force would come out to fight, but they never did. Instead, they just packed up and left New Jersey altogether."

"Can we celebrate now?" Carter asked.

"I'm afraid not," I replied. "Washington again was worried. He knew that there was a reason for them leaving. The question was, where did they go, and why?"

"Before long, Washington had his answer. The British had sailed south into Chesapeake Bay. Within a day, a huge force of British and Hessian troops came ashore only 55 miles south of Philadelphia.

"In the meantime, a young member of French nobility – the Marquis de Lafayette – presented himself to Congress to join the Continental Army. He arrived full of revolutionary spirit and letters of recommendation from several colonials in France, including Ben Franklin. The Continental Congress commissioned him as a Major General and sent him to Washington's camp."

"Gomps, a French guy they didn't even know, a Major General?" Carter blurted.

"That's right," I replied. "Franklin thought that Lafayette's connections with the French King might help get French support. And he may have been right.

"Lafayette was the son of a rich, well-connected family. Orphaned at age twelve, he inherited it all. He showed up on Congress's doorstep with a few assistants when he was only 19 and offered to serve for free."

"Nice guy," Carter remarked.

"I'll say," I agreed. "And it shows how committed he was to the cause of freedom.

"Washington was so impressed with Lafayette that he made him one of his aides right away. The more he saw of the young Frenchman, the more Washington liked and trusted him, and it wasn't long before he gave Lafayette a regiment to command.

"Washington included Lafayette in the action as he rushed his troops from New Jersey to intercept the advancing British. But they were defeated in the Battle of Brandywine Creek and again in the Battle of Paoli's Tavern."

"Paoli's Tavern?" laughed Hannah. "Was that a battle or a bar fight?"

We all laughed, but then I became serious. "Actually, it was a massacre," I said. "Sadly, the Continentals were resting after a long day of fighting when the Hessian and British troops came out of the woods and slaughtered them.

"With the Continental Army defeated, the British marched right into Philadelphia. They arrived to a warm welcome from the Loyalists who lived there, while the Continental Congress was forced to escape to the town of York, Pennsylvania.

"Through that fighting season, Washington's troops harried the British, but lost one battle after another and never did them damage.

"Winter was coming again, and General Howe, the commander of the British forces, located his winter headquarters right in Philadelphia. He placed some of his troops in the city and the rest of them just outside the city, in a town named Germantown.

"On October 3, 1777, Washington received reinforcements from the north. They marched all night and attacked the British settlement in Germantown at dawn. The Continentals nearly won, but the British counterattacked and they had to retreat, beaten once again.

"While the British were occupying Philadelphia, their northern forces were marching south from Canada under General Burgoyne. Their plan was to sweep down Lake Champlain, retake Fort Ticonderoga, march south past Lake George, and meet up with Howe's British forces coming north from Albany. It almost worked, but ended in disaster for the British."

"Wasn't Howe in Philadelphia?" Carter frowned.

"You spotted their blunder," I said. "Good thinking. Let's see how it happened.

"The British coming from Canada met no resistance, not even at Fort Ticonderoga. The two Continental generals who were assigned there, Schuyler and Gates, were jealous of one another, and rather than protect the Fort, they were busy arguing. The British marched right in and took the Fort without even a single shot.

"The next part of Burgoyne's plan got the British in trouble, though. Thinking that the colonials would have a lot of boats patrolling Lake George, Burgoyne decided to bypass it and travel overland instead. Since everyone wanting to go north and south went by boat, there were no good roads. So the British had to cut their way through the forest and over the mountains.

"Seeing this, the colonials used a different tactic. General Schuyler had loggers cut down trees across the British path. They dug deep ditches. They destroyed bridges. They drove farmers' cattle away and burned their crops so that the British could not scavenge for food. Soon, the British were penned up and exhausted.

"At that point, several battles broke out between different Continental and British regiments. The Green Mountain Boys were victorious . . ."

"Yay, the Green Mountain Boys again!" Carter exclaimed.

"But at Fort Stanwix in Saratoga, things were not going so well. The British had surrounded it. General Schuyler asked his assistants for a volunteer to lead the reinforcements, and General Benedict Arnold volunteered.

"Benedict Arnold was a man with a huge ego," I said. "He thought that he should be in charge of the whole Continental Army instead of Washington."

"Instead of Washington?" Hannah said. "How could he have been better?"

"He had had some experience," I replied. "He was the commander of the force that originally took Fort Ticonderoga. Then he had led troops in a failed attack on Quebec.

"At Ticonderoga, his commanding officer, General Gates, took all of the credit for Arnold's success, and Arnold was angry. In the attack on Quebec, he was blamed for the loss when he had in fact fought bravely. This made him even angrier. So, by the time the chance came in Saratoga, he was ready to clear his name.

"General Arnold started out for Fort Stanwix with his regiment and two Indian scouts. He sent the scouts out ahead to warn the British of a big force of Continental troops. Then he marched his men so as to make as much noise as possible. The British became so frightened that they quickly retreated, and the Fort was saved.

"While Arnold was on this expedition, Congress decided to replace General Schuyler with General Gates. So when Arnold got back to headquarters, there was his old enemy, General Gates, in overall command.

"Meanwhile, the British General, Burgoyne, had expected to be reinforced by General Howe coming from the south. Unbeknownst to Burgoyne, however, Howe had gone to Philadelphia instead, as you spotted, Carter. That left Burgoyne with only one choice – fight to the finish.

"The two sides met outside of Saratoga. The battle went one way and then the other for an entire day. General Arnold and his men made a bold attack and broke through.

"That night, Gates sent a report to Congress about the advantage they had gained. He credited all the senior officers except Arnold. The next day General Arnold confronted Gates, and Gates stripped Arnold of his command.

"Arnold was furious, but still determined to show his ability. On the third day of battle, against Gates' orders, he rode out and led his men. Arnold's troops defeated a key British position, and in the fighting, Arnold had his leg broken.

"Burgoyne's forces had to retreat. Then, on October 17, 1777, exhausted, without supplies, and surrounded by Continental forces,

Burgoyne surrendered his entire army. The 5,000 surviving British troops were sent to a prisoners' camp in Charlottesville, Virginia, and the northern half of the British Army was no more."

"Yay," the kids shouted. "Benedict Arnold turned out to be a hero," Carter said.

"You would think so," I said, "yet, as things turned out, he was anything but. I'll tell you the rest of his story later.

"The important thing to remember is that the Battle of Saratoga became the turning point of the war. When the French heard about the surrender of the British northern army, they became much more willing to help us.

"The year before, in September, 1776, the Continental Congress had sent Ben Franklin to France to bolster Silas Deane's negotiating efforts, but even Franklin was able only to get secret loans until the news of the victory at Saratoga arrived. After months of persuasion, Franklin was finally able to work out an alliance with the French.

"The alliance took the form of two treaties: the Treaty of Alliance and the Treaty of Amity and Commerce, drafted by John Adams. They were signed on February 6, 1778, and the flow of military and financial support increased.

"Now, back to Washington in Pennsylvania."

"After his loss in Germantown in October 1777, Washington was forced to set up winter quarters for the Continental Army. He chose Valley Forge, Pennsylvania, as the place. It was 18 miles to the northwest of Philadelphia, not far from Germantown. From there, he would be able to keep his eye on both the British command and their main body of forces.

"By this time, Washington had as many as 12,000 troops, and he had the same problems with supplying them as before. While they were able to build crude shelters from local forests, they had little food or clothing. Boots were in such short supply that bloody footprints were again seen everywhere in the camp.

"As in Morristown, disease spread. Frostbite was common. Washington supervised the construction of an army field hospital to care for the sick and dying. And here is where his wife Martha, 'Molly Pitcher' and other wives set up their camp. In spite of everyone's best efforts, though, as many as 3,000 soldiers died during that winter."

"Wowww," Carter breathed.

"And, as before, Washington repeatedly begged Congress for money and supplies. And, as before, the Congress could not or would not do anything beyond the loans from France and from wealthy colonists."

"That is so sad," Hannah said. "Did the British know how bad off we were?"

"Probably," I replied, "but it wouldn't have mattered. In those days, the British strategy of war was not to fight during the winter. The officers escaped to the warmth of Philadelphia, while the troops lay low in Germantown."

"Couldn't Washington have attacked them again?" Carter asked.

"He could have," I replied, "but his army was in no condition to fight."

"Oh, yeah," he said.

"There was one shining moment at Valley Forge, though," I said. "In February, a Prussian General named Baron von Steuben appeared out of nowhere to offer his services."

"Prussian?" Carter asked. "What's that?"

"Prussia was an area of Germany," I replied.

"Von Steuben had heard about the Declaration of Independence and wanted to fight on the side of freedom.

"It turned out, though, that von Steuben was not all he claimed to be. He wasn't really a General. He wasn't even a Baron. But he did have fighting experience in Europe, and he did know how to train soldiers.

"So, through the rest of the winter of '78, he taught the troops to march and maneuver together and to use bayonets. He also showed the officers how to write a training book so that all the regiments could operate under the same orders."

"Is that how Molly Pitcher's husband learned how to fire the cannon?" Carter asked.

"Yes, it was, Carter," I replied. "He learned during that training.

"Then, in the spring, the King – George III - had seen enough of General Howe. The King could not understand why the colonials had not been defeated by this time. Of course, King George was as nutty as a fruitcake, so his judgment was often wrong, but that's what he thought."

"What do you mean nutty, Gomps?" asked Hannah.

"King George III apparently suffered from mental illness," I replied. "He seemed determined to continue the war when he knew he couldn't afford it. He ranted and raved at his advisors, and they had to obey him.

"So, to the king, Howe had caused the loss of his northern army at Saratoga, even though it was Burgoyne's fault. General Howe was brought back to England and replaced by General Clinton, Howe's second in command.

"General Clinton saw that Philadelphia had been worthless to the British. He ordered a complete withdrawal to New York City, and in

June 1778, the British forces crossed the Delaware and became strung out across New Jersey. This was just the kind of mistake that Washington was waiting for.

"Washington ordered the attack at Monmouth, but his General, General Lee, had failed to set up any plan of action. His men, not knowing what Lee wanted, were soon defeated and in retreat.

"Upon seeing this, Washington removed Lee from command and raced to the battle line. Riding his horse in front of the retreating soldiers, Washington was able to stop them and turn them around.

"At the end of the day, Washington ordered a general charge at the British line, with Molly Pitcher firing her cannon all the while. They broke through, and the British turned and ran."

"Oh, Gomps, I'm exhausted just hearing about it," Hannah said. "But I'm happy, too. Can I ask a question?"

"Sure."

"You said that the Continental Congress passed the Declaration and the Articles of Confederation," she said. "Did they do anything else?"

"Good question, Hannah," I replied. "But you're going to have to wait until next time to find out. I'm also going to tell you about treason high in the officers' ranks."

"What's treason?" Carter tried to entice me to continue.

"Next time. You two look like you're ready to go back out and play."

36

CONGRESS STARTS
THE COUNTRY AND
AN OFFICER COMMITS
TREASON

"Hannah, last time you asked what the Continental Congress did, but I wasn't sure what you meant," I asked the following Wednesday evening.

"Yes, did the Congress do anything after writing the Articles of Confederation?" she continued.

"Oh. Yes. I get it now," I replied. "Yes, they did. They had a choice. They could wait until all the colonies approved the Articles before they set up a government, or they could act as if the Articles had already been approved.

"To save time they decided to begin operating as if the Articles had been approved. They appointed ambassadors, worked on international trade, arranged for loans and the printing of money, and so forth."

"Why couldn't they help Washington, then?" Hannah asked.

"Oh, I see where you were going with your question," I replied. "You spotted the big problem. The Articles formed a central government of sorts, but the structure of it was very weak. It changed the colonies to States, but it really couldn't require them to do much of anything. It wasn't much more than an agreement that the States would work together. The States still had all the power, and if they didn't want to tax themselves to support Washington, there was nothing in the Articles to make them do it."

"But some of them must have wanted to," Hannah insisted.

"Ah," I replied, "here is where the ugly head of self-interest rises. Let me ask you a question. Suppose you are Massachusetts. You want to pass taxes in your State to send to General Washington, but you know that the State of New York will not do the same. What would you think to yourself?"

"Why wouldn't New York want to?" asked Carter.

"There were a lot more Loyalists in New York than there were in Massachusetts," I replied.

"Is that true?" Hannah asked.

"Yes, it is," I replied.

"Even though the English soldiers were fighting us in New York, too?" Carter continued.

"Even though," I replied.

"If I were Massachusetts, I'd feel like I was fighting New York's war for them," Hannah observed.

"What do you mean, Hannah?" Carter asked.

"If I sent money, some of it would be used to defend New Yorkers," she continued. "The New Yorkers would be getting defended for free."

"I get it," Carter said. "That wouldn't be fair."

"Exactly," I said. "So, Carter, would you send the money or not?"

"Hmm," he replied, "probably not."

"And that's just what all the States did," I said. "They held back.

"In addition to these weaknesses, the Articles didn't provide for courts, or a President, or government departments. It was as if each State was its own country. They had different money, different laws, different taxes, and different tariffs.

"The Articles did little to bind them together, but it was a start, and in the next few years, the States would learn what worked and what didn't."

"Now, I want to go back to a guy you've met - Benedict Arnold. Remember that he was the Continental General at Saratoga who had his leg broken? When it healed, he still wasn't ready to go back to fighting, so he was given what we call a desk job — away from the battlefield.

"In 1778 Benedict Arnold was put in charge of running Philadelphia after the British left. He still resented his commanders, and at being put in this desk job, his resentment grew even more.

"At the same time, it turned out that Arnold was dishonest. While in Philadelphia, he made money from his dealings in city business. Congress investigated, discovered what he had done, and removed Arnold from his assignment.

"Arnold believed he had done nothing wrong and became bitter at his treatment. He felt that the country had treated him unfairly at every turn, and he decided to do something about it. He decided to go over to the British side."

"No way!" Carter shouted.

"That's what you meant by 'treason'!" Hannah shouted.

"Absolutely," I replied. "Here's how he did it. He secretly contacted the British to see what they would want in return for making him a General. They told him that they wanted a key location on the Hudson River. The deal was struck.

"Arnold then got himself assigned to the command of West Point – the U.S. Military Academy. It is on the banks of the Hudson River about halfway between New York City and Albany. It was just what the British wanted.

"Even after we found out that he was corrupt?" Hannah interrupted. "Why would we give him any more assignments? I would have kicked him out."

"You have to wonder, don't you?" I said. "I think it was because of two things: first, he was still a talented general. He had shown his ability in battle. And, second, they thought he couldn't do much harm at a training school. It probably never entered their minds that he was capable of treason."

"Still . . . " Hannah let her voice trail off.

"As soon as he arrived, Benedict Arnold drew up a map of the Academy and of the lookout positions. Then, over time, he began to cut back on the lookout schedule until the Academy was open to attack.

"When the time was right, he gave the map and the schedule to a spy who was to take it to the British in New York City. On his way, though, the spy was stopped by Continental troops and searched. The plot was uncovered, and West Point was saved."

"Phew!" Carter exclaimed, "But what happened to Benedict Arnold?"

"He found out about the capture of the spy and escaped before the Continentals could catch him," I replied. "He snuck through Continental lines and made it to the British side."

"That rat!" Hannah exclaimed.

"He should have been shot!" Carter shouted.

"If they had caught him, he would have been," I said. "But ever since, Benedict Arnold has been thought of as the ultimate traitor. When someone calls another person a Benedict Arnold, they are calling him a traitor. And that's all that need be said about him for now. And, for that matter, that's all that will be said tonight.

"Next week we'll end the war, and we'll do it with the southern Continental Army. I'll tell you about General 'Light Horse' Harry Lee and about how Lord Cornwallis stepped into his own trap. So, good night to all, and I'll see you next week."

37

WE WIN OUR FREEDOM

As usual, we gathered in the living room after dessert.

"Let's see if we can end this war, shall we?" I began. "The key action was to take place in the south.

"On December 29, 1778, British Lieutenant Colonel Archibald Campbell, under the command of General Clinton, sailed into Savannah, Georgia, and captured it with 3,500 troops. He was joined by the forces of Brigadier General Prevost, and they set up a command post for the south.

"Seeing the advantage that Campbell and Prevost had gained, General Clinton came from New York to lead them. From there, they marched north, putting Charleston, South Carolina, under siege and capturing it on May 12, 1780. They now occupied the two most important ports in the south."

"Hold on, Gomps," Carter said. "What happened to 1779?"

"What do you mean, what happened to 1779?" I asked.

"The British captured Savannah in 1778 and Charleston in 1780, right?" he asked.

"That's right," I said.

"So what did they do in 1779?"

"I see what you're asking," I replied. "The British were bottled up in Savannah under a Continental Army siege with the help of some French troops and ships, but it failed. That opened the door for the British to march north to Charleston.

"Once General Clinton led the capture of Charleston, he thought Lord Cornwallis could take it from there. He put Cornwallis in command and went back to New York to run the overall war.

"At the same time, George Washington put General Horatio Gates in charge of the Continentals in the south, but Cornwallis quickly defeated him at the Battle of Camden, South Carolina. Then he chased the Continental Army north into North Carolina, where the British won several small battles.

"Finally, back in Philadelphia, the Continental Congress had had enough of General Gates. On October 5, 1780, they gave Washington permission to replace him. Washington wasted no time and chose Major General Nathaniel Greene.

"Greene got right to work and marched his troops to Kings Mountain, North Carolina. There, he set a trap and waited. The British forces marched right into the trap and the Continentals won the battle.

"The victory at Kings Mountain was considered the turning point in the southern campaign, and maybe in the whole war. Rather than risk further losses, Cornwallis ordered his troops back to South Carolina to regroup. But the Continentals were not finished, and they won the Battle of Cowpens, South Carolina, by springing the same kind of trap.

"This defeat made Cornwallis angry, and he became determined to fight back. He planned to chase the Continentals, corner them, and wipe them out. To do this he equipped his troops lightly so that they could move fast. No heavy wagons, no cannons, no tents.

"After he wiped out the southern Continental Army, Cornwallis planned to free the British northern army being held in Charlottesville, Virginia. Then, with this added strength, he was going to link up with General Benedict Arnold and march to the north."

"Benedict Arnold?" Carter exclaimed. "Was he fighting for the British already?"

"That skunk!" Hannah shouted.

"Yes, he was," I said. "He no sooner changed sides than the British made him a general and gave him a command. His forces were landed in northern Virginia by British gunboats, and he was in business.

"But Cornwallis would have to reach him first — and that never happened. First, the British chased the Continentals through North Carolina and fell into a third trap."

"What was that, Gomps?" Hannah asked.

"Not what, but who," I said. "General Greene had 'Light Horse' Harry Lee."

"Ha, ha," the kids laughed. "Was that his real name?" Carter asked.

"His name was Henry Lee, and Light Horse Harry was his nickname," I replied.

"Light Horse," Hannah said. "What, did he ride a pony?"

Everyone laughed at that.

"That was a good one, Hannah," I said when the laughter died down. "No, he was a skilled horseman. They called him that because he chose light, agile horses that allowed him to fight with a saber nimbly.

"Light Horse Harry Lee was in charge of a regiment of horse cavalry, and General Greene put him in the rear of his forces. As Cornwallis was chasing them, Lee and his riders kept pecking away at them and slowing them down. This gave the main army the time they needed to get across a key river into Virginia.

"Once they reached the river, Cornwallis's forces could go no further. They had no boats and were exhausted. So they retreated back into North Carolina.

"Over the next 8 months, Greene and his troops kept pecking away at Cornwallis's forces, always avoiding a direct battle.

"By August 1781, Greene and his troops had reoccupied almost all of the southern territory, and Cornwallis was low on troops, morale, and supplies. He decided to bypass General Greene and march up to Virginia as fast as he could to join forces with Benedict Arnold and pick up the prisoners at Charlottesville."

"That sounds not so good for us," Hannah said.

"You're right, if his plan had worked," I said. "But it didn't."

"Whew! What happened, Gomps?" Hannah asked.

"The French came to the rescue!" I exclaimed.

"Finally," sighed Hannah. "It took them long enough."

"Well, better late than never," I said. "Before the British had captured Charleston, South Carolina, our old friend the Marquis de Lafayette had gone back to France to get reinforcements and to talk the French government into giving more help."

"You mean he wasn't with the French government?" Carter asked.

"No," I said, "he had been doing this all on his own.

"Franklin had been right about Lafayette. He had a lot of pull with the King of France and the King gave Lafayette six French ships and 6,000 soldiers.

"When Lafayette returned, Washington sent him and his forces to Virginia. Washington had heard that Benedict Arnold would be landing there, and he wanted Lafayette to be his welcoming committee."

"Yay," shouted the kids. "We know what's going to happen."

"You do?" I asked.

"Yup," said Hannah. "I bet Lafayette surprised him."

"He sure did," I confirmed. "No sooner did Arnold arrive than Lafayette put his forces between him and the advancing Cornwallis. Now there was no way the two British armies could join up, and the end was in sight."

"Yay," the kids shouted again.

"But it took one more blunder by the British to bring the war to an end," I said. "When General Clinton heard that Cornwallis and Benedict Arnold would not be able to join forces, he ordered Cornwallis to set up a defensive position that could be supplied from the ocean.

"So Cornwallis marched himself right into his own trap. He set up his defenses in Yorktown, Virginia, a town on the York River. This was a place that was easily closed off from escape by land, and Washington wasted no time in ordering the Continental and French troops to set up a siege.

"At the same time, Washington had learned that the French had given him more naval support than the six ships that came back with Lafayette. Their whole Caribbean fleet suddenly appeared off the Virginia coast.

"In September 1781, they attacked the British fleet and defeated them in the Battle of Chesapeake Bay. Cornwallis's means of supply and escape was cut off, and it became a matter of time.

"The Siege of Yorktown began in October with Continental and French forces bombarding the British continuously. It wasn't long before Cornwallis could see that his cause was lost. He surrendered his entire army on October 17, 1781."

"Wahoo!" Carter yelled. "Did that end the war?"

"Pretty much," I said. "There were some sea battles in the Atlantic and the Caribbean, but no more fighting in America. The British still had about 30,000 troops stationed in New York, Charleston, and Savannah, and they were brought back to England.

"Finally, on September 3, 1783, a peace treaty was signed in Paris, France. Properly enough, it was called The Treaty of . . . ?"

"Paris?" Carter ventured.

"That's right!" I replied, "A brilliant deduction, Carter. And the Treaty was approved by Congress on January 14, 1784. We were finally free."

"Yay," we all shouted. We got up and marched around the living room, waving our arms and hugging.

When everyone calmed down, Hannah asked, "Is that the end of the story?"

"Not by a long shot, Hannah," I said. "In the . . ."

"Then I have a question," she interrupted.

"OK, Hannah," I said. "What is it?"

"I saw on TV that slaves fought in the war," She said. "Is that true?"

"To some extent, yes, Hannah," I replied. "Let's back up and look at the black people in the colonies at that time. There were slaves, of course, but there also may have been as many as 40,000 free blacks. These were blacks who had been freed by their owners, or were runaway slaves, or were free blacks who immigrated to the colonies from other countries.

"Just about all of the free blacks were in the northern colonies. Some served in militias. One of them – Crispus Attucks – was in the Boston Massacre, and is said to have been the first person killed. Blacks are believed to have served in militias in the battles of Lexington and Concord.

"The Continental Army recruited blacks to serve with New England forces. In addition to the free blacks who joined, slaves were also recruited in exchange for their freedom, but we don't know how many.

"Some have guessed that there may have been as many as 5,000 black soldiers who fought for the colonies at one time or another. By the end of the War, the Continental forces in the north may have been as much as one-fifth black.

"On top of that, the British tried to get colonial slaves to run away and fight for them . . . "

"Slaves fought for the British?" Carter interrupted. "How could that be?"

"That's right," I said. "The British figured that, if slaves could get across battle lines, they would fight the colonies in exchange for their freedom. So the Royal Governor of Virginia at the time, the Earl of Dunmore, offered to free any slaves who joined the British Army."

"I didn't know that, Gomps," Hannah said. "Did it work?"

"Apparently not very well," I replied. "Only 1,000 or so are believed to have taken him up on it. He created a separate unit for them called Dunmore's Ethiopian Regiment. But within a year, most of the Regiment died of smallpox. In the end, only about 300 slaves gained their freedom that way.

"All told, there may have been as many as 20,000 blacks who fought for the British, but this would have included runaway slaves and blacks from other countries, in addition to the Dunmore group."

"You would think that blacks could have been used more than that," Hannah concluded.

"Maybe," I said, "but both the colonists and the British were wary of giving guns to free blacks or to slaves. They were afraid that the blacks would carry out a rebellion of their own and overthrow all whites. Remember that there were about 700,000 blacks in the colonies by this time, and most of them were very unhappy with their situation."

"I see what you mean, Gomps," Hannah said. "It wasn't as simple as I thought."

"Unfortunately so," I continued. "By this time, the colonies had become a very complicated society. Any more questions about slaves in the army?"

"Nope," said Hannah. "I understand."

"Carter?" I asked.

"Nope," he replied. "I'm fine, too."

"Back to our story, then," I said. "The Treaty of Paris was signed and the Revolutionary War was over, but in the coming months and years, it all almost came apart."

"Oh, no," Hannah exclaimed. "What happened?"

"I'm afraid you're going to have to wait until next time," I said. "This is a good stopping place for tonight. But don't forget your question. We'll take it up as soon as we start next week."

38

THE ARTICLES OF CONFEDERATION CREATE A MESS

"Gomps, last time you asked me to remember my question," Hannah began. "So here goes: what happened that the country almost came apart?"

"The trouble pretty much stemmed from the Articles of Confederation," I replied. "It worsened all the divisions and jealousies among the States. Rather than bring the States together, it split them apart.

"As it was, the States continued to be quite different from one another. The southern States were still agricultural, with few cities. Their economy was still based mostly on tobacco, cotton, rice, and indigo, and their wealth rested on big plantations and dealers in their products.

"The northern States still were more industrial, with many cities. The northern geography was too hilly and rocky for big farms, so their economy was still based mostly on small factories and home businesses, warehouses, shopkeeping, and international trade. Wealth in the northern States rested mostly in the hands of manufacturers, merchants, and importer-exporters.

"The southern States did not trust the northern States. They believed that businesses in the north controlled both prices and the flow of goods from the south to other States and countries. The northern States didn't trust the southern States, because the plantation owners could withhold their products from the market when they didn't like the prices. Also, by this time many northerners hated slavery.

"The Articles of Confederation had no power to fix any of that. There was no central government that could govern the States. The States even printed their own money! How'd you like to take a Maryland dollar bill into New York and try to buy something with it?"

"Not!" answered Carter.

"Also, the Articles didn't provide for an executive branch — a President and departments to govern things — or a court system," I continued. "The Articles gave power to the Congress to enter into treaties with other countries, but so could each State."

"Gomps, a State could have a treaty with another country?" Hannah asked.

"That's right," I replied. "Under the Articles, they could."

"Oh, that doesn't sound good," she replied.

"You got that right," I said, "especially when the other countries found out about it. They played one State off against another. They would secretly talk to one State and get the best deal they could. Then they would go to another State and ask for a still better one. The States were cutting each other's throats!

"And, what's worse," I continued, "each State could collect tariffs. Remember, tariffs are taxes that are charged for international trade. So, if you were a cooper selling your barrels for $2.00 and a cooper in the next State wanted to sell his barrels in your State for $1.00, your

State could vote for a tariff of $1.10 on each of his barrels, making his barrels more expensive in your State."

"Did that actually happen?" Carter asked.

"It sure did," I said, "a lot. And it didn't end there.

"Under the Articles, each State was free to decide its own rules of navigation. Let's say that a ship was sailing to Connecticut to unload goods in New Haven harbor. To do that, they would have to sail through Rhode Island waters. Rhode Island could pass a navigation law that extended the Rhode Island State waters for 200 miles from shore. What do you think Rhode Island could do under that rule?"

"Charge a tariff on the ship?" Hannah offered.

"Exactly right," I said. "If you're bringing those goods into our country, would you order the ship to go to New Haven knowing you'd have to pay a tariff to Rhode Island? Remember, you've bought the goods, paid for them, and paid for the ship."

"No way," answered Carter.

"Of course not," I said. "What would you do?"

"Probably unload in Rhode Island," he continued.

"Right," I said. "And, as a result, business in Rhode Island goes . . . ?"

"Up," they chimed.

"And, business in Connecticut goes . . . ?" I continued.

"Down," they moaned together.

"Do we have a mess?" I asked.

"We have a big mess," they concluded.

"But," I said, "as they say in the steak-knife commercials, 'Wait, there's more.'"

"How can it get any worse?" Hannah exclaimed. "It's a miracle that the States didn't go to war with each other."

"It seems like it," I said, "but there were also problems left over from the Revolutionary War.

"Remember the loans and promises that were made to pay for the Continental Army? The Continental Congress had borrowed money from other countries and from private citizens. And so had the colonies. And the debt didn't stop there.

"Remember the promises that were made to the men who enlisted in the regular Continental Army? Those soldiers were now coming forward to demand their pay."

"Can't blame them," Hannah observed.

"No, you can't," I concurred.

"So what did we do?" Hannah continued.

"We did what we've done off and on ever since," I said. "We printed money, lots of it. The Congress printed money called Continentals, and the States printed more of their own money."

"So?" asked Carter. "Didn't they have the right?"

"They had the right," I concurred, "but that didn't mean it was a good idea. They printed so much money that it became worthless."

"Why is that, Gomps?" Carter continued. "It was real money, wasn't it?"

"Yes, it was real money, but it had no value," I replied. "It sounds like we need a quick session on money. You up for it?"

"OK," replied Carter reluctantly. "Sounds boring, though."

"C'mon, Carter," Hannah said. "If I can do it, you can do it."

"I'll try to make it interesting," I said. "I promise to stop if it starts to get too complicated, OK? You let me know."

"Deal," said Carter.

"All right," I said. "A long time ago, real gold and silver were about the only form of money. Each country would make gold and silver coins, and people would carry around the coins to buy things.

"But gold and silver are heavy, especially gold, and it was hard to carry around more than a few coins. So a country, probably China, had an idea. Instead of coins, they gave out pieces of paper, and on that paper they printed a promise that whoever had the piece of paper could trade it for real coins whenever they wanted to.

"Then, that country gave people the paper and the people turned in their gold and silver. So the country kept the gold and silver in a safe place, and every piece of paper had gold or silver waiting, in case the person wanted their coins back. Any questions so far?"

"Why were gold and silver used for money?" Hannah asked.

"Good question," I replied. "Both metals were scarce, and they were hard to get. So, the amount of gold and silver in the world at any one time didn't increase much. Also, the metals were very stable, especially gold. They didn't rust or deteriorate, so the amount didn't go down much either. A certain amount of gold, a coin, say, would weigh the same now as in 50 years."

"I never thought of that," admitted Hannah.

"Why would anyone give up their gold?" Carter asked.

"That's the most important question." I replied. "You had to be sure that your country had enough gold to give yours back to you if you asked for it. You would be willing to accept the convenience of paper money if you had confidence that you could get the same amount in gold if you ever needed to.

"And that's all we need to say about money to understand where trouble starts," I said.

"That's it?" Carter asked.

"That's it," I confirmed.

"Wow, that was easy."

"Hannah?" I asked.

"That was interesting," she replied. "I'm good."

"So, here's what happens," I continued. "A country prints up more money than they have gold or silver to back it with. And they keep printing more and more. Pretty soon, people begin to wonder how much, if any, gold they can get if they ask for it back.

"In our case, in the beginning the United States and the States themselves didn't even have gold and silver to back up the paper money. They were just printing it, like the Continentals. If more was needed, they just printed more. So, the value of the money went . . . ?"

"Down?" Carter ventured.

"Right," I replied.

"And, the people's confidence in our country's money went down. Pretty soon, shopkeepers refused to accept the paper money because they didn't know how much it was worth. Banks and other lenders refused to accept it to pay debts. People refused to accept it because they couldn't buy anything with it. And, maybe worst of all, countries to which we owed money refused to accept it as repayment of their loans. And they refused to loan us any more.

"Finally, in 1785 we adopted the U.S. Dollar, based on the value of a Spanish silver coin, and that put us on a gold standard of a sort. But it didn't get us out of the woods.

"We were a free country, all right, but our country was in trouble, and we were on the verge of losing the whole deal."

"That's scary," Hannah said.

"What did we do?" said Carter.

"Not what," I said. "Who. James Madison came to the rescue!"

"Yay," exclaimed Carter.

"Wasn't he one of the Super Six?" Hannah asked.

"Yes, it's been a long time since I mentioned his name, so good for you for remembering," I said. "He is the last of the Super Six, but I'm a little tired tonight, so I'll tell you about him next time.

"Let me get my hugs and I'll be on my way."

39

SUPER JAMES MADISON TO THE RESCUE

"Hannah, last time you picked up on James Madison as one of the Super Six," I began. "Let me introduce him before I tell you what he did.

"Madison was born in 1751 in central Virginia and grew up on a tobacco plantation called Montpelier, owned by his father and mother. He was the first of twelve children."

"Wow," Hannah interrupted. "You were right when you said that they had big families back then."

"There you go," I said. "Madison was just about the most unlikely person you could imagine becoming one of the Super Six. He was small and frail as a child and was always sick. He grew only to about 5 feet 4 inches and maybe 110 pounds.

"From an early age he had frequent seizures, so much so that some doctors believed that he might have epilepsy."

"What's a seizure, Gomps?" Carter asked.

"Oh, you know, Carter," interrupted Hannah, "that's when someone falls down and foams at the mouth."

"Is that right, Gomps?" Carter asked.

"That's one way to put it," I replied. "Their body might go stiff or they might shake or go unconscious. Seizure is a general word that covers a lot of things like that."

"Then what's epilepsy?" he continued.

"Well, as I understand it, epilepsy is a brain disease," I replied. "It's like little electrical storms in the brain. At unexpected times, the person has seizures. Then, after a period of a minute up to maybe fifteen or twenty minutes, they return to normal."

"Weird!" Hannah concluded.

"Sounds scary," Carter said. "Is there a cure?"

"You'd have to talk to a doctor about that," I replied, "but I don't think so. I think it's a condition that can be controlled, and there may be things that set it off that can be avoided, but I think people have it for life. Maybe you can look that up on your own.

"Later in his life, Madison's doctors changed their minds and decided that he didn't have epilepsy after all. But he still had seizures, and he had a bad digestive system, too. Some wondered if the two were caused by the same disease, but no one ever found out.

"To make it more complicated, it appears that Madison also may have been a bit of a hypochondriac."

"What's a hypochondriac?" Carter asked.

"That's someone who constantly worries that he is sick and thinks he is sick even when he isn't," I replied. "It's a kind of mental thing."

"You're right, Gomps," Hannah observed. "Madison doesn't sound like he would turn out to be super at all."

"You wouldn't think so," I replied, "but maybe his weaknesses brought out other things in him.

"Madison's sickness and frailty prevented him from doing much work, but he was strong enough to read. He started school with a local Scottish minister when he was eleven. At 16, he began two years of study for college under another minister. Then he entered the College of New Jersey, or what we now call Princeton University.

"There, he studied very hard, some said too hard, and his health suffered the whole time. He took courses in Latin, Greek, philosophy, math, science, and debate. He did so well that he ended up studying under the President of the College - another minister."

"Gomps, it sounds like all his teachers were ministers," Carter said. "Is that what he wanted to be?"

"That may be what his family wanted," I replied, "but he didn't know what he wanted to be at the time. Since religion was so widespread in daily life, it was common for ministers to be teachers."

"I see," he said.

"Madison graduated in 1771 and stayed at the College for two more years, studying Hebrew, theology, and more philosophy. At the end of his stay, he finally decided that he wanted to become a lawyer, but not in the practice of law.

"I don't get it," Hannah interrupted. "If he wanted to be a lawyer, why wouldn't he want to practice law? Makes no sense."

"It seems so, doesn't it?" I replied. "But there was one other odd thing about him. He was painfully shy. The idea of standing in front of a court and presenting a case frightened him. That's why he took debate classes, but they were not enough."

"Still," she continued, "what else was there for a lawyer to do?"

"Write the U.S. Constitution," I replied.

Both kids fell silent. I stayed quiet, giving the idea time to sink in.

"But," I finally interjected, "we're getting ahead of ourselves. Madison didn't write it out of the blue. He did other things that, looking back, got him ready for it."

"Remember that in 1774, the First Continental Congress banned trade with England?" I asked.

"Yeah, I think so," Hannah declared while Carter was quiet.

"Well, at the same time, they recommended that each city and county in the colonies create a Committee of Safety to make sure that people weren't sneaking around the trade ban. Madison was elected to the Committee for his county.

"Then, in April, 1776, two years later, Madison was elected to the Convention that wrote the Virginia State Constitution. The Convention met in Williamsburg, and the first thing they did was to tell the Virginia representatives in the Continental Congress to vote for independence from England.

"The next thing they did was to form a committee to write a plan of government for Virginia as a State. They called it the Declaration of Rights. Madison was put on that committee, and he worked on the paragraph for freedom of religion."

"Why did they need that?" Hannah interrupted. "Wasn't there freedom of religion already?"

"Excellent question," I replied. "In some colonies there was, but over the years, freedom of religion had been fading away in the others. In fact, by this time, six of the colonies had established the

Church of England as their official religion, and Virginia was one of them."

"But that was one of the big reasons that the Pilgrims came in the first place, wasn't it? To get away from the Church of England?" Hannah pressed.

"True," I agreed, "but there were many Loyalists in those six colonies, and they wanted the Church of England to be the official religion. In those colonies, taxes were collected and given to the Church to pay for ministers, church buildings, and other things, just as they had been in England."

"That wasn't fair to the other religions," Hannah concluded.

"No, it wasn't, Hannah," I said. "And it went even further than that. In Virginia, all ministers who weren't Church of England had to pay for a license to preach. Among them were the Baptists. In fact, some Baptist ministers had been jailed for preaching without a license. They complained to Madison, and he saw the unfairness of it.

"Madison didn't think that the government should be involved in religion at all. He believed that even just the approval of a religion by a government would interfere with people's natural right to believe what they wanted to believe. And he thought that it was too easy for an official church to hold sway over government business.

"So the Virginia Convention finished the Declaration of Rights on July 5, 1776, one day after the Declaration of Independence was approved in Philadelphia. Madison went back home, but was immediately elected to the Virginia Assembly, so it was back to Williamsburg in October.

"There he got on the Committee on Religion and was successful in ending the payments by Virginia to the Church of England. Without the money, the Church had no power in the government. And that ended official religion in Virginia.

"Then, less than a year later, the Governor of Virginia had a vacancy in his Council of State . . . "

"What's a Council of State, Gomps?" Carter interrupted.

"Yeah, I was wondering that, too," Hannah added.

"The Council of State was a small group of advisors that the Governor chose to help him make decisions," I replied. "Most heads of organizations have groups like that, even the President of the United States."

"Are they elected?" Carter continued.

"Nope," I replied, "they are 'appointed,' meaning that the governor or President could choose whomever he wanted."

"Did they get paid?" Carter asked.

"These days they do," I said, "but they may not have back then."

"How could they have afforded to do it, then?" he persisted.

"Well, they had other sources of money," I said. "Some would have been plantation owners or owned businesses or factories."

"What about a poor person?" Hannah asked. "They can be just as smart as a rich person."

"Intelligence was only part of it, Hannah," I replied. "Most believed that only opinions from people who had been successful, or who had something to lose, should count."

"What do you mean, Gomps?" Hannah asked.

"If you own something like a business or a farm and you make a bad suggestion, your suggestion might result in your losing what you have," I replied. "You are going to be careful not to make a suggestion that would be too risky or that can't work.

"If you don't own anything, then you can suggest anything, and if it fails, you haven't lost.

"And that's why the Virginia Governor chose people who owned things. They wouldn't make careless suggestions, and they wouldn't even make good suggestions and then just walk away. They'd have a reason to put their own personal efforts into making their suggestions work. It is called having a stake in the outcome. Some people call it 'having skin in the game.'"

"I get it," said Hannah.

"Me too," said Carter.

"So the Governor named Madison to his Council of State . . ." I said.

"Because he had a plantation," Carter broke in.

"Right, Carter," I said, "and why did having a plantation matter to the Governor?"

"If he made a bad suggestion, the State might make a mistake that would hurt his farming business," he replied.

"What kind of mistake?" I asked. "The State couldn't do anything about the soil or the insects or the weather, could it?"

Carter thought a moment. Then Hannah jumped in. "They could make a bad deal with France or someone on tariffs, couldn't they?"

"Yeah," Carter said. "Cost Madison big bucks."

"Two business-minded kids, if ever I saw them," I replied, as they both beamed. "Madison had a stake in the outcome — his plantation.

He had to be careful not to make recommendations that might end up hurting that.

"As a member of the Governor's Council, Madison was part of the day-to-day operation of the State. He was involved in everything from awarding military ranks to military supplies to border disputes to treaties.

"Then, in June 1779, our old friend Thomas Jefferson was elected Governor of Virginia, and he and Madison struck up an immediate friendship and political partnership that lasted until Jefferson's death."

"You mean Madison lived longer than Jefferson?" Carter asked.

"You're a smart one to pick that up, Carter," I said. "Even though Madison seemed sick just about every day of his life, he lasted 85 years, far outliving Jefferson."

"Huh," Carter remarked.

"So, back to our story," I went on. "Madison was still on the Virginia Council of State when Jefferson took office. From there, Madison could see what terrible shape the State's and the country's finances were in.

"Then Madison wrote a paper on the causes and solutions of the financial crisis. He titled it simply 'Money' and it was printed and sent all over the country. In it, he said that the States and the federal government must stop printing money without anything to back it up. Otherwise, he said, other countries wouldn't loan money and the people would stop using it."

"Hey, Gomps, that's just like what you said before!" Hannah exclaimed.

"How do you mean, Hannah?" I asked.

"That people need to have confidence that they can get their money in gold when they want to," she replied.

"That's right. Isn't it nice that Madison agreed with me?" I joked.

"Now, it wasn't long after Jefferson became Governor that Madison's life changed again. Just six months later, one of Virginia's delegates to the Continental Congress was removed for poor performance, and Madison was named to replace him. In 1779, at 28 years old, Madison was now a Congressman in the Continental Congress."

"Wow," exclaimed Carter, "he had already done so much and he was only 28."

"Yeah," Hannah agreed, "just like the other Five, but in a different way. So, what happened next, Gomps?"

"Unfortunately, not much, at first," I said. "We had won our freedom through the Revolutionary War, but our new country was a shambles because our first try at a constitution, the Articles of Confederation, didn't work. For the next few years, things just got worse and worse."

"What about the Super Six?" Carter asked. "Couldn't they do anything?"

"Great question, Carter," I replied. "Let's catch up with what the other five were doing.

❧

"Let's start with Benjamin Franklin. He had been in France negotiating loans and the Treaty of Paris. He didn't return to the United States until September 1785. Although he was 80 years old by that time, he was elected the Governor of Pennsylvania just two months after he got back. So his main job was to run the State of Pennsylvania, but he couldn't overlook the mess that the country was in. He wrote to a friend, 'We discover, indeed, some errors in our . . . constitutions [meaning the Articles and States] . . . But these we shall soon mend.'

"George Washington resigned from the Continental Army in December 1783, just months after the end of the War. He went back to his Virginia plantation to become a farmer. Nonetheless, he, too, saw what was happening to the country, and he wrote to Alexander Hamilton that unless more power was given to a central government, " . . . the blood we have spilt . . . will avail us nothing." In another letter, he called for another constitutional convention. Still, his plantation had gone into big debt, and he worked full-time to pay it off.

"John Adams had been in Europe since 1778. He went to France and then to Holland, Spain, and England to get loans and to help in the negotiation of the Treaty of Paris. He didn't get back until 1788, having been away for ten years. Although, on a quick trip home in 1779, he wrote the Massachusetts State Constitution."

"Amazing," Hannah concluded. "How long did it take him?"

"Two months," I replied.

"Unbelievable," seconded Carter. "I think I'll take a little time off to write a constitution," he continued, speaking tongue-in-cheek in admiration.

"Thomas Jefferson was Governor of Virginia for two years, leaving in 1781," I continued. "He returned to his plantation, which by this time had also fallen into deep debt. Jefferson had hopes of retiring from public life and bringing his plantation back from debt, as Washington was doing.

"But after the death of his wife, Jefferson went back to public life, and Virginia elected him to the Confederation Congress in 1783."

"The Confederation Congress? What's that?" Hannah asked.

"Good, Hannah, you're really paying attention," I said. "In 1781 all the States had finally approved the Articles of Confederation, and the Articles officially named Congress the 'Congress of the Confederation.'

"Six months later, Congress named Jefferson the Minister to France, and off he went to Paris, where he stayed until 1788.

"Alexander Hamilton had last fought in 1781 as the commander of three infantry battalions in the defeat of the British at the Battle of Yorktown. After the War, he went back to New York and was immediately elected to the Confederation Congress. He had seen, first-hand, the financial problems that the Articles of Confederation had caused, and he tried to fix them. But after being frustrated by New York's refusal to give up the Articles, he resigned from Congress and returned to New York to practice law and, a year later, to found the Bank of New York.

"So the stage was set. All of the Super Six well understood the failures of the Articles of Confederation, and each had tried in various ways to improve it. But it was not to be.

"They all knew to one degree or another that something new was needed. First and foremost, they all believed that people had the natural, God-given right to freedom from control by their government. We know that because they all supported the Revolutionary War and the Declaration of Independence.

"But they also knew that people, by nature, could fall prey to temptation and do bad things. In the case of government, the temptation was to use government power to tell people what to do.

"And they knew from experience and from their studies that no form of government yet created had been able to protect the people's freedom. Even the English government still had a King who could do whatever he wanted.

"It was time to do something different, but the Super Six didn't just sit down and dream something up. They had 175 years of colonial history to rely on. But the rest of that story will have to wait until next time. This is a good place to stop.

"You guys have been very patient tonight, because I've rambled on too long. So I'll just say good night."

40

FREEDOM IS BORN

Wednesday night came again quickly, and everyone gathered around. It was mid-May and the evenings were staying light longer, so it wasn't yet dark when we finished dessert. The children's choosing story time over outdoor playtime encouraged me that they were still interested.

"Last time," I said, "we caught up with what the Super Six had been doing in getting ready to form our nation. And, I said that the Super Six didn't just dream something up. Ever since the first ships came, settlers had written rules for themselves. Remember the Charters that started each colony?"

"Weren't they what the King gave to the adventurers to get them started?" Hannah asked.

"That's about right," I replied. "Those Charters had rules for how the colonies would get going, including elected Councils. They were a form of constitution.

"Then, there was the Mayflower Compact — the first constitution, as simple as it was. That was written by the Pilgrims.

"Then, the Articles of Confederation between Plymouth Plantation and the Massachusetts Bay Colony in 1643 described how the two colonies could work together.

"Also, don't forget that the colonies had elected legislatures, and they wrote constitutions and passed laws. We had been passing laws locally for over one hundred years.

"Then there was the Albany Congress of 1754. Do you remember that?" I asked.

"Not me," Carter replied.

"Sounds vaguely familiar," said Hannah.

"That was during the French and Indian War," I said. "The British commanded the colonists to meet in Albany, New York, to work out ways to fight the French together."

"Oh, yeah," Hannah said, "wasn't that when Benjamin Franklin wrote a plan for the colonies to join forces? Ahh, wait a minute, now I see what you're getting at."

"What?" Carter asked.

"Different plans for a country had already been tried over the years," Hannah replied. "The Super Six had some ideas about what would work from what the colonies had done before."

"Oh, I see what you mean," Carter said. "The colonies had been using laws and constitutions already."

"That's right!" I exclaimed. "We had been making rules for ourselves from the beginning. And it didn't end there. Remember the Stamp Act Congress of 1765, when Sam Adams organized meetings to fight the Act?"

"Oh, I remember that one," Carter interjected. "I did the report on the Boston Tea Party. The Stamp Act Congress was about the same thing. Wasn't that when they said, 'No taxation without representation?'"

"It sure was, Carter," I replied. "Well done."

"Yeah, good catch, Carter," Hannah confirmed, while Carter beamed.

"And how about the Second Continental Congress, the Declaration of Independence, and, of course, the Articles of Confederation?" I continued. "The Articles showed them mostly what *not* to do.

"Then, you have plans that members of the Super Six had written. Each one, except Washington, had written his thinking on what a government should and should not be, and their writings had been studied at length by one another and by many other Founders.

"Franklin had written his Albany Plan and his Articles of Confederation and Perpetual Union that came from it. Adams had his 'Thoughts on Government' and his 'Defence of the Constitutions of Government of the United States of America' as well as the Massachusetts Constitution. Jefferson, of course, had written the Declaration. Hamilton had published 'A Full Vindication of the Measures of Congress's and 'The Continentalist,' both of which described the need for a strong central government. And, of course, Madison had the Declaration of Rights and the Virginia State Constitution.

"So the writing of the Constitution was the result of a process that had been moving toward this moment for 175 years or more.

"Even at that, there had to be a buildup to it. If they had just announced another Convention, they probably wouldn't have been able to get enough people to come."

"So how did they do it?" Carter asked.

"First, George Washington had a little get-together of five key Maryland and Virginia people at Mount Vernon in March, 1785. It came to be called the Mount Vernon Conference. Among those invited was James Madison, but he had been informed too late to go.

"The reason for the Conference had been differences between the two States on commerce, fishing, and navigation rules on Chesapeake Bay and the surrounding waters. These differences were not covered by the Articles of Confederation, but were the source of disputes that were interfering with good interstate relations.

"The Mount Vernon Conference ended with agreement on 13 points, all of which were approved by Maryland and Virginia. Then Pennsylvania and Delaware were invited to sign on.

"The success of this Conference encouraged Madison and Hamilton to get started on the problems of the entire Articles of Confederation. They called a meeting, but just to recommend that another Convention be held," I continued.

"In 1786, Madison sent letters to all the States, calling for a meeting to discuss the problems that the Articles were creating. He called it a 'Meeting of Commissioners to Remedy Defects of the Federal Government.' The Meeting came to be known more simply as the Annapolis Convention of 1786, because they met in . . . ?"

"Annapolis?" suggested Hannah.

"That's right!" I joked. Both kids laughed.

"As meetings go, this one wasn't very successful. Representatives of only five states showed up — New York, New Jersey, Pennsylvania, Virginia, and Delaware. Massachusetts, North Carolina, Rhode Island, and New Hampshire had named representatives, but they got there after the meeting ended. And Connecticut, South Carolina, Georgia, and Maryland didn't even name anyone to go.

"The Meeting didn't have enough members to do anything except write a report and set a date for the Constitutional Convention. It was to be in Philadelphia in May, 1787. In fact, some say that all Madison wanted to get out of the Annapolis Convention was to call the Constitutional Convention. In this light, Annapolis was a success."

☙

"So, here we go with the Constitutional Convention. It started on May 14, 1787. Four of the Super Six were there: Washington and Madison from Virginia; Hamilton from New York; and Franklin from Pennsylvania. The other two were in Europe: Jefferson was Minister to France, and Adams was Minister to Great Britain. Today we would call them ambassadors.

"There were 55 representatives from all the colonies except Rhode Island. They met . . ."

"Gomps, why wasn't Rhode Island there?" Carter interrupted.

"Rhode Island wanted to stick with the Articles of Confederation," I replied, "and they figured if they stayed home, any changes wouldn't get enough votes. They also thought that even if a new plan was approved there, they could defeat it when it got to the colonies."

"Were they wrong?" Carter continued.

"Yes, they were," I replied, "and I'll explain why a little later in the story.

"So, the representatives met in Independence Hall in Philadelphia – the same place where the Declaration of Independence had been approved - and elected George Washington as President of the Convention.

"Knowing that the Convention was coming up, some of the representatives had prepared plans to submit. One of them was Madison. He had discussed his ideas with Jefferson in advance and then wrote a plan that he called the Virginia Plan.

"The Virginia Plan answered the basic problems that were in the Articles of Confederation. It preserved individual freedoms and kept power out of the hands of any one person."

"How did it do that, Gomps?" Carter asked.

"First," I said, "it took John Adams's idea of limited powers, that the central government must have only those powers set out in the Constitution and couldn't decide for itself what additional powers it should have. And it gave all other powers to the States and to the people.

"There were three parts or branches of the central government in the Virginia Plan – the Congress, the President, and the courts. The Congress could only make laws. The President could only run the government under those laws. And, the courts could only decide whether the laws had been followed.

"In addition, because lawmaking was so important, the Virginia Plan had the Congress divided into two parts or houses – the Senate and the House of Representatives. And the two houses had to agree for a law to be passed. All of this was called the system of checks and balances."

"Gomps, it sounds like this would make it awful hard to do anything," Hannah observed.

"There, my dear, you have hit on the beauty of the system," I said. "They *wanted* it to be awful hard to do anything. They knew that if it was easy to do things, some part of the government would quickly overstep its powers. In the Virginia Plan, the need for a law would have to be clear to everyone."

"But what about things like poverty?" she persisted. "Should the government let people starve because the word poverty isn't in the Constitution?"

"So individual people should not be responsible for earning their own living?" I said.

"Of course they should, but what about the people who can't?" she asked.

"Can't earn their own living because . . . ?" I replied.

"Like they don't have an education or they are disabled," she replied.

"Do you think they didn't have people in that situation back then?" I asked.

"No, I guess they must have," she replied, "but how did they help them back then?"

"Voluntarily," I said, "mostly through churches and the contributions of private citizens. Also, when people realized they would have to take care of themselves, they worked harder to survive. People we might have thought needed help really didn't.

"Remember the settlers in Jamestown and the Plymouth Plantation who discovered that they could take from the central warehouse and not do any work? As soon as their governors did away with that system, what did they do?"

"Worked," Carter interjected. His facial expression showed little sympathy for Hannah's line of concern.

"It's not as simple as I make it out to be, I realize," I said, "but the Super Six knew that it was much more dangerous for a central government to have the power to rule everyone's lives than to make people look to their States or to do it themselves. See what I mean?"

"I think so," Hannah said, "but I'm still going to have to think about it."

"I get it, Gomps," Carter interjected again, sneaking a derisive glance over at his sister.

"Just you wait!" Hannah exclaimed. "Mister smarty pants."

"Hey, knock it off!" I shouted. That quieted them down, so I continued.

"So Madison had the Virginia Plan, Charles Pinckney of South Carolina came with a plan, William Patterson of New Jersey brought his plan, and to no one's surprise, Alexander Hamilton had a plan, too.

"Madison introduced his Virginia Plan first, and it became the starting point for debate. In this plan, the numbers of Representatives each State had in the House were proportional to its population. The more voters a State had, the more Representatives it would have. Each State would have two Senators.

"In Madison's plan, the Representatives to the House would be elected by the people and the Senators would be elected by the House of Representatives. The President would be elected by representatives of each State in what was called the Electoral College. Judges would be appointed and would serve for life.

"Madison's plan for proportional representation caused as much debate as anything. The less populous States fought hard against this idea. They argued that New York, Massachusetts and Pennsylvania had such large populations that it would take very little for them to join forces in each of the houses and make a majority. This would leave the smaller States powerless.

"As soon as this disagreement arose, Charles Pinckney of South Carolina offered his plan. It was designed to favor the States with smaller populations. Unfortunately for him, he had not written his plan in advance and only delivered it in a speech. It was assigned to a committee and was not considered further.

"Next was William Patterson of New Jersey. He submitted the New Jersey Plan — a plan that looked more like the Articles of Confederation. Under the Articles, there was only one house of Congress and each State had one vote in it. Patterson's plan copied that. In effect, the New Jersey Plan proposed to fix the Articles rather than throw them out.

"This Plan caused the most heated debate in the Convention. The small States backed this Plan because it protected them from domination by the big States through the one State-one vote rule.

"Seeing the disagreement among the delegates, Hamilton chose this as the time to submit his plan. It came to be known as the British Plan. In it, Hamilton proposed a structure more like a monarchy than a republic. It did away with States altogether, limiting the country to only a national government. The President and members of the Senate would serve for life, and the President would have absolute veto power over all proposed laws."

"What's veto power, Gomps?" Carter asked.

"That's the power to reject what Congress passes before it becomes law," I replied. "Hamilton's Plan gave the President the last word. Madison's Plan made it possible for the Congress to pass the law over the President's veto, if they had enough votes.

"Which way did we end up with?" I asked. "Does the President have the last word on laws or does Congress?"

"I think Congress," Hannah said.

"Me, too," added Carter, "but I don't know how it works."

"It's not too complicated," I said. "If both Houses of Congress agree to pass a law, the President either signs it or turns it down — vetoes it. If he vetoes it, the law can still be passed if both the House of Representatives and the Senate vote to approve it by two-thirds majority. It's called overriding the veto.

"As for Hamilton's plan, it was defeated, and unfortunately for him, it branded him as a monarchist for the rest of his days."

"Was he a monarchist?" Hannah asked.

"No, I don't think he was, although he sounded like one," I replied. "He insisted that he was loyal to the Revolution and just thought that the country would need a strong leader."

"The debate over the various plans, especially the Virginia and New Jersey plans, lasted two months - until July 16. Then someone stepped forward to solve the problem."

"How did they solve it?" Hannah asked.

"A Connecticut representative by the name of Roger Sherman offered a compromise," I said. "It came to be called the Connecticut Plan. In it, Sherman kept the House of Representatives and the Senate. The House would have representatives based on the population of each State, and they would be elected by the people. The Senate had two spots for each State, and they would be elected by each State's legislature. If there were disagreements between the two houses over a law, they would have to get together and reach agreement, or the law would not be passed."

"That sounds like what we have now," Hannah observed.

"You're close, Hannah, it is, with one exception: how the Senators are elected," I said. "But the rest of it is what we've still got."

"So it's lasted all this time?" Carter asked.

"Yes, it has, Carter, with a few changes," I said. "For example, in 1913 an amendment changed the election of Senators to a popular vote, like the House of Representatives."

"So, was that it?" Hannah asked.

"Not by a long shot," I replied. "One more serious problem had to be taken up — a problem that no one had been willing to face."

"What was that, Gomps?" Carter asked.

❧

"Slavery," I replied.

"The southern states refused to be a part of the country if slavery was made illegal. The opponents to slavery could see that the southern states would not budge — no slavery, no country. So, slavery was not made illegal in the Constitution.

"There were two other slavery questions that were debated, though. The first came up, not in connection with who could vote, but with who was to be counted for the purpose of deciding how many representatives a State would have in the House of Representatives. Remember that the Connecticut Plan provided that the number of each State's seats would be based on its population - the more people, the more seats. And, obviously, each State wanted as many seats as it could get.

"By this time, there were about 700,000 slaves in the United States. Most of them were in the South. During the debate on proportional representation, the southern states argued that their slaves should be counted as part of the population in figuring the number of seats each of their States would get. Incidentally, they argued at the same time that their slaves should *not* count in figuring their populations for purposes of taxation.

"The northern states argued just the opposite. They claimed that slaves should not count for figuring the number of their Congressmen, but should count for taxation purposes.

"James Wilson of Pennsylvania and Roger Sherman of Connecticut came up with the solution. It was called the Three-Fifths Compromise. They said that, for the purposes of figuring the number of seats a State would get in the House of Representatives *and* in figuring taxes, three-fifths of the number of slaves in that State would be added to the population of the free inhabitants.

"Second was the question of the slave trade. It was already against the law in ten States, but Georgia and North and South Carolina threatened to stay out of the union if the Constitution made the slave trade illegal.

"In the end, the Convention did not want to sacrifice the new country over the slave trade problem, either, so they sidestepped it. A committee was formed and they came up with another compromise: the Congress could make a law on the slave trade, but not until 1808 – 20 years later. That compromise was approved by all, and that ended the debates on slavery. In the final Constitution, the word 'slavery' was not used."

"What about that three-fifths rule, Gomps?" Hannah asked. "Was that in the Constitution?"

"Yes, it was, Hannah," I replied. "It is in Article I, Section 2. It uses the term 'other persons' to refer to slaves in stating the three-fifths rule."

"Oh," she said. "What about voting? Would only three-fifths of the votes of slaves be counted?"

"Voting is a different matter," I said. "The Constitution left voting rules for each State to decide. It doesn't make any rules on who can or can't vote."

"I didn't know that," Hannah continued. "Doesn't the Constitution give voting to women and minorities?"

"Yes, it does," I replied, "but only through amendments that came much later. At the time the Constitution was passed, they left it up to each State to make their own rules.

"Now, as a matter of fact, no State allowed slaves to vote, but they withheld voting rights from many other classes of people, too. With some variation from State to State, the general rule was that only property holders were given the right to vote."

"Why was that, Gomps?" Carter asked.

"Remember our conversation about people having a stake in the outcome?" I replied.

"Sort of," he said.

"It was when we talked about how Madison was named to the Virginia Governor's Council of State," I said. "The Governor appointed only people with something to lose if they gave bad advice."

"Oh, yeah," he replied, "people with skin in the game. I remember now."

"Well, the same thing applied here," I continued. "The leaders didn't want people voting who had nothing to lose with their votes. Otherwise, they feared that some people would vote themselves benefits out of taxes paid by other people. They wanted people who were more likely to have some education and some interest in good government."

"So what counted as property?" Hannah interjected.

"Count as property how?" I asked.

"You said only property holders could vote," she continued. "What property would you have to have in order to vote?"

"I see what you're asking," I said. "The rules varied from State to State. In some states, you had to own land. It could be a minimum amount of land or land worth a minimum amount of money. In a few states, paying rent or owning livestock counted."

"I take it women could not vote at all," Hannah continued.

"This may surprise you, but the answer is, not exactly," I replied.

"In a few States, women who owned land could vote. Look up Lydia Taft of Massachusetts and read her story. She inherited land from her husband, and she could vote. And all women in New Jersey from 1776 to 1807 had the right to vote. There were also earlier examples in Maryland and New York."

"Huh," Hannah concluded. "Maybe I should do some research."

"Now back to the Convention," I continued. "The members took a week off at the end of July while Edmund Randolph of Virginia, an old friend of Madison's, and James Wilson of Pennsylvania wrote a first draft of the Constitution. It was Madison's Virginia Plan with the compromises we've talked about.

"When the members returned in August, there was further debate over some minor issues, and then a committee was named, including Madison and Hamilton, to write up the final version. That took them three days. Then the Convention debated it for another three days before it was ready for signing. The Constitution was done."

"Phew!" said Hannah. "What's next?"

"Approval," I replied. "The Convention had only written it. It still had to be approved. I'll save that for next time. This has been a long session, and you two have been very patient to listen to all this."

"You're right, Gomps," Hannah said, "it's been hard to follow sometimes, but it helps us to know why they did what they did."

"Glad to hear it," I said. "And with that, I'll say good night. See you next week."

41

APPROVAL – A TOUGH ROW TO HOE

It turned out that we had to skip a week while I was traveling on business. So it was two Wednesdays later that I started in.

"Last time, the Convention had written the Constitution, and it was ready for signing," I began, "but not all of the Convention delegates signed. Thirteen left before signing. Three refused to sign. One of them, George Mason of Virginia, refused because it did not have an Article granting individual rights – what we now call a Bill of Rights.

"The other two members refused to sign because they still wanted to go back to the Articles of Confederation. The 13 who left did so for the same reason. But enough of the members did sign it - 39 of the original 55. Then, they sent it to the Continental Congress on September 17, 1787.

"The Congress debated the Constitution for three more days. The opponents, basically the small states, could not get agreement to reject it or to amend it, so the Congress sent it to the States for approval – they used the word 'ratification.'

"Gomps, you didn't say anything about the Congress approving it," Hannah said. "Didn't they have to approve it first?"

"Believe it or not, Hannah, the Constitution didn't call for Congress to approve it," I said. "Madison and the others knew that if Congress were asked to approve it, they would have made one change after another."

"Couldn't they have just asked them to vote yes or no?" Hannah asked.

"The writers knew that you can't ask representatives as smart as those to vote on something and expect them not to say something about it," I said. "So they didn't ask.

"The writers also knew that the State governments would see that this Constitution would take away some of the power they had under the Articles. So the Constitution didn't provide for the State legislatures to approve it, either."

"I don't get it, Gomps," Carter interjected. "If the Congress couldn't approve it and the States couldn't approve it, who could?"

"The people," I replied. "The Constitution was written so that all the States could do was set up ratifying conventions. The people in each State would elect representatives to their State ratifying convention, and their representatives would vote to approve or not.

"The final piece of the plan was that only two-thirds of the States would need to approve it in order for the Constitution to apply to all of them. So only nine of the 13 States' conventions would have to approve, and the Constitution would go into effect for all."

"Smart," Carter concluded.

"That's amazing that they could think of that," Hannah observed.

"I'll say, and yet, ratification was still not certain," I continued. "Once the Constitution was taken up in each State, the elections to the ratifying conventions became hotly contested.

"As soon as word got out that the Constitution was in the hands of the people, everyone talked about it. Newspapers wrote articles about it and gave opinions. Ministers preached sermons about it. Politicians gave speeches. People who ran into one another on the street talked about it. And families talked about it at the dinner table."

"Sorta like us," Carter blurted.

"That's right, Carter," I said, "sorta like us.

"Against it were the people who feared a powerful central government. They were called the Anti-Federalists — that is, they were against a strong federal government. They remembered how the British passed taxes without asking them and tried to control them in other ways. They didn't want their own government to be able to do the same thing.

"In favor of the Constitution were the people who saw what a weak central government had already done under the Articles. They were called the Federalists. They believed that the country needed a stronger central government than what they had, while guarding against its getting too much power.

"As Federalists, Madison and Hamilton led the fight to get the Constitution ratified. One of the things they did was to write opinion columns that were published in newspapers. They took the various parts of government and wrote explanations of how the Constitution was the best way of doing them. They split up the subjects between them and asked one of their allies — John Jay — to write a few of the columns, as well.

"Over just six months, between 1787 and 1788, they wrote 85 columns, each one usually several pages long. The subjects covered everything from the Greek and modern political philosophers to the nature of human beings and their shortcomings to the proposed branches of government to the reasons why they chose the method of ratification that they did.

"The goal of Madison, Hamilton and Jay was to persuade people to support the Constitution and to vote for representatives to their state ratifying convention who would approve it.

"But after they finished the last column, people looked at the collection of their writings and realized that it was one of the best explanations of government and republican principles ever seen. It is now called *The Federalist*, or *The Federalist Papers*, and even today, it is still one of the best. You can buy it in book form, and I hope someday you will read it.

"As persuasive as *The Federalist* was, though, the Anti-Federalists were still strong. One of the questions that they raised was a Bill of Rights. That was a list of individual rights that the Constitution would grant to the people. George Mason refused to sign the Constitution because it did not have one."

"What was the big deal about a Bill of Rights, Gomps?" asked Carter. "I don't get it."

"Well, some people felt that the Constitution was giving powers to a central government and that individual people needed to be protected from government going too far. They felt that the Constitution should spell out the areas where the government didn't have powers over private citizens. They felt that we had fought the Revolutionary War to gain these rights and that we risked giving them up to our own government. They pointed to the Declaration of Independence as the best example of that. Even Jefferson wanted a Bill of Rights, as he wrote in a letter to Madison."

"Sounds like a good thing," Carter said. "What did Madison say about it?"

"At first, he was against a Bill of Rights," I replied. "He thought that the Constitution protected the people perfectly through the principle of limited powers. All powers not granted to the government would be reserved for the States and the people.

"Madison opposed a Bill of Rights for another reason, too — the timing of it. He knew that the ratification of the Constitution would be tough. The Anti-Federalists were powerful. If the Federalists agreed to open up the wording of the Constitution for a Bill of Rights, it would give the Anti-Federalists a chance to propose all kinds of other changes that would ruin it. So Madison thought he had to push for ratification of the Constitution as it was, at all costs.

"Seeing widespread interest in a Bill of Rights, though, Madison began to soften his position. He certainly had shown in his other writings, like his work on freedom of religion, that he favored strong protection of individual rights. But how to do it?"

"He was stuck between a rock and a hard place, wasn't he, Gomps?" Hannah asked.

"Yes, he was," I replied. "He was right about keeping the proposed Constitution intact. There is no question that, if they had reopened the Constitutional Convention, the Anti-Federalists would have proposed one change after another until they killed it. On the other hand, Madison faced the possibility that the Constitution would not get the nine States needed for ratification without a Bill of Rights."

"Well, we know that it got passed," Hannah said. "How did he do it?"

"He got the idea for a compromise from the Massachusetts ratifying convention," I replied.

"The Massachusetts Federalists and Anti-Federalists lined up against one another. But then, through debate and meetings, they came up with a way out. The Anti-Federalists would write a list of rights that would be amendments to the new Constitution, and the Federalists promised to present the list to the first Congress AFTER the Constitution was ratified.

"Madison now had the solution, and all other States except Maryland adopted that compromise in their ratifying conventions. Each one decided which amendments they wanted and made them part of their approval.

"Still, the ratification took time. It was up to each State to decide the timing of its election and convention. One by one over the next three years, each State held elections to their ratification convention, and then each convention met and debated.

"Three States ratified in December 1787 – Delaware (the first), Pennsylvania, and New Jersey. Georgia and Connecticut ratified soon after, in January 1788. Then Massachusetts ratified by a narrow vote margin in February, and then only because of the Bill of Rights Compromise. Maryland and South Carolina ratified in May, and that made eight States. Only one more was needed to put the Constitution over the top.

"That vote came from New Hampshire in June of 1788, and that made nine States. The Constitution was ratified."

"Gomps, what about the other four?" Hannah asked.

"One by one, they saw the light and ratified," I replied, "although it took Rhode Island two more years, until May 1790, to do it. By that time, the new government had been operating for over a year.

"I'm exhausted just hearing about it," Hannah said.

"Yeah," said Carter. "I didn't know that some people were against it."

"Me either," said Hannah.

"Have either of you read it?" I asked.

"Nope," they both replied.

"Well, I'm not going to read it to you," I said, "but . . ."

"Whew," interrupted Hannah, "we were worried that you might."

"No, you can do that on your own when you're ready," I said. "Besides, you already have a good idea of what's in it. But, as I was saying, I would like to sum up the main sections. Let's start with the Preamble — next time."

42

WE SUM UP

Wednesday evening came around again and we gathered as usual.

"Last time I ended by promising to sum up the main sections of the Constitution," I started. "Let's begin with the Preamble."

"What's a Preamble, Gomps?" Carter asked.

"A Preamble is like an introduction," I replied. "It's not a part of the actual document and gives no powers, but it sets the tone and explains some things in advance, such as why it was written.

"The Preamble to the Constitution starts with probably the three most important words in all of political history – 'We the People.' Think about that: 'We the People.'" I paused to let it sink in.

"For the first time, the people were setting up their own government," I continued. "That was a revolution in political action. The philosophers had talked about it for over 100 years. But we did it.

"The Preamble says, 'We the People of the United States, in Order to form a more perfect Union, establish Justice, insure domestic Tranquility, provide for the common defence, promote the general Welfare, and secure the Blessings of Liberty to ourselves and our Posterity, do ordain and establish this Constitution for the United States of America.'"

"That's it?" Carter asked.

"That's it," I confirmed. "That's the whole introduction to likely the most important document in political history."

"I'm not sure what it all means, Gomps," Carter continued. "Could you go over it for us?"

"Sure," I said. "'We the People' sounds simple, but it's saying that it's not the Founders who are creating the nation, it's the people who are creating it.

"Then, there are phrases that say why the people are doing this. The first is, 'in Order to form a more perfect Union . . . ' That was put in to give respect to the Articles of Confederation. The idea was to say that, although the Articles were perfect, this Constitution was even better – *more* perfect. It was put in to try to make peace with the Anti-Federalists.

"Next, 'establish Justice' meant that the Constitution aimed to treat everyone equally so that everyone got what they deserved under the law.

"Then, 'insure domestic Tranquility' meant to keep the peace within the new country.

"Next, 'provide for the common defence' meant to pay for a military to protect us against attack by foreign countries.

"Then, 'promote the general Welfare' meant to provide the freedom for people to work for a good life; to do what's good for everybody. Notice that it doesn't say 'promise' the general welfare or 'give the right' to the general welfare. This phrase is like the 'Pursuit of Happiness' phrase in the Declaration in that way.

"Finally, 'secure the Blessings of Liberty to ourselves and our Posterity' meant to protect the freedoms that God had given for those living and for their children and grandchildren. That's what Posterity means — the generations of families that live after us."

"What about 'ordain,' Gomps?" Hannah asked. "What does that mean?"

"You may have heard that word in relation to religious ministers, but in this case, it means to give the go-ahead," I replied. "By ratifying the Constitution, the People were giving the go-ahead to set up the new government."

"Did Madison write the Preamble, Gomps?" Hannah asked.

"No, the historians don't think so," I replied. "They think that it was probably written by Gouverneur Morris, who was a member of the committee that drafted the Constitution in the Constitutional Convention.

"Now, a few words about the main parts of the Constitution. Each part is covered by an Article. Article One creates lawmaking, that is, the Congress. It creates the House and the Senate and explains how each is elected, how long they serve — two years in the House and six in the Senate - how each is to be run, and what powers each has.

"Article One also lists the things that Congress can make laws about. These include taxes, borrowing money, regulating interstate commerce, printing money, creating post offices, declaring war, paying for the military, providing for State militias, and providing for law enforcement."

"That's all Congress can make laws for?" Hannah exclaimed. "That's not much."

"That's all, Hannah," I replied. "The Founders gave the Congress only those things that were required for a national government."

"But Congress makes laws about way more than that," she continued. "Where do they get the power to do it?"

"There are two answers to that question – a specific answer and a general answer," I replied. "The specific answer is that Congress gets power from the interstate commerce clause, as an example. Under the commerce clause, the power to make laws regulating interstate commerce has been interpreted to cover a lot of the laws that Congress now passes.

"The general answer comes from that specific one. It is that, in writing the Constitution, the Founders couldn't write down every detail, so we have to be able to interpret what they wanted it to mean. Those are called 'implied' powers."

"Could you give us an example?" Carter asked.

"Sure," I replied. "Let's stay with the Congress's power to regulate interstate commerce. Did the Founders mean for the members of Congress to go to State borders personally and to watch goods being shipped back and forth?"

"You mean Senators and Congressmen?" he asked.

"Yeah," I replied.

He thought for a moment. "No," he said, "that's ridiculous."

"Exactly," I said. "So, we interpret that the Founders must have meant for a law on interstate commerce to include how the regulation would be done. It's implied that people other than members of Congress would do the regulating. Get it?"

"I see," he said.

"Hannah? You get it?" I asked.

"Got it," she said. "But, who interprets these things?"

"Good question," I replied. "In the end, the Supreme Court interprets the Constitution based on cases that it decides."

"Got it," she said.

For now, I thought.

"Great," I said, "so let's move to Article Two. Article Two covers the President. It gives the President executive power, that is, the power to set up departments and run the government according to the laws passed by Congress. It says that the President is elected by the votes of the Electoral College and serves for four years at a time. And it makes the President the Commander In Chief of the military. This means that he has overall power over it.

"Article Three covers the court system and its powers. It creates the Supreme Court and lower-level courts. It explains what kinds of cases the courts can judge and how the courts are to hear those cases. It makes the Supreme Court the highest court. It also gives the right to a trial by jury."

"What kinds of cases can the Supreme Court judge?" Hannah asked.

"Article Three says the judicial power covers all cases arising out of the Constitution, both criminal cases and civil cases – lawsuits. The Supreme Court also covers treaties with other countries and other international cases. And, it covers cases between States and between citizens of different States. Those are the main ones."

"Where does it say that the Supreme Court decides what laws are constitutional?" she continued.

"Well, it doesn't say that directly," I replied. "Again, it has been interpreted that the Supreme Court has that power."

"Who did the interpreting this time?" Hannah asked.

"You mean who decided what powers are implied for the Supreme Court?"

"Yeah."

"The Supreme Court interprets its own powers," I replied. "That was basically decided in two of the first cases the Supreme Court heard — first, in the Hylton case where they found a law to be constitutional and second, in Marbury versus Madison where they found a law to be unconstitutional."

"Lotta power," Hannah observed. "And, those judges serve for life?"

"Yup."

"Hmmph," she mumbled.

"All right, then," I continued. "Moving on, Article Four explains that the States and the people who live in them are considered equal, and that each State's laws are to be accepted by every other State.

"Article Five explains how the Constitution can be changed. Changes are called Amendments.

"Article Six says that the Constitution is the highest law in the nation. When treaties or State laws are different, the Constitution rules. It also says that only treaties made through Constitutional rules are valid. This voided all treaties made by States. And, it says that all judges must treat the Constitution as the highest law.

"And, finally, Article Seven explains the rules to be followed for ratifying the Constitution.

"And that's it."

"That's it?" Hannah asked.

"Yup," I said. "The whole thing was handwritten and signed by those 39 members. I have a copy of it on my wall. You can look at it any time you want."

"Is that the end of the story, Gomps?" Carter asked.

"Almost," I said. "We still have the Bill of Rights."

"Oh, yeah," he said, "I remember – Madison promised the States he would write one."

"That's right," I said, "but I'll tell you about that next time. To-night was pretty heavy going, and I'm glad you stayed with me. I think that's as much as any of us can take in. Someone once said that the brain can absorb only as much as the behind can withstand.

"Now, I'd like seconds on dessert. How about you?"

43

MADISON KEEPS HIS PROMISE

The next Wednesday, I called on Carter to start off.

"Carter," I asked, "will you tell me where we left off last week?"

"Sure, Gomps," he replied. "You finished telling us about the Constitution, and I remembered that Madison had promised to write the Bill of Rights."

"That's right," I said. "Although the Constitution was now ratified, Madison had promised to write a Bill of Rights immediately afterward, and that's what he did.

"Let's start with the Bill of Rights itself. The first time anything like this had been done was probably the English Bill of Rights. This was a law passed by Parliament in 1689. It was a reaction to the widespread complaints of the English people that the King had been treating them unfairly.

"The English Bill of Rights granted a number of protections to the English people. It gave freedom of speech in Parliament - not on the streets, just in Parliament. It gave the people the right to ask for things, called the right to petition. It required regular elections to Parliament. It gave the right to a trial by jury. It gave the right to own and use guns — called the right to keep and bear arms. And it prevented cruel and unusual punishment of criminals.

"The colonists had known about the English Bill of Rights and had written at least some of those rights into their laws in the colonial Assemblies. And, of course, as colonies became States, their legislatures had written bills of rights in different forms, too. Remember, for instance, the Declaration of Rights that Madison had written for Virginia.

"So by the time of the State Ratification Conventions, a Bill of Rights was a well-known idea. So much so that it didn't take long for the individual conventions' members to write lists of rights to go with their ratification votes.

"Madison gathered up all these lists sent to him by the State Conventions. The lists were long and had subjects of all kinds. It would be up to Madison to pick out the ones that everyone wanted, and to write them up.

"Elections to the first Congress and to the first Presidential Electoral College were held in the fall of 1788 . . . "

"Wait, Gomps," Hannah interjected. "I had a question about that last week, but you went by it too fast. What's the Electoral College?"

"That's not an easy one," I replied. "Remember how one idea behind the Constitution was that representatives of the people would make the laws rather than the people themselves?"

"Yeah," replied Hannah.

"This was to prevent mob rule, right?" I continued.

"Yeah," she replied again.

"Well, the election of the President was designed in the same way," I continued. "The people don't elect the President; they elect Electors.

These are like their representatives in the election of the President. The Electors then meet about five weeks after the election in what is called the Electoral College and elect the President among themselves."

"Really?" Carter asked. "I thought he is elected by the people."

"Indirectly he is," I said. "Each candidate has Electors who promise before the election to vote for that candidate in the Electoral College. When the people vote for a candidate, they are actually voting for the Electors who support that candidate. It seems like the people's votes elect the President because the Electors vote pretty much the way they promised."

"Huh," said Hannah. "I didn't know that."

"Me, either," said Carter. "You said, 'pretty much' they keep their promise. Don't they always?"

"They are not required to under the Constitution," I replied. "Some States require it, but for those that don't, on rare occasions, an Elector will vote for the other candidate."

"Why would he do that, if he promised?" Carter persisted.

"Suppose people found out something about a candidate after the election, but before the Electoral College meets?" I replied. "Or what if the candidate dies?"

"I see," Carter replied.

"Any questions, Hannah?" I asked.

"No," she replied. "At first it sounded too complicated, but now I can see the reason."

"Good," I said, "so, back to our story. The votes for the first Congress were in, and Madison was elected to the House of Representatives. Their first day of business was April 1, and their first item of business was to count the votes of the Electoral College to see who would be our first President. Guess who won?"

"George Washington!" they shouted together.

"Right!" I said. "Now, what percent of the vote did he get?"

"That's not a fair question," Hannah said. "How can we know that?"

"I think it's fair," I said. "It's the only answer that you could guess correctly."

The kids looked at each other uncertainly. "All of them?" Hannah offered.

"What do you think, Carter?" I continued.

"That's all I can think of," he said.

"Well, you're right!" I said.

"No way," Hannah exclaimed.

"Really?" Carter added.

"Really," I confirmed. "The vote was unanimous."

"It figures, I guess, if you think about it," Carter concluded. "Everyone thought he was a great man."

"I agree," I said. "Next question – who was elected Vice President?"

"I have no idea," Hannah said.

"Me, either," said Carter.

"Well, it was our old friend John Adams," I said. "He came in second."

"He didn't run for Vice President?" Hannah asked.

"Nope," I replied. "In the early years, the second-place finisher in the vote for President became the Vice President."

"Huh," Hannah said.

"Then, once the vote counting was done, Madison proposed a set of laws for foreign trade, tariffs, and taxes. Four days later, debate on his proposals was stopped in order to hold George Washington's Presidential inauguration. Then it was back to business. The laws passed.

"Madison's next move was to submit a Bill of Rights for debate. By this time, he had become convinced through his discussions with Jefferson and others that a Bill of Rights would actually make the Constitution stronger, as long as it didn't undo the Constitution itself.

"Congress debated through the summer. By the end of August, they had reduced the proposal to a statement of twelve Articles, and those passed both Houses. The proposed Articles were then sent to the States for ratification. Under the wording of the Constitution, amendments to the Constitution would have to be passed by three-quarters of the States. So 11 of the States would have to ratify."

"Wait a minute, Gomps," Carter said. "Three-quarters of 13 isn't 11." He looked at the ceiling, calculating. "It's less than 10."

"Pretty sharp, Carter," I said, "but what's three-fourths of 14? Because while all this was going on, a new State joined the Union: Vermont."

"Ah hah," said Carter. "I get it."

"The process for State ratification of the Bill of Rights was the same as for the Constitution. Each State held a convention with delegates elected by the people. They took up each Article separately. In the end, two of the twelve Articles were not passed by the States, and they were dropped from the Bill of Rights.

"The ratification took almost two years. Virginia was the eleventh State to ratify, completing their vote on December 15, 1791. At that point, the ten Articles became the first ten Amendments to the Constitution. Our Constitution now had the Bill of Rights, and the foundation of our nation was in place.

"Next time, we'll go over them."

44

THE BILL OF RIGHTS

This week, I picked up on the Bill of Rights right where I had left off.

"The Bill of Rights has become a vital part of how we run our country. Do you know any of them?"

"Freedom of speech, freedom of religion . . . " Hannah said, and paused. "That's all I can think of."

"How about you, Carter?" I asked. "Do you know any?"

"Freedom to own guns?" he offered.

"Figures," Hannah muttered.

"Hey, I'm right, aren't I, Gomps?" Carter insisted, sticking up for himself.

"Yes, you are, Carter," I confirmed. "You're both right. But let's go over each of them before we finish this story.

"The First Amendment says, 'Congress shall make no law respecting an establishment of religion, or prohibiting the free exercise thereof; or abridging the freedom of speech, or of the press; or the right of the people peaceably to assemble, and to petition the Government for a redress of grievances.' Now, that's a mouthful for one Amendment, so let's see if I can break it down for you.

"The whole Amendment is about preventing Congress from making laws that infringe on various rights. They used the word 'respecting' as you would the word 'regarding,' to mean 'about.' Congress can't make laws about these subjects.

"The first subject is 'an establishment of religion, or prohibiting the free exercise thereof.' Do you remember what they meant when they used the word 'establishment' in talking about religion?"

"Wasn't that making one religion the official religion?" Carter asked.

"Very good," I replied. "This section says that Congress can't make any law that makes any one religion the official religion. Then, they used the phrase 'or the free exercise thereof.' That meant that Congress also can't make any law that keeps anyone from following in any way their chosen religion. People can build churches. They can hold worship services. They can organize their religious congregations as they choose."

"What if the religion says to break the law?" Hannah asked.

"That's a tricky one," I replied. "Most religions accept that their members are still part of a country that has laws. They accept that, if their members break those laws, they should be punished under those laws. A few countries have official religions that also govern the country. There, the religious beliefs are the law and the religious leaders make decisions on the law. Ours is not one of them. Did that answer it?"

"I guess so," Hannah replied, "but there have been a lot of court cases about the freedom of religion, haven't there? I mean, people argue about this a lot, don't they?"

"Yes, the meaning of this section of the Amendment has been argued ever since, both in court and just about everywhere else," I replied.

"What do you think, Gomps?" Carter asked.

"What I think is one thing, but what's also important is for you to think about it as you grow older and make your own decisions," I replied.

"C'mon, Gomps," Hannah chided, "you're dodging the question."

"OK," I said, "but you can't just take what I say as final. You have to think about it for yourselves. Deal?"

"Deal," they both replied.

"I think the Founders, not just the Super Six, meant what they wrote in the Constitution. We cannot put words in their mouths just because we don't agree with them. When they spoke plainly, we have to accept what they said.

"We know what they meant when they used the word 'establishment' in regard to religion. They meant that there should be no one official religion. But I don't think that meant that religion should be made illegal. There were strong religious beliefs and practices in our country from the beginning. The Founders didn't mean to abandon that.

"The phrase that goes along with the 'establishment' phrase has equal importance, and I think that second phrase has been ignored or downplayed in the arguments over the 'establishment' phrase.

"The second phrase says that people must be free to practice their religion however their religion says to do. If they want to practice their religion in public, such as praying in public or putting a religious symbol on their property, no law can keep them from doing it. And, if a church congregation wants to pray in public or put up a religious symbol on their property, no law can keep them from doing that, either.

"It's just that the government can't pay ministers' salaries or pay for the building of churches, and churches can't tell Congressmen what to do – things like that. That's what I think."

"But what about something like prayers before high school football games?" Carter asked.

"I think that as long as the prayer doesn't promote one religion over another, it's OK," I replied. "The Amendment says ' . . . establishment of religion,' not freedom 'from' religion. The Founders fought for God-given rights and I don't think they would turn right around and take God out of it."

"Hmmm," said Hannah. "Hadn't thought about it that way."

"I see what you're saying," Carter concluded.

"Now, on to the next part of this Amendment," I said, "and I promise that it won't take as long."

"Whew," Carter exclaimed.

"I know," I said. "Thanks for hanging in there."

"We asked," Hannah observed.

"Still, it's complicated stuff," I replied. "So we can combine the next two phrases: 'or abridging the freedom of speech, or of the press.' This means that you can say whatever you want and that the newspapers and TV and radio and internet blogs can investigate and report freely without government preventing them from doing it."

"Except you can't yell 'fire' in a crowded theater," Hannah interjected.

"That's right, Hannah!" I replied. "You've been studying! In deciding cases, the courts have said that there have to be a few practical limits on free speech, such as saying things that you could predict would cause injury to other people - like yelling 'fire' in a crowded theater.

"Now, I want you to think about the free speech phrase and connect it to the free exercise of religion phrase. Does free speech include the freedom to speak about your religion in public?"

"Hm, never thought about it," Hannah replied. "That sounds ridiculous. Of course it does."

"Carter, how about you?" I asked.

"Can you curse in public?" he asked.

"Yes, you can," I replied, stunned at the simplicity of the thought.

"Then you ought to be able to pray in public, too," he concluded.

"That's the connection I was trying to make," I said. "I think the freedom of speech phrase further makes clear what the Founders meant about freedom of religion.

"Now, let's go on to the next phrase: 'or the right of the people peaceably to assemble.' This means that people can meet or get together in public in large groups as long as they don't riot or disrupt things. Any questions on that one?"

"So people can demonstrate in the streets as long as they do it peacefully?" Hannah asked.

"That's right, although stopping traffic may not be peaceable," I said. "And, since they have free speech, they can demonstrate against the government . . ."

"And if they break windows and burn cars?" Hannah asked.

"That's definitely not peaceable," I replied.

"Good," she concluded.

"And the last phrase in the First Amendment says, 'and to petition the Government for a redress of grievances.' This means that the people can ask the government to hear their complaints and the corrections they want made. Any questions there?"

"Nope," said Carter, "that one's pretty obvious, once you know what the words mean."

"Next, the Second Amendment," I continued. "It says, 'A well regulated Militia, being necessary to the security of a free State, the right of the people to keep and bear Arms, shall not be infringed.' This Amendment has also been the subject of a lot of disagreement over the years, so let's take a closer look.

"Let's start with the first phrase, 'A well regulated Militia, being necessary to the security of a free State . . .' We know what the Founders meant by Militia. They meant the ability of ordinary citizens to grab their guns when they might need to defend themselves.

"Some have said that it refers to defense against another country, but I don't think so, except for invasion. By this time, the Continental Army had fought and won the Revolutionary War. Militias had fought with the Army here and there, but they were not our main military force, and the Founders knew the difference.

"So, the Founders weren't referring to the need to have militias to fight against other countries. They were referring to the need for people to be able to use their guns when local troubles arose. That meant that people needed to have guns at hand to be able to use them at a moment's notice."

"But what would they need them for?" Hannah asked.

"To defend themselves against Indians, against criminals, and even against the government," I replied.

"Against the government?" Carter exclaimed.

"That's right," I replied. "Sounds crazy, doesn't it? But, if you think about it, the Founders were worried to death about a government becoming too powerful. That's the main reason they were writing the Bill of Rights. They knew what the King's army had done. And I think they wanted the people to be able to defend against any attempt at a takeover by a government that overstepped its bounds.

"You mean fight the Army?" Hannah asked.

"I do mean that," I replied. "Have you noticed that you never see the Army patrolling our streets?"

"But what about riots and floods?" Carter interjected.

"If you look and listen closely," I replied, "you will see that those are National Guard, or soldiers of a State. Those are not our national Army. We have been very careful about the national Army coming in on local matters. And that's the reason.

"The Second Amendment preserves that right by saying that the people can keep and use guns. And, since you never know when you might need your gun, the government can't make them illegal or put restrictions on them — that's what the word 'infringed' means."

"Don't you need a license for a gun?" Hannah asked.

"Yes, in most places you do," I replied. "The Supreme Court has decided that the government can keep track of who has bought a gun, but you can't keep them from buying it, unless it's a criminal who predictably would use it to break the law."

"But criminals have guns all the time," Carter exclaimed.

"Yes, but they are breaking the law when they do," I replied. "When they are caught with a gun illegally, they can be charged with that as a separate crime. Anything else?"

"Nope, I got it," Carter said.

"Me too," said Hannah.

"OK," I said, "for the rest of the Amendments I'm just going to sum up what they say and not read them word for word. You good with that?"

"Fine," said Hannah.

"Yeah," said an obviously relieved Carter.

"Then, the Third Amendment is next," I said. "It says that the government can't force the people to house soldiers in their homes."

"That's it?" Carter asked. "Why would they make a whole Amendment just for that?"

"I think that shows how careful they were about avoiding the kind of abuse that the King had put the colonies through," I replied. "Remember the Quartering Act?"

"Yeah," he said. "I guess you're right."

"Next, the Fourth Amendment," I continued. "It requires the government to have a search warrant before searching you, your house, or your belongings in a criminal case. It also requires that the government has to have probable cause to get the warrant."

"What's a search warrant and what's probably cause, Gomps?" Carter asked.

"Probable cause, not probably cause," Hannah corrected. "It's probable cause, Carter."

"Hah, hah," Carter laughed, "got you again."

"That's enough," I said, "or we'll be here all night.

"A search warrant is written permission from a court of law for the government to search you," I replied. "Probable cause means the government has to have some evidence or reason to ask for the warrant, and the court has to decide that the evidence is good enough to make the search legal."

"Got it," Carter said, "but what if they search without a warrant?"

"Good question, Carter," I replied. "If the government searches without a warrant or probable cause, then anything they find cannot be used against you in court."

"That seems fair," Carter concluded.

"Next, is the Fifth Amendment," I said. "This is another of the catch-all Amendments, like the First. This one has to do with the rights of people accused of crimes. The first phrase says that a separate jury, called a Grand Jury, has to review the evidence when someone is accused of a crime and decide if there is enough evidence against them for a trial.

"The second phrase says that you can't be tried for the same crime twice. If the first jury finds you innocent of that crime, the government can't try you again. It's called double jeopardy.

"The next phrase says you can't be forced to testify against yourself. Have you heard of people taking the Fifth Amendment?" I asked.

"Yeah," said Hannah, "but I thought it was in a joking way."

"Well, some people use it that way, I suppose," I said. "Maybe one of your friends might do something bad and their mother asks if they did it. They might say, 'I'm taking the Fifth.' Under the Fifth Amendment, a person accused of a crime can 'take the Fifth' legally.

"The next phrase says that you can't be penalized under the law unless your case has gone through all the necessary steps. That's called going through 'due process of law.' People might say, 'He didn't get due process,' or 'He didn't get his day in court.'

"The last phrase of the Fifth Amendment says that, if the government wants to take your private property, they have to put it to public use and they have to pay you what it's worth."

"The government can take your property, Gomps? How can they do that?" Carter asked.

"Well, suppose you owned a house at the beach," I replied, "and it was in a place that the government wanted for a national park. The government couldn't just take it from you. They would have to get it appraised and pay you what the appraisal said."

"But, what if you didn't want to move, even though the government was willing to pay you?" Carter said.

"Good question," I replied. "You could take the government to court, but it wouldn't be easy. You might win if the government doesn't really need your house or if it really wants to sell your property to a private company or if the government's appraisal is unfairly low. But the government has to be able to buy land that it needs to do its business. And the government can decide that its needs are more important than yours. See what I mean?"

"I see," he replied, "but I don't think it's fair."

"If it makes you feel any better," I said, "there are more than a few people who feel the same way. Still, it's in the Constitution.

"Next is the Sixth Amendment," I continued. "This is another catch-all, and it's about criminal prosecution also. The first phrase says that a person accused of a crime has to get a speedy trial. They can't be kept in jail forever before they get a trial. It also says that the person has a right to a jury trial by an unbiased jury.

"The next phrase says that the government must show an accused person all of the evidence against him and he must be able to face any witnesses against him.

"The last phrase says that the accused person has a right to have a lawyer to defend him in court. And that's it on the Sixth. Are we OK with it?"

Both nodded.

"Great," I said. "The rest will go quickly. The Seventh Amendment says that if you are sued, you have a right to a jury trial.

"The Eighth says the government can't charge excessive bail or fines and that it cannot give you cruel and unusual punishment."

"What's bail, exactly, Gomps?" Carter asked.

"That's money the court makes you put up to make sure that you show up for your trial," I replied. "If you don't show up, you lose your bail money. Questions?"

"Could you get away, then?" Carter asked.

"No," I replied, "the police would come and get you."

"Would you get your bail back after they brought you in?" he continued.

"No," I replied. "You would still lose it."

"Good," he concluded.

"Hannah?" I asked. "You get this?"

"I'm good," she replied. "But what about cruel and unusual punishment? What did they mean there?"

"They meant torture and lengthy jail sentences," I replied. "You couldn't starve a person or give them physical punishment, and you couldn't keep them for ten years for stealing a candy bar, say. Questions on that?"

"Nope," she replied.

"Carter?" I asked.

"Nope," he replied.

"OK," I continued. "The Ninth Amendment says that the people have other rights in addition to those written in the Constitution. That is, just because one of those rights is not written in the Constitution doesn't mean the people don't have it. And, that a right, written in the Constitution, can't take away other rights of the people."

"I'm confused on that one, Gomps," Hannah said. "Could you give an example?"

"Yeah," Carter said, "I'm confused, too."

"I understand," I replied. "That's a tough one.

"Let's use this example: Do you have a right to sleep at night?"

"Sure," they both chimed.

"Is that right mentioned in the Bill of Rights?" I asked.

"'Course not," Carter said.

"Correct," I concurred. "So, could the government pass a law that said you couldn't have more than six hours of sleep at night, just because your right to sleep isn't mentioned there?"

"'Course not," they both chimed.

"Or, could the Constitution be amended to limit you to six hours of sleep?" I asked.

"No," they agreed.

"That's the Ninth Amendment," I concluded.

"But, what if the government passed that law anyway?" Hannah persisted.

"Someone would have to take the government to court," I replied, "and the court would look at the Constitution and the Bill of Rights to see if they intended for the government to have the power to do that. If not, the court would declare the law unconstitutional and it would be eliminated."

"I see," Hannah said. "Thanks, Gomps."

"And, finally, the Tenth Amendment says that any power not given to the government by the Constitution belongs to the States or to the people," I continued. "This is John Adams's enumerated or limited powers principle. Before the government can have the power to do something, the Constitution has to say that it can do it."

"Kind of like the Ninth, isn't it?" Carter asked.

"They seem to go hand in hand, don't they, Carter?" I replied. "The Ninth says that the government can't take on power that isn't in the Constitution and the Tenth says that the government can only have the power that is in the Constitution."

"Sounds like different ways of saying the same thing," Carter observed.

"The Founders were that afraid that someone could get elected and take over the country," I said. "They made sure that they covered all the bases that they could think of.

"So, at that point, our government was now in place, ready to do business. In fact, George Washington was already doing business, as President."

"Is this the end of the story, Gomps?" Carter asked.

"Well, I don't want to leave it there," I replied. "I'm going to tell you what happened to each of the Super Six and then kind of wrap things up. So we have a little more to go."

"Good," said Hannah. "I'm going to be sad for this to end."

"Me too," said Carter.

"So am I," I said, "but I'm not too sad that this particular part of the story is over. This has been a long night, and I thank you for hanging in with me. I hope I've made it bearable."

"I didn't realize the time," Hannah said. "It hasn't seemed long at all."

"Same here," added Carter.

"Good," I said. "That's nice to hear. Next time, Franklin will die peacefully, ever the scientist, while Hamilton is shot."

"Oh no, Gomps," Hannah complained. "You're not going to leave us hanging like that, are you?"

"Yes, I am," I replied. "See you next week."

45

FRANKLIN DIES PEACEFULLY; HAMILTON IS SHOT

"Hannah and Carter," I started, "last time you said that you would be sorry when the story ended.

"Me too, but let me finish the story of each of the Super Six. I'll start with Franklin.

"Franklin saw the Constitution ratified, but he never lived to see the ratification of the Bill of Rights. He was 81 when he was appointed by Pennsylvania as a member of the Constitutional Convention. Despite continuing ill health, he was active in every part of the Constitution's design. In fact, he actually made the formal motion to approve Roger Sherman's Connecticut Compromise.

"But Franklin was still not done with service to the people. After the Convention, he was elected to another term as Governor of Pennsylvania and served it through. By this time, Franklin was already the President of the Pennsylvania Abolition Society as well."

"What was that, Gomps?" Carter asked.

"That was an organization of people in Pennsylvania who worked to free the slaves," I replied. "Abolition meant abolishing slavery."

"Oh, OK," Carter said.

"Franklin had owned one or two slaves for a brief time many years before," I said, "but he quickly became opposed to the practice. In 1757, while he was in England, he had been introduced to a group of church people who were abolitionists. He served on their board of directors and helped them to set up schools for freed slaves.

"Over the next thirty years, Franklin wrote publicly against slavery. He had led the effort in the Pennsylvania legislature to pass a law for the freeing of slaves and for the end of slavery. Then, in 1789, he became President of the Abolition Society, and in 1790, he called for the end of slavery in a memorial he wrote to Congress.

"The memorial was his last public act, coming just two months before his death. He died peacefully at home at the age of 84. He continued his practice of science right to the end, commenting to his daughter on his dying condition as he grew weaker.

"He also continued his practice as a philosopher, commenting on his belief that God creates both our souls and our bodies. He believed that the body dies but the soul lives on. In his Autobiography, he wrote, 'I never doubted, for instance, the existence of the Deity; that he made the world, and govern'd it by his Providence; that the most acceptable service of God was the doing good to man; that our souls are immortal; and that all crime will be punished, and virtue rewarded, either here or hereafter.'"

"He was a great man," Hannah concluded.

"Yeah, he was," Carter agreed.

"We were lucky to have had him," I said, "as we were to have had Hamilton.

"Hamilton is probably the least known and celebrated of the Super Six. Not many know of his heroism in the Revolutionary War. Nor of how much George Washington had relied on him as an advisor both during and after the War. But it was after the War that Hamilton did the most for our country.

"Hamilton had been working for some time on an answer to the problem of the national debt and the debts of the States following the Revolutionary War. Part of the problem was that there was no national banking system. To help solve it, he founded the Bank of New York in 1784, and that provided the basis he needed to design a national banking plan.

"President Washington made Hamilton the first Secretary of the Treasury in 1789, and one of the first things that Hamilton did was to create the first national bank and the first Mint, so that official money could be centrally coined and printed to be used throughout the States. He also set up the budget system for the new government."

"Ah, Gomps," Carter interrupted, "I thought mint was something you put in iced tea."

"It has a different meaning here," I said. "Here the Mint refers to the government's system of making coins and printing paper money. Ever hear someone say, 'That guy made a mint of money'?"

"I got it," Carter said.

"Then, Hamilton designed plans for trade, tariffs, customs, and manufacturing," I continued.

"Whoa, Gomps," Carter interrupted, "you're going too fast. I know what trade and tariffs are, but what's customs?"

"Customs tracks goods being imported into our country and exported out of it," I said. "In addition to collecting tariffs, Customs also controls shipments, chases smugglers, and generally acts as the police of trade with other countries."

"What about manufacturing?" Carter continued.

"We're talking about factories making things," I said. "Hamilton presented to Congress a plan for encouraging and supporting manufacturing, especially to compete with English manufacturing, and to produce things that would be needed should we have to go to war again."

"Wow," Carter exclaimed. "It sounds like Hamilton did just about everything."

"Well, not quite," I replied, "but he did a lot more than most people know about. And it didn't end there.

"In order to enforce the trade and tariff laws, Hamilton created what was called the Revenue Cutter Service. This was a system of ships that patrolled the coastline to prevent smuggling. Today, it's called the U.S. Coast Guard. Because he set up all these things, some people call him the Father of the U.S. Government.

"While he was doing all this, he continued to try to solve the public debt problem. As we have seen, there was debt just about everywhere. The national government owed money to foreign governments and to individuals, like those who had fought in the Continental Army. Many States owed money to foreign governments and to people, too. The total debt was staggering, and as long as it was allowed to go unpaid, no one would loan money to anyone else and foreign governments would not loan to us.

"The problem was made worse by the fact that some States had paid off a lot of their debt, while others had not. So a good solution for one State might not be good for another. And that meant that the States started arguing with one another all over again.

"Hamilton presented a plan that had the federal government taking over the debt for all the States. It was called assumption – the federal government would assume the debts. It called for the debt to be paid at a small percentage of the amount still owed and to use the federal government's new taxing power to get the money to pay it off.

"This debt payoff plan did not sit well with the States that had paid their debts. They felt that their citizens would be punished for having done the right thing. They would be paying taxes to the government that would then be used to pay off the debts of the States that had done nothing.

"One of the States that had paid off its debts was Virginia. When Hamilton revealed his plan, Thomas Jefferson was furious, and he got Madison to help him oppose it. Two sides in Congress lined up against each other.

"Finally, a compromise was reached. Jefferson and Madison agreed to support Hamilton's debt payoff plan, and Hamilton agreed to support their plan to move the national capital to Virginia, on the banks of the Potomac River. Shortly after that, in July 1790, Hamilton's plan passed the Congress by a narrow margin."

"Gomps, wait a minute!" Hannah interrupted. "Are you talking about Washington, D.C.?"

"I am," I replied.

"You mean that putting the capital there was part of a deal on debt payoff?" she continued.

"That's right," I said. "Until then, the capital was to have either stayed in Philadelphia or moved to New York City, but the southern States weren't happy about it. To them, this would be another example of the northern States having control over them. Jefferson and

Madison were the leaders of a southern group that wanted it closer to them. The place they chose was in the South, but still reasonably close to most of the northern States."

"But I heard it was a swamp," Hannah observed.

"It was," I said, "and to some extent it still is. But there was nothing there at the time, so it gave the planners the chance to design a city from scratch. Nonetheless, a part of Washington D.C. is still called 'Foggy Bottom.'"

"Foggy Bottom!" Carter exclaimed. "That's funny. Is that because it smells like farts?"

"Never mind," I replied sternly, as I winked at him. His father, normally quiet during our sessions, tried so hard to keep from laughing that he snorted and snot flew out of his nose. The tears were streaming down his mother's face, but she was able to not make a sound. "Let's get back to Hamilton."

"After all the difficulties that Hamilton had gone through in helping to form the new government, he was tired of public life. He had suffered from false accusations that he had been having a love affair with another woman. And his wife had just suffered a miscarriage. He resigned as Secretary of the Treasury on December 1, 1794 and returned to New York to a law practice.

"Once back in New York, Hamilton ran into his old enemy, Aaron Burr. In fact, Burr was operating his own law firm just down the street. They could not avoid each other."

"Hold it, Gomps," Hannah interrupted, "I remember the name Aaron Burr, but that was a long time ago."

"Yes," I replied, "it has been a while since I mentioned him, hasn't it. Aaron Burr was the officer that had tried to get the job as George Washington's chief advisor. Burr had schemed to try to get it while Hamilton was fighting on the front lines. Hamilton had seen Burr for the opportunist that he was and never forgot it.

"As the years went by, Burr then tried to get himself appointed to other jobs and, in fact, did manage to become the Attorney General for the State of New York. In every case, Hamilton publicly opposed him.

"Burr tried to undercut John Adams's campaign for President, and then ran against Thomas Jefferson for President, too. In the Jefferson election, Burr came out tied with Jefferson and schemed to get some of Jefferson's Electors to switch their votes. In the end, he became Vice President since he came in second.

"Hamilton worked against Burr, knowing what kind of person he was. We know that Burr lost against both Adams and Jefferson, so his hatred toward Hamilton grew and grew.

"Finally, Hamilton and Burr ended up competing for some of the same clients in their law practices in New York City. One day, Hamilton made some harsh remarks in public about Burr, and Burr saw his chance to get revenge.

"Burr challenged Hamilton to a duel for what he had said, and . . . "

"Wait, Gomps!" Carter exclaimed. "What do you mean by duel?"

"For years and years before this time, men would sometimes settle their arguments with a duel," I replied. "Before there were guns, they would have a sword fight. Once there were guns, they used pistols. They would stand back to back, take ten or so steps, turn, aim, and fire."

"I've heard of that," Hannah said. "Was that really done, really?"

"Yes, it was," I replied.

"That was barbaric!" she concluded.

"If it makes you feel any better," I continued, "duels were rare by this time, and people had adopted a way of dueling without risking injury.

"It was called 'throwing your shot.' Each duelist would bring along an assistant who would carry their pistol and hold other belongings during the duel. They were called 'seconds.' The seconds would meet in private beforehand and agree to tell their guy that the other guy would miss on purpose. So, each guy would aim at the sky, fire, and purposely miss. That would end the duel without anyone getting hurt.

"Now, Burr and Hamilton went to the woods on Staten Island to have their duel. The details of what happened there are shrouded in mystery. Some believe that their seconds met and agreed that both men would throw their shots.

"Hamilton shot first, shot high and missed. Did he throw his shot? We don't know. Nor do we know whether Burr had agreed to throw his shot, too. What we do know is that Burr then shot Hamilton, and he died the next day."

"Oh, no!" Carter shouted.

"That's terrible!" Hannah exclaimed. "That Burr was a rat, wasn't he?"

"That's how it looks," I said. "And that's all we'll say about him.

"It was a sad end to a brilliant career for Hamilton. He packed a lot of accomplishments into his 47 years of life, but by this time, he probably wouldn't have been able to do much more. He was a highly judgmental man who publicly criticized anyone he thought was wrong. By that time, he had made enemies of Jefferson, Adams and Madison. Only George Washington defended him, but Washington's power and influence were, by this time, fading."

"Only 47!" Carter observed. "With all that he did, I thought he would be much older. Did he ever run for President?"

"No, he didn't," I replied. "The Constitution said that only a person born in the U.S. could be President. He was born on a Caribbean island."

"Oh, yeah," Carter replied. "I remember now."

"Why did they put that in the Constitution, Gomps?" Hannah asked.

"What, that you had to have been born here to be President?" I replied.

"Yeah," she said, "wouldn't Hamilton have made a great President?"

"Well, let me answer your first question first," I replied. "The Founding Fathers were afraid that a foreign-born person might not be completely dedicated to the best interests of the country. They were well aware of the divided loyalties and secrecy that people from other countries were capable of. They felt that it would take someone born and raised in our culture to be able to operate the government patriotically. Make sense?"

"Makes sense," Hannah concluded.

"As to your second question, many people were at least suspicious of Hamilton, if not his outright enemy. I'm not sure he could have been elected. And I think that's all I want to say about Hamilton for now. You guys have any other questions about him?"

"No," Hannah said.

"Same here," Carter chimed.

"OK, then," I said. "I'd like to finish the James Madison part next, but it will take longer than we have left tonight, so I'll stop here and get to him next time."

46

MADISON OUTLIVES THEM ALL

"Do you guys realize what holiday it is this week?" I started by asking.

"Yeah, the Fourth of July," Carter replied.

"That's right," I said. "And what were we doing a year ago?"

"Oh, yeah," he continued. "We had our first story time!"

"It's been one year?" Hannah said. "It doesn't seem like it. Time goes fast."

"Yeah!" Carter concurred. "Is tonight the last?"

"No," I replied, "but we're getting close. Tonight I'm going to start with the end of Madison's story.

"Starting in 1789, Madison was reelected to Congress three times, finishing his last term in 1797. He was a leader in many areas during that time. Probably the most important were the national and State debts and the formation of the national bank. The solutions to these resulted in his philosophical breakup with Alexander Hamilton.

"As we know, Hamilton submitted a plan that called for the payment of all those debts by the new federal government. It also required the creation of the national bank to do it. Madison saw how, in Hamilton's plan, Virginia and other States that had already paid some of their debt would lose out. But he also saw that the plan might give too much power to the federal government. The debt problem was one thing, but a takeover by the federal government went against every limited-government belief that he held dear.

"So, Madison lined up with Jefferson who felt the same way. Madison, having had the biggest role in writing the Constitution, knew that the creation of a national bank was not mentioned there. He insisted that, under the enumerated powers principle, if the Constitution did not specifically state that the federal government could do it, then the national bank was unconstitutional, and therefore couldn't be created.

"Hamilton, on the other hand, argued that if the Constitution gives you the power to do something that requires another power that isn't given, it would be impossible to use the power that is given."

"I'm still a little confused on that, Gomps," Carter said.

"OK," I said, "I'll use an example.

"Suppose you had some friends over to play and your Mom said that you could go out to play baseball. When you went to get the ball and bat, she stopped you and said, 'I never said that you could take the ball and bat.' What would you say?"

"How can we play baseball without a ball and bat?" Carter replied. "I get it now."

"I knew you would," I said. "Hamilton called those unstated things implied powers. By being allowed to go out and play baseball, it was implied that you had to use a ball and bat. Otherwise, Hamilton argued, the Constitution would have had to spell out every possible power you might ever need to carry out its instructions.

"Madison, Jefferson and Hamilton could not resolve their differences, so they met with President Washington for a decision. Washington heard both sides and decided that Hamilton was right.

"Madison and Jefferson were successful in getting Hamilton to make concessions, though. He agreed to a compromise on the debt payoff plan and to limit the national bank's charter to only twenty years. And, of course, we already know that he agreed to support the relocation of the national capital to the Potomac River in Virginia.

"Nonetheless, the differences between Madison and Jefferson, on the one hand, and Hamilton on the other resulted in the formation of two political parties – the Federalists, with Hamilton leading, and the Democratic-Republicans, with Jefferson and Madison leading. But the national bank question was not over, and Madison stood at the heart of it.

"Madison was elected as the fourth President in 1809 and again in 1813. During his terms of office, we went to war with Britain. It was called the War of 1812 . . . "

"Gomps, didn't we just beat them in the Revolutionary War?" Carter interrupted.

"Yes, we did, Carter," I replied, "but Britain did not just go away. In addition to their resentment over our having beaten them, they also treated us as they did every other foreign country. They were out to maintain their power in the world, and they saw us as no different than France or Spain in that regard – just weaker."

"What does that have to do with the national bank, Gomps?" Hannah asked.

"Here's what," I replied. "The charter for Hamilton's First Bank of the United States ran out in 1811. As President, Madison had the power to renew the charter, but he refused. Then along came the War of 1812, and Madison's Secretaries of the Treasury couldn't find a way to pay for it without the bank. Finally, Madison found out what Hamilton had been talking about – the country really did need a national bank. President Madison approved the Second National Bank in 1816.""Now, in telling that part of Madison's story, I've jumped over several years. Let's backtrack a little bit."

"After leaving the House of Representatives in 1797, Madison returned to his home to strengthen himself physically and financially.

"As in other times of hard work, Madison's health had worsened. His seizures continued, and he suffered from digestive failure as well. He needed a rest.

"In addition, in his absence, his tobacco plantation, Montpelier, had been losing money. His service to his country had cost him financially, and he was now deeply in debt. He needed to get the operation back on track.

"So, for the next four years, Madison took care of his health and tried to bring Montpelier to profitability. Oh, and one other thing: he finally married."

"He wasn't married?" Hannah exclaimed. "How old was he?"

"He was 43," I replied, "and his bride was 26. She was a Quaker from the Richmond, Virginia area and a widow. Her name was Dolley Payne Todd. After their marriage, Dolley became well known as a valuable helpmate to James and an able hostess of parties and visitors at Montpelier and, later, in the White House.

"In spite of the debt that Madison found himself in, Montpelier did return to profitability, due in large part to good fortune in the marketplace. While his tobacco crops had become increasingly weak, the market for wheat in the Old World went up dramatically. With Jefferson's advice, Madison was able to switch to food crops, and that turned his financial fortunes around.

"Then Jefferson was elected the third President, and he immediately named Madison as his Secretary of State. So Madison was off again to serve his country.

"Madison stayed on as Secretary of State from 1801 to 1809, through both of Jefferson's terms. His greatest achievement during this time was the negotiation of the Louisiana Purchase."

"I've heard of that, Gomps, but I couldn't understand it," Hannah said.

"The Louisiana Purchase was probably the single biggest triumph in the growth of our country," I said. "It was pretty simple, but hard to imagine because of the huge amount of land involved.

"Remember when we got the eastern half of France's Louisiana holdings at the end of the Seven Years' War?" I asked.

"Yeah, Carter thought you meant the eastern half of the State of Louisiana," Hannah replied.

"Yeah, I remember," he confirmed. "It was really everything east of the Mississippi River, wasn't it?"

"Oh, good memory, Carter!" I exclaimed, as he beamed with pride. "Well, that left Spain with everything west of the Mississippi. They held it until 1800, when the French took it back, but it gave the French problems."

"What kind of problems, Gomps?" Carter continued.

"France was no better off financially than Spain was," I replied. "In fact, because of civil war in France, they were probably in even worse shape.

"Territory this size was costing them a fortune to control. This was money they had to borrow, and they were having a hard time finding a loan.

"France's other problem was England. The French knew how valuable their Louisiana land would be to the British, and they wanted to keep it from them at all costs.

"Jefferson and Madison saw what was going on and had an idea. They would buy the rest of Louisiana from France for the United States. Madison and his diplomats handled the negotiations, and they ended up getting it in 1803 for $15 million, which is next to nothing. And, the United States then had enough land for decades of growth.

"Then, in 1808, Madison was elected our fourth President. He served two terms, ending in 1817. During his presidency, he was primarily concerned with relations with other countries, especially Britain, and then with the War of 1812.

"I talked about the financing of that War already, but you should also know what a threat it was to our new country. We hadn't really built a big enough military to hold off Britain, and they nearly took us over.

"In fact, they landed on the Virginia shoreline and captured Washington D.C.! Both Madisons fled from the White House just before the British troops set fire to it."

"I didn't know that," exclaimed Hannah.

"Me either," Carter said. "But we didn't lose, did we?"

"No, we didn't lose," I confirmed. "But I don't think we won, either,"

"Then how did it end?" he persisted.

"Well, Britain had also been fighting France at the same time," I replied, "and I think all three of us ran out of money and lost the will to fight any longer. Everyone just stopped fighting."

"I wish it had been permanent," Hannah interjected.

"Don't we all?" I concurred. "But at least the peace that followed gave the country a chance to grow and get out of debt.

"When his second term as President ended, Madison went back, again, to Montpelier to live out the rest of his days. He ran his plantation and edited his letters and essays for history and served as President of the University of Virginia.

"He died in 1836 at the age of 85, the last and oldest of the Super Six to die."

"Gomps, isn't it amazing that he was so sick for his whole life and still lived so long?" Hannah observed.

"Yes, I am still amazed every time I think about him," I concurred. "There's no doubt that he deserves being called Super.

"So, we've closed the chapters on Franklin, Hamilton and Madison. Let's do John Adams and Jefferson next. Their last days became one of the most amazing coincidences in history."

"What was that, Gomps?" asked Carter.

"For that, you're going to have to wait until next time," I said. "I don't want to skimp on that mystery in any way."

47

AN AMAZING
COINCIDENCE

As it turned out, the kids had to wait two weeks for the great mystery, as I had to go away on business for a week.

"Last time, we closed the chapter on James Madison," I began. "Then, I teased you with a hint about a coincidence in this week's story. The coincidence has to do with John Adams and Thomas Jefferson. Let's start with Adams.

"Remember that Adams had twice been seeking loans in Europe. The first trip ended in failure.

"His second trip was more successful. He persuaded the Dutch to recognize the United States as a country and to negotiate a loan. He also negotiated a trade agreement with them - our first treaty with a foreign country.

"In 1785, Adams was named our ambassador to Britain, and he served there for another three years, during which he was able to restore good relations with them.

"Adams returned from England in 1788, right into the Presidential election. He was on the ballot with George Washington.

"Washington was elected President, and Adams became the Vice President. For the next eight years, he found out what every other Vice President has found out since then – there is little for the Vice President to do, except to cast a vote in the Senate when there is a tie.

"At the end of Washington's second term, the Federalist party made Adams their candidate for President. He narrowly beat Jefferson in the election to become the second President and the Federalist party gained control of Congress. That made Jefferson the Vice President.

"As President, Adams didn't make many changes to what Washington had done. He kept Washington's department heads and continued his policies, including the financial programs of Hamilton. But he thought Hamilton was power-hungry, and the two ended up opposing one another.

"Probably the most important thing Adams did as President was to keep us out of war between Britain and France. They began to fight each other over trade issues, and each tried to get us to take their side. But Adams knew that a war would bankrupt us, so he kept us neutral.

"Just in case, though, he built up the Army and Navy, to be ready should war become necessary. And in order to pay for that, he had to raise taxes.

"Jefferson and the Democratic-Republicans pushed Adams to take France's side in the war, but he refused. This angered the Democratic-Republicans so much that some States controlled by them refused to obey federal laws and even threatened rebellion. In response, the Federalists threatened to put down the opposition with military.

"The arguments and threats became so heated that some feared the country might come apart. To try to stop these attacks, the

Federalist Congress passed the Alien and Sedition Acts in 1798. One of them, the Sedition Act, made it a crime to write anything 'False, scandalous, and malicious' against the President or Congress.

"The Alien and Sedition Acts angered Adams's opponents even more. To them it was an unconstitutional violation of free speech. Jefferson is said to have secretly drafted a resolution for Kentucky to officially ignore federal law if they decided that Congress had gone beyond its enumerated powers. While the resolution was not adopted, it showed the depth of the Democratic-Republicans opposition.

"Cooler heads eventually prevailed and the showdown was avoided, but the Alien and Sedition Acts became a key issue in Adams's second Presidential campaign. As a result, he was defeated by Jefferson in the election of 1800. The vote was close, 65 to 73, but Adams was out.

"With that, Adams went back home to Braintree, Massachusetts, and retired from public life. He ran his little farm and wrote letters and essays about government and current events.

"Then, some years later, a curious thing happened. A mutual friend saw that Adams and Jefferson were still at odds with one another. He found it sad that these old allies of the Revolution had kept up their grudge for so long. So he began writing to them, asking each to forgive the other, and it worked.

"In 1812, Adams sent a short, friendly letter to Jefferson. Jefferson replied in kind, and that was the start of what became a total of 158 letters exchanged between them for the rest of their lives. They mended fences with one another and went on to discuss government, philosophy, farming, and families."

"Did they ever see each other again?" Carter asked.

"No, Carter, they never did," I replied. "Kind of sad, isn't it? Their friendship was limited to letter writing from then on.

"There are only two other things to say about Adams," I said. "The first is that his son, John Quincy Adams, was elected the sixth President. But that's part of another story.

"The last thing to say has to do with Adams's death. It is probably the most unusual coincidence in all of history, but I'm going to save it for the end of Jefferson's part of the story. And, to save you the suspense, that's who we'll finish up next."

"We know that Jefferson was in France while the Constitution was written and ratified. In fact, Washington had already been elected President by the time Jefferson returned in November 1789. No sooner did he get back than he was told that Washington had named him Secretary of State."

"Gomps, what does the Secretary of State do?" Carter interrupted.

"Good question, Carter," I replied. "Sounds ordinary, doesn't it?"

"Yeah," he concurred.

"In the case of our government, though, the word 'Secretary' means the head of," I continued. "And the word 'State' means country or nation. So, the Secretary of State is the head of our dealings with other countries — what we now call foreign relations. Got it?"

"Got it," he said.

"Hannah, you OK on that?" I asked.

"Yeah, I knew that," she replied.

"So, back to Jefferson," I said. "He was sworn in as Secretary of State in March of 1790. First, he set up his department so that we could negotiate treaties and trade agreements. But there were other things that concerned him more — the decisions that Alexander Hamilton was making about the debt and the setup of the government.

"Jefferson was in many ways a farmer at heart. He liked the idea that someone could take a piece of land and live on it independently. To Jefferson, this was the ideal kind of life, and he thought everyone should live that way."

"Wasn't that kind of unrealistic?" Hannah asked.

"Yes, I think it was," I replied, "but Jefferson could be a little unrealistic at times. He was more of a dreamer, a big-picture guy. That's part of what made him able to write such a beautiful Declaration of Independence. He could take various ideas and say them with style and inspiration. He didn't get bogged down in details.

"So, as Jefferson saw what Hamilton was doing, it was just the opposite of the kind of life he supported. To him, the banking and debt and factories and warehouses and businessmen were a threat to the independent farmer who just wanted to feed his family and be left alone."

"In his mind," Hannah observed.

"Yes, in his mind," I concurred. "Part of his way of looking at things may also have been because he wasn't a very good businessman himself. He tried various little business ventures over the years, and he failed every time. For example, he set up a nail-making factory on his plantation and it never turned a profit. As a result, he borrowed money regularly and rarely paid it back. By the time of his death, he was deep in debt.

"That's why Jefferson worked so hard to defeat Hamilton's actions. In fact, he spent probably more time opposing Hamilton than he did running the State Department. And he was the chief organizer of the Democratic-Republican party.

"Tired of the detail-plagued kind of life that running a government department required, he resigned as Secretary of State in 1794 and went back to Monticello, which had fallen into what he called 'degradation' during his absence. He spent the next three years there bringing the soil and plantation operation back to working order.

"In spite of his love of the land, Jefferson could not overlook the news of Hamilton's further development of the federal government. In 1796, Madison visited Jefferson to urge him to oppose the Federalists by running for President. He eventually agreed.

"We know that Jefferson ran for President first against John Adams and lost narrowly, 68 to 71. So Jefferson became the Vice President.

"Even before he took office, Jefferson knew what John Adams had learned — that the Vice President has little power and nothing much to do. So he turned his attention to Adams and the programs of the Federalists.

"Jefferson wrote frequently in opposition to the Alien and Sedition Acts. He felt they were an unconstitutional limit on free speech and submitted a proposal to Congress to remove them. His party didn't have the votes, though, and the laws remained on the books. Nonetheless, people disliked the Acts so much that it changed the balance of power from the Federalists to the Democratic-Republicans.

"As we've said, in 1800, Jefferson ran again for President against John Adams, and this time he won. Along with Jefferson, the voters elected a majority of Democratic-Republicans in both Houses of Congress. And that began the death of the Federalist Party.

"Jefferson was sworn in as the third President. By this time, the national capital had been moved to Washington, D.C. While there were very few buildings, Hamilton had made good on the national bank deal, and the new location was official.

"Jefferson served two terms as President, finishing in 1809. In his first four years, with the help of Congress, he undid what he saw as the worst of the Federalist policies. He did away with many federal government programs and jobs, calling them unneeded. He cut back on the sizes of the Army and Navy. And he did away with all taxes, leaving only tariffs."

"He eliminated taxes?" Hannah asked. "Completely?"

"All of what he called 'internal' taxes, Hannah," I replied. "That meant taxes on factories, warehouses, businesses, products, and the like."

"But, how could we pay for the government?" she continued.

"He also cut government expenses way back," I said. "There were enough foreign goods being bought here that the tariffs on them covered the rest."

"Wow," she exclaimed. "I wouldn't have thought that was possible."

"As bold as these early successes were, Jefferson is best known for three big moves. The first, the Louisiana Purchase, we have already talked about. The second was winning a little war that is often forgotten — the Barbary War. Have you heard of it?"

"Never," Hannah said.

"Me either," Carter added.

"The Barbary War was a war against pirates along the Barbary Coast of North Africa," I said. "For years, pirates there had been capturing merchant ships and keeping them or holding them for ransom."

"What's ransom, Gomps?" Carter interrupted.

"That's the money that a kidnapper demands in return for what he has kidnapped," I replied. "The Barbary pirates kidnapped ships, goods and sailors and demanded money from the countries from which they had sailed. They often sold the sailors into slavery in North Africa."

"Slavery?" Hannah interrupted. "Our guys?"

"That's right, Hannah," I said. "Remember, I said that slavery has been practiced in many places in many different ways over time, and this was just another example. Carter, you get all this?"

He looked at me with a squint and said in a pirate voice, "Aye, matey."

After a good laugh all around, I continued. "This piracy had not been a big problem for us until we became an independent country. While we were a colony, the British Navy protected us against the pirates, and during the Revolutionary War, the French did the same. But once we became independent, we were on our own, and the Barbary pirates knew it.

"By the time Jefferson became President, he had seen enough of the pirates. He built up our naval forces and defeated them."

"So, what was the third thing, Gomps?" Hannah asked.

"What third thing?" I replied.

"The third thing that Jefferson did as President," she continued. "When you started telling us about Jefferson's Presidency you said he did three main things — the Louisiana Purchase, the Barbary War and something else, but you never said what it was."

"Oh, yes," I replied, "I got so worked up over those pirates that I lost track.

"The third thing Jefferson did was to keep the promise of Madison about the slave trade. In a December 1806 speech to Congress, Jefferson called for a law to make the slave trade illegal. Then he guided a bill through Congress. It passed in 1807, and Jefferson signed it. The law took effect on January 1, 1808, the first day it would be constitutional. It was one of his last acts as President.

"At the end of his last term, Jefferson went back to Monticello, although, as with the rest of the Super Six, he could not stop his public service entirely. During his later years, Jefferson designed the University of Virginia campus and its first buildings. It opened in 1825, and he became its first President at the age of 81.

"Otherwise, Jefferson spent his remaining years as a gentleman farmer. Unfortunately, he was never able successfully to change from tobacco to food crops, as Madison had done, so he was never able to get out of debt.

"Jefferson's health began to fail in 1825, and he began to suffer from pneumonia, among other diseases.

"Now for the coincidence of his and Adams's deaths: both of them died on the same day."

"No way," Carter exclaimed.

"Way," I said. "Within a few hours of each other — Jefferson first and then Adams. In fact, not knowing that Jefferson was already dead, Adams's last words were, 'Jefferson survives.'"

"Amazing," Hannah uttered. "You were right, Gomps, that was a big coincidence."

"But that's not all," I said and paused for effect. "The year was 1826, and the date was none other than . . . July 4!"

"You can't be serious!" she shouted.

"No waaaay!" Carter shouted.

"I am perfectly serious," I insisted. "Exactly 50 years from the Declaration of Independence, those two old war horses of the Revolution went out together."

"You were right, Gomps," Hannah continued. "That's got to be the greatest coincidence in history."

"Yeah," agreed Carter, "you couldn't make that up."

After pausing once more, I said, "So that's it for all the Super Six except George Washington. I'll close the chapter on him and wind up the story next time.

"For tonight, I'll say good night. And I'll see you next week for our last story time. Sleep tight and don't let the bedbugs bite."

48

WASHINGTON'S LAST BREATH

In honor of our last story time, Mandy and Mark put up quite a feast. We had all of my favorite foods, including lobster. After a yummy dessert of chocolate cake and ice cream, I started in.

"Well, we're coming to the end of this story. I can't believe it, but it's been over a year since we started.

"Let's see George Washington through to the end, and then I'll have some last thoughts.

"Washington took office as President in April 1789. The thing you have to keep in mind about his presidency is that he had no history to fall back on. He had to make every decision from scratch. At the same time, States and other countries began immediately to make demands.

"His choices of Hamilton for Secretary of the Treasury and Jefferson for Secretary of State were masterful. As we know, Hamilton understood how to set up the government's structure, while Jefferson had years of experience in European diplomacy.

"Once the government was underway, Washington took two tours of the country to meet the people and to assure them that the Constitution and the new government were up to the task of building the new nation. He first went to the northern States, beginning in the fall of 1789. Then, in the spring of 1791, he toured the southern States. As you might imagine, he was greeted as a hero wherever he went.

"By the end of his first term, Washington began to think of retirement. He was 60 years old and his health was beginning to fade. He even went so far as to have James Madison write a farewell speech for him.

"But all his supporters, led by Jefferson, Madison, and Hamilton, insisted that he run for a second term. Washington said nothing more about it and allowed his name to be entered in the election of 1792. When the votes were counted, he was, again, elected unanimously.

"Washington was faced with more problems in his second term than in his first. The running feud between Jefferson and Hamilton became more intense, both France and England tried to drag us into their quarreling, and there was resistance to taxation at home.

"Meanwhile, starting in 1789, the French were in the midst of their own political revolution. In answer to the power of their King and to his massive war debts, the King's citizen advisory group, the Third Estate, declared itself in charge of the country.

"This started the French Revolution. Mobs formed everywhere, and the bloodbath began. The King, his royal family, nobles, and wealthy people were murdered by out-of-control peasant groups. The Catholic Church's authority as the official religion was abolished almost overnight, and new governments of a supposed democratic form were tried, one after another. All failed.

"Washington faced pressure to support the French people against the King. Things were changing fast in France, and the Revolution seemed out of control. Further, the French were attacking British islands in the Caribbean.

"Our finances and military forces were in no condition to go to war. So, Washington decided to stay out of it. He issued the Neutrality Proclamation of 1793. Friends of Britain, such as Hamilton, supported the proclamation, but friends of France, such as Jefferson, opposed it. Nonetheless, Washington stood firm, although the disagreement took its toll on his health.

"Meanwhile, resistance to taxes in this country was growing. In 1790, Hamilton had started a tax on whiskey as one of the ways to pay off our debt. Whiskey makers complained, and in 1794, a group of them in Pittsburgh, Pennsylvania, attacked a tax collector and those who tried to rescue him. Their action became known as the Whiskey Rebellion.

"When Washington heard about it, he sent his representatives to reason with the rebels. At the same time, he sent word to the States to recruit militias, should force be needed. Washington saw the Rebellion as a threat to the authority of the federal government, and he knew that if he didn't get the rebels to back down, others would try the same thing.

"As he feared, the rebels were not to be reasoned with. Washington's representatives reported that the rebels were standing firm, so he turned to force. As many as 60,000 militiamen had volunteered to march on Pittsburgh, and from them, Washington put together a force of 18,000. He oversaw their preparations in eastern Pennsylvania and personally led them in a march to Pittsburgh.

"After a month of marching, Washington left them in the command of our old friend General Light Horse Harry Lee. Lee led them the last few miles while Washington went back to Philadelphia for the start of the new session of Congress.

"Once they saw 18,000 militiamen, the rebels surrendered without a fight. Eighteen of the leaders were arrested and tried. Two of them were sentenced to death for treason, but Washington pardoned them. He had proved his point about the authority of the government, and the militiamen went home.

"The final achievement of Washington's second term was a treaty with Britain on trade and merchant shipping. The British had been attacking our merchant ships, taking the shipments, and capturing our sailors."

"That sounds like the Barbary pirates," Hannah observed.

"Very similar," I replied. "The difference was that the British were not asking for ransom. They were just taking everything. Hundreds of ships.

"In response, Congress had ordered that all British merchant ships and goods be banned from entry into our ports. At the same time, Washington sent a representative, John Jay, to England to work out a deal.

"The result was a treaty in which the British agreed to peace, but said nothing about the actual attacks on our ships. The treaty was opposed as soon as it was made public, and Washington was criticized bitterly.

"Washington wasn't happy with the treaty either, but he thought it was the best that could be gotten at the time. He supported it in Congress, and after months of debate and public argument, it was approved.

"The treaty turned out to have kept peace with England, but Washington never recovered from the personal attacks that were heaped on him for it. By this time, he was 63 years old and in failing health. He completed his second term as President and did not run again.

"Washington retired to Mount Vernon in hopes of living out his days in peace and quiet, and it almost worked. In 1798, France threatened to attack us again. John Adams named Washington to put together and command the military forces that would be necessary to defend us.

"Washington went ahead with the preparations, but the French backed down, and no military action turned out to be needed. This was Washington's last public action. He went back again to Mount Vernon.

"Then, in December, 1799, Washington went out for a horseback ride in bad weather. He caught a cold that quickly worsened, and a few days later he died. He was 67 years old.

"He was not the last of the Super Six to die, by any means, but he was the heart and soul of the Revolution, and it was up to those who remained to pick up the cause and continue it."

"How sad," Hannah said. "I think he was a great man."

"Yeah," Carter added, "funny how it happened so quick. Did he say anything at the end, like Adams?"

"Yes, he did, Carter," I said, "but, it was just typical George Washington humility. He said to his doctor, 'I feel myself going. I thank you for your attentions, but I pray you to take no more trouble about me. Let me go off quietly; I cannot last long.' And, at ten o'clock that night, he breathed his last."

We all sat quietly for a moment and I finally broke the silence. "There are just a few more things I'd like to talk to you about."

"First, we can't finish the story without a last look at slavery. We know that Congress had kept Madison's promise by banning the slave trade. But that didn't end slavery by any means. It only banned the importation of slaves.

"Most States passed their own laws to end slavery in the years that followed, but not all. It took President Lincoln and a bloody Civil War to do that almost 60 years later. And we know that the results of slavery persisted beyond that.

"There is no question that slavery was a problem that divided our country more than any other. Once slavery started, no one could find a peaceful way to stop it. It was such a big problem that the Founding Fathers had to choose between putting our new nation together or not. They chose the new nation in the hope that the issue of slavery could be solved later."

"Gomps, why couldn't the Army have just gone into those plantations and set the slaves free?" Hannah asked.

"It would have been great had that been possible, Hannah," I replied, "but there were 700,000 slaves by that time. Where would they live? How would they have been fed and clothed? Where would they have been educated? And once they had been freed, where were the jobs for them?

"And what of the plantations? Would the plantation owners have been willing to pay wages to their slaves? That would have bankrupted them, and then where would our food and cloth have come from? If the slaves had not stayed on the plantations, where would the owners have found other farm workers? And wouldn't they have bankrupted themselves just the same in paying *them*?

"We have to face the fact that the southern plantation system was the economy of the southern States. If the plantations had failed, the whole economy of those States would have collapsed. As it was, many plantations were not very profitable anyway.

"Jefferson said of slavery that we have a wolf by the ears and we cannot hold onto him or safely let him go. I think that the way it played out – taking so many years and then a war to do it – was probably the only way we could have ended it and still had hope for saving our country."

"I see what you mean, Gomps," Hannah said.

"There is no doubt that slavery is a stain on our history," I concluded.

"Now, I'd like to finish up our story by looking at the big picture. Some say that our country was dreamed up by a few old white men. They say that their ideas may have worked at the time, but there is nothing sacred in what they created. Therefore, we should be able to change whatever stands in the way of modern times.

"For example, President Theodore Roosevelt said that limited government '. . . is a bit of outworn academic doctrine . . . It can be applied with profit, if anywhere at all, only in a primitive community such as the United States at the end of the 18th century.'

"President Woodrow Wilson said of constitutional government, 'It does not remain fixed in any unchanging form, but grows with the growth and is altered with the change of the nation's needs and purposes.'

"President Franklin D. Roosevelt, FDR, said regarding the Interstate Commerce Clause, '(It was written) in the horse-and-buggy age . . . since that time . . . we have developed an entirely different philosophy.'

"And, FDR wrote to a Congressman urging him to pass a law, 'I hope your committee will not permit doubts as to constitutionality, however reasonable, to block the suggested legislation.'

"Others have tried to question the religious faith of the Founders. They claim, for instance, that Washington was not a Christian. Nothing could be further from the truth.

"These people insist that if the Founders' belief in God is questionable, then the Founders could not use God as the source of our basic rights. And, if God is not the source of our rights, human beings must be. Which humans would be the ones to grant those rights or take them away? Those in power, of course.

"Do not listen to them. Our country is not just a concoction put together over a few years. It is the result of the determination of generations of our ancestors during a 200-year period to make a better life for themselves and, ultimately, for you and me.

"Our ancestors suffered through conditions that are unthinkable today. Picture the crude dirt-floor huts at the Plymouth Plantation. Picture the bloody footprints, starvation, and disease of the Revolutionary War.

"Our ancestors fought and died for the right to make a living as they chose, to worship as they chose, and to associate with whom they chose. Outgunned and outmanned by the British, they kept fighting until the British could fight no more.

"Our forefathers designed and tested various new forms of government over the 200 years – the Charters, the Mayflower Compact, the New England Confederation, the Albany Congress, the Stamp Act Congress, the colonial Assemblies and laws, the State constitutions, and the Articles of Confederation. Then, the Founders took the best parts of those forms and forged a system that maintains our rights and protects us from power-hungry politicians at home and from foreign enemies abroad.

"Sure, they made mistakes. Their treatment of Native Americans and slaves was wrong. But they were in uncharted waters, having to decide the right things to do with no history to fall back on. Think about that – there was no ancestor that they could look back to for answers, no country that had done this.

"In the end, they gave us a great gift – the gift of a way of life where we have the chance to pursue our dreams without someone in authority saying we can't or forcing us to do something else. And they put their reputations, their money and their lives on the line to do it.

"The generations that came after them have defended our system and applied it to their lives. It has continued to work so well that it has become an ideal that people all over the world admire and seek. From the beginning, we have welcomed those who want to work for the same freedoms and are willing to take the same risks to preserve them. And that is part of the greatness of the United States.

"From time to time, some people have tried to go around the Constitution for their own purposes. Most of the time, they do it to gain power that they should not have. We have to watch out for that and oppose them when they do. In that regard, we are part of that original Revolution to this day, walking hand in hand with the Super Six and the rest of the Founding Fathers to preserve our way of life.

"And that is how our freedom was born."

"Is that the end, Gomps?" Carter asked.

"Of the Founding story, yes, Carter," I replied.

"I don't want it to end," he said.

"It doesn't," I said.

"I know, but I don't want story time to end," he continued.

"Story time won't end," I said, "but I've told all I have to tell about this story. That's why I'm stopping. There'll be other stories and other story times, I promise."

"OK," he said. "Thank you for this one. I didn't always understand everything, but I learned a lot and had fun, too."

"Yes, thank you, Gomps," Hannah said. "I've learned so much, and you've made it fun."

"Bearable, at least," I said. "It's been my privilege to tell it. And I hope that you'll read more about it. Pick an event or person that interests you, and try to find eyewitness descriptions or the person's diary or letters so you can see for yourself."

"I'm going to miss it," Hannah continued. "I'll always remember your story on Wednesdays."

"Me too," I said.

"Gomps, I think I can speak for us all when I say what a great gift you have given us," Mark said. "We have learned a lot and have looked forward to this time every week. Thanks so much."

"Yes, thank you so much, Dad," Mandy said. "We'll remember this forever."

"You're all very welcome," I replied. "It's been my pleasure.

"Now, where's my dessert?"

LEARN MORE

I hope that reading this book about how our country came to be has made you want to learn more. Rather than list the many books, articles, journals, and letters that I studied for this book, I thought it would be more helpful to list the ones that might be the most interesting. These fall into two types: original or primary sources, and interpretations of primary sources, also known as secondary sources.

Original or primary sources are documents that the subjects themselves wrote. These include diaries, letters, journals, essays, books, and more. Many of the writings of George Washington, for example, exist in their original forms or as copies, and are, therefore, primary sources. We are lucky that the writings of many of the subjects in this book have survived the centuries.

Interpretations or secondary sources are, for all practical purposes, history books and articles. This book is a secondary source. Secondary sources are written by people who study primary sources (and other secondary sources, for that matter) and quote or interpret them in telling the story.

Any truth about a historical subject is more likely to come from the person who wrote or said it than it is to come from a person who interprets it. So it's often better to read a primary source. The problem with primary source material from early America, for historians and casual readers alike, is that there is so much of it. George

Washington's writings alone take up more than 100 volumes. This is a good problem to have.

Nonetheless, anyone, be it a historian or an interested general reader, must limit the amount of primary source information that they choose to include in their studies of any historical subject. What they include and exclude depends on a number of things: their choices of topic; why they are reading in that topic area or what readers they are writing for; their reasons for reading or writing that work; and their personal filters or biases. If you have not already, you may see some of my choices (as best I know them) in the Foreword to this book.

Primary Sources – See For Yourself

One of my mottoes has always been, "See for yourself." This probably came from my early years in the study of science. In science, nothing is taken for granted. Hypotheses are only "confirmed" (or not) by findings. Nothing is "proven, once and for all." To attempt to confirm a hypothesis, all students run experiments to see for themselves if they get the same results that others have.

The best way to be sure of historical accuracy is to "see for yourself." If you wonder whether something in this or any other book of history is true, look it up. Don't necessarily take anybody's word for it, including mine. That's what I did in my studies of early American history: I got things from the horses' mouths, as much as possible.

To help you to do that, I have listed below the most interesting primary sources (to me). Most are published and can be purchased. Most are now also online. Virtually all can be borrowed at a library. A few must be seen at the Library of Congress. See for yourself.

The Online Library of Liberty http://oll.libertyfund. org/#founders

Look here first if you want direct access. Most of the primary sources below are carried here, as in a clearinghouse.

George Washington, *The Writings of George Washington*. John C. Fitzpatrick, ed. (Washington: U.S. Government Printing Office, 1944), 39 vols. The full text is online at http://etext.virginia. edu/washington/fitzpatrick/, and if you dip into it almost anywhere you will meet the man face to face and be plunged into his times. Also, the University of Virginia has an edition of *The Papers of George Washington* – his diaries, his correspondence including letters to and from him, and other documents and maps – in progress: http://gwpapers.virginia.edu/project/index.html. It is two-thirds done and will be about 90 volumes when complete. You can browse this collection (read George Washington's diary!) through the Mount Vernon website: http://rotunda.upress.virginia.edu/founders/GEWN.xqy

Benjamin Franklin, *The Papers of Benjamin Franklin*. Yale University has been working on this scholarly edition of Franklin's voluminous writings since 1954, and it has now reached 40 volumes, which are published in physical book form by Yale University Press, at least some of which your local library may have. You can also browse and search the complete papers online for free: http://franklinpapers.org/franklin/ Start with this introductory essay which will walk you through Franklin's life, with links to many of his writings. http://franklinpapers.org/franklin/framedMorgan.jsp

John Adams, *The Works of John Adams, Second President of the United States: with a Life of the Author, Notes and Illustrations, by his Grandson Charles Francis Adams* (Boston: Little, Brown and Co., 1856). Charles Francis Adams, ed. (Boston: Little, Brown & Co., 1856), 10 volumes. All online at the Online Library of Liberty: http://oll.libertyfund.org/2098

Alexander Hamilton, *The Works of Alexander Hamilton* (Federal Edition), Henry Cabot Lodge, ed. (New York: G.P. Putnam's Sons, 1904), 12 vols. Online at the Online Library of Liberty: http://oll.libertyfund.org/title/1712

Thomas Jefferson, *The Writings of Thomas Jefferson*, Albert Ellery Bergh, ed. (Washington: The Thomas Jefferson Memorial Association of the United States, 1907), 20 vols. Online at http://www.constitution.org/tj/jeff.htm. Another edition, *The Works of Thomas Jefferson*, Federal Edition, Paul Leicester Ford, ed. (New York and London, G.P. Putnam's Sons, 1904-5). 12 vols., is available at the Online Library of Liberty, http://oll.libertyfund.org/1734.

James Madison, *The Writings of James Madison*, Gaillard Hunt, ed. (New York: G. P. Putnam's Sons, 1900), 9 vols. Online at the Online Library of Liberty, http://oll.libertyfund.org/title/1933

John Smith, *The Complete Works of Captain John Smith (1580-1631)*, Philip L. Barbour, ed. (Chapel Hill: University of North Carolina Press, 1986), 3 vols.

William Bradford, *Of Plymouth Plantation, 1620-1647*, Samuel Eliot Morison, ed. (New York: Alfred A. Knopf, 2004). There are several editions out there. Morison has written an excellent introduction, and I recommend his version.

John Winthrop, *The Journal of John Winthrop, 1630-1649,* Richard S. Dunn, James Savage, and Laetitia Yeandle, eds. (Cambridge, MA: Harvard University Press, 1996).

Thomas Paine, *Common Sense, Rights of Man, and Other Essential Writings of Thomas Paine,* Sidney Hook, introduction (New York: Signet Classic, 2003).

The Constitution of the United States with the Declaration of Independence and the Articles of Confederation, R.B. Bernstein, introduction (New York: Fall River Press, 2002). This is a pocket-size edition that includes all of the Amendments with an excellent introduction and timeline. The texts of all three add up to less than 80 pages. Read them.

Alexander Hamilton, James Madison, John Jay, *The Federalist,* Benjamin F. Wright, ed., (Cambridge, MA: Belknap Press of Harvard University Press, 1961; New York: Barnes & Noble Books, 2004). The 2004 edition has the subtitle *The Famous Papers on the Principles of American Government.* Wright has compiled these 85 "letters to the editor" (also known as *The Federalist Papers*) brilliantly. He maintained their 18th Century writing style, but the arguments shine through.

Secondary Sources

Why do people write history? We trust that they love the period and the subjects about which they write. Writing history honestly requires virtual obsession and unending hard work. Scholars bear the additional burden of "publish or perish." Most, if not all, hope that they earn money from book sales. Some may seek acclaim, although writing history may be one of the least likely roads to it.

Some hope to interpret and present history so as to influence social trends.

So, writers of history read primary documents and the writings of others, sort out the story they want to tell, and write it. Consciously or subconsciously, the personal baggage they bring to their writing finds its way into their writing. I'm no different.

For the reader and student of history, the question arises, "What is true?" That you have to figure out for yourself. Some writing is very persuasive. That is why primary sources are so important, but even then, any one source may not be enough. There is evidence that, in retirement, James Madison rewrote or revised many of his papers because he wanted to improve or strengthen how he would be remembered.

The best single piece of advice, then, is to read a lot on the period or subject that interests you. Read different authors' versions. Read about related periods or subjects that bear on your favorites. Read. As you go, a clearer picture will begin to form and you will be able to separate the wheat from the chaff.

There are a few dead giveaways, though, that an author is trying not only to paint a picture of what happened, but to tell you what you should think about it. If an author uses words such as "What other conclusion is there?" a warning light should go on in your brain — a signal to seriously think about what other conclusions there indeed might be, and not just allow the author to persuade you.

If the author writes of a historical personage, "He would have said or done such and such (or worse yet, "thought such and such" or "felt such and such"), that is fiction, not history. The author doesn't have evidence on which to base the statement. The author may just be trying to liven up the narrative — responsible historians will tell you when they are imagining a scene or speculating about a character's thoughts – or, more dangerously, he or she may be using a historical figure as a mouthpiece to promote the author's point of view.

I used such a method in this book. On occasion, I wrote words or motives as the "King's." The intent was to help the reader to understand the general forces behind certain actions and to keep the history moving along at the same time. Also, I put words into the mouths of the Duke of York, William Penn and Lord Baltimore to show the kind of thinking that can lead up to a lawsuit of this kind. In both instances, I tried to make clear that I was not quoting them as historical "fact." If I failed, I offer my apologies. I had no intention of trying to promote a biased point of view.

A special word about television and film: beware. Both are produced primarily to earn money through entertainment (and to some extent to educate and influence broad groups of people). If the ratings are low or the box office is not there, they fail. So producers plan their productions for high ratings or box-office receipts. General story lines are filled in with what they want or what they think the viewer wants the history to have been, and historical honesty is left at the wayside if it might discourage viewership.

Here are books on early American history that are worth reading. There are many others, some perhaps more worthy. Some are recent; some less so. Some are more "scholarly"; some less so. All would be good additions to your learning and to your library.

Andrew M. Allison, Jay A. Parry and W. Cleon Skousen, *The Real George Washington: The True Story of America's Most Indispensable Man* (Malta, ID: National Center for Constitutional Studies, 1991 and 2008). Easy reading. Includes over 200 pages of quotations from

Washington's writings on a wide range of subjects, grouped by subject. This is volume 3 of the publisher's American Classic Series.

Andrew M. Allison, W. Cleon Skousen and M. Richard Maxfield, *The Real Benjamin Franklin: The True Story of America's Greatest Diplomat* (Malta, ID: National Center for Constitutional Studies, 1982 and 2008). Easy reading. Includes over 200 pages of quotations from Franklin's writings on a wide range of subjects, grouped by subject. This is volume 2 of the publisher's American Classic Series.

Andrew M. Allison, M. Richard Maxfield, K. DeLynn Cook, and W. Cleon Skousen, _*The Real Thomas Jefferson The True Story of America's Philosopher of Freedom*, 2nd ed. (Malta, ID: National Center for Constitutional Studies, 1983 and 2008). Easy reading. Includes over 200 pages of quotations from Jefferson's writings on a wide range of subjects, grouped by subject. This is volume 1 of the publisher's American Classic Series.

David A. Price, *Love and Hate in Jamestown: John Smith, Pocahontas, and the Start of a New Nation* (New York: Vintage Books, 2005).

Francis J. Bremer, *John Winthrop: America's Forgotten Founding Father* (New York, Oxford University Press, 2003).

Peter A. Lillback with Jerry Newcombe, *George Washington's Sacred Fire* (West Conshocken, PA: Providence Forum Press, 2006). Certain historians have attempted to define Washington as an unbeliever: a Deist (believing at best that a creative force or "God" set the world in motion long ago and then left it alone) or even an agnostic. With the extensive use of Washington's own words and first-person observations of him, this well-researched and reasoned book refutes such claims completely. He was a Christian — an Episcopalian - of deep faith.

Joseph J. Ellis, *His Excellency: George Washington* (New York: Alfred A. Knopf, 2004). Ellis is a controversial scholar who tells a good story. He is, however, one of those who attempt to paint Washington as a Deist. Although he doesn't make that claim directly here, he weaves it into the book through suggestion and innuendo. Worth reading nonetheless.

Carl Van Doren, *Benjamin Franklin* (New York: Viking Press, 1938; PenguinBooks, 1991). This is a rigorously researched and written book in the tradition of the 19th Century historical scholars. It is heavy going, but the writing is supported by extensive quotes from Franklin's works. Your effort will be rewarded.

David McCullough, *John Adams* (New York: Simon & Schuster, 2001). As good a combination of serious history and storytelling as you will find. McCullough brings Adams to life as no one has before. He has received well-deserved recognition for this work.

Ron Chernow, *Alexander Hamilton* (New York: Penguin Press, 2004). A clear and complete biography, this book raises Hamilton to a deserved level. Chernow manages to weave Hamilton's words with those of his contemporaries into a rich and vivid portrait of the man and his times.

Joseph J. Ellis, *American Sphinx: The Character of Thomas Jefferson* (New York: Alfred A. Knopf, 1997; Vintage Books, 1998). Ellis seems to capture the essence of Thomas Jefferson — a mysterious character in many ways. Here Ellis treats fairly Jefferson's apparent religious contradictions. He proclaimed himself a Christian while rejecting the dogma and discipline of the Church.

Ralph Ketcham, *James Madison: A Biography* (Charlottesville, VA: The University Press of Virginia, 1990). Generally recognized to be the preeminent work on Madison. This is a scholarly tour de force covering his entire life in detail.

Richard Labunski, *James Madison and the Struggle for the Bill of Rights* (New York: Oxford University Press, 2006). Labunski deftly weaves together Madison's leadership and the story of the development of the Bill of Rights.

Joseph J. Ellis, *Founding Brothers: the Revolutionary Generation* (New York: Alfred A. Knopf and Vintage Books, 2000). Here Ellis abbreviates the history to tell a compelling story while maintaining the historical foundations.

David McCullough, *1776* (New York: Simon & Schuster, 2005). A history of the critical year of the Revolution. McCullough keeps in balance the many events that occurred at the same time in different places.

ABOUT THE AUTHOR

A Bachelor's in Political Science and a Master's in Public Administration both from the University of California, Berkeley, launched Mr. Bugaeff on a 40 year career in organizational consulting and teaching, during which he wrote and published over 100 manuscripts and technical manuals privately for his clients. Along the way, he continued the serious study of early American political history, concentrating on primary source materials. Bugaeff and his wife, Pinny, have a son, a daughter and two grandchildren and live in Stafford Springs, Connecticut.

ABOUT THE TYPE

Pilgrims To Patriots was set in Centaur MT, 13 point. Centaur lends a nobility and power to an easy-to-read typeface, thus befitting colonial times. Designed in 1912 by Bruce Rogers for the Metropolitan Museum of Art, Centaur traces its roots to the 1469 Eusebius typeface by Nicholas Jenson of Venice, Italy.

THANK YOU

The idea for this book came to me as my wife, Pinny, and I drove home from a visit with our dear friends, David and Billie Kapp. I had recently left my employer to begin what I thought of at the time as retirement.

During our visit, we discussed what I planned to do with my new-found freedom. I had told them that I wanted to pass along to my grandchildren in some way an appreciation for the founding of our country and for the heritage that has passed to them.

Having been a student of early American History for my adult life, I felt the need to share what I had learned. I knew that my grandchildren would be unlikely to get the story as accurately or as fully anywhere else. But, as we chatted during that visit, I had only a vague idea of how to get it across to them.

Then, about halfway home, it hit me. I would tell them the story in a book. I spent the rest of the trip blurting ideas to Pinny as I drove. By the time we got home I had the rough outline for the project and, after parking the car, I rushed to my office where I spent the next several hours getting it down.

So, my first Thank You goes to David and Billie Kapp. Without that visit and discussion, who knows what, if anything, would have come of this? They created the conditions under which the critical mass of thoughts could take shape and I thank them for their accepting and nurturing way.

I happily and gratefully thank my editor, Annie Gottlieb of New York City, for her expert and enthusiastic work on my manuscript. From the concept through the usage down to every comma and period, she understood instantly what I was trying to do and she maintained her belief in it throughout. She steered me with an experienced hand, helping me to navigate past unseen shoals and undercurrents. More than once, she saved me from myself and I appreciate it.

I prevailed upon two special people to read my manuscript and to give me feedback. My loving daughter, Mandy, took time from her busy schedule to read it from beginning to end when it was still in rough shape and way too long. She showed patience and forbearance in her responses to it at a time when I needed encouragement, not skepticism, and I thank her for it. And, her feedback was invaluable.

The other special person is David Kapp. Eighteen months after that formative visit, I prevailed upon him to read a revised manuscript. An accomplished writer and editor himself, David graciously put other work aside and gave it a careful reading. His insights were important additions to my approach and made the book better. I am most grateful to him for his friendship and for his wise counsel.

For her help in so many ways, I thank my wife, Pinny. In the midst of writing her own book, she always made time to listen, guide, suggest, and console. She is my cheerleader, confidante and sage. In addition, she also made time to read my manuscript and her many observations, suggestions and warnings helped me immeasurably, not only with my writing, but also with my understanding of the publishing business. I am in her debt in ways too numerous to count.

Finally, I cannot close without recognizing my son, Gregor, for the love and support I needed, even when he was immersed in his sculpture. He was always encouraging, always there for me with a

"Semper Fi." His steadfast belief in me was more important than he knew and his artistic input on the "look" of the book was invaluable.

After all the input I got along the way, it was still my responsibility to decide what to write and not to write. I am most appreciative for all the help I got, but in the end, any and all omissions, factual errors and errors in interpretation are mine alone.

25866081R00265

Made in the USA
Middletown, DE
12 November 2015